US INTERNATIONAL LAWYERS IN THE INTERWAR YEARS

In the interwar years, a group of reform-minded American scholars of international law, such as Quincy Wright and Manley Hudson, challenged traditional international law and strove to establish a 'new' international law in which outlawry of war was institutionalized. They highly valued the Covenant of the League of Nations and the Kellogg–Briand Pact, and presented legal arguments in support of them. These scholars were activists in their efforts to promote their views to policy makers and the public. In the US international law community, however, a different group of scholars, notably Edwin Borchard, vehemently opposed the progressive scholars. *US International Lawyers in the Interwar Years* chronicles those involved in the debate and provides a detailed account of their scholarly works and activities that hitherto have not had the recognition that they deserve.

HATSUE SHINOHARA is a professor of international relations at the Graduate School of Asia-Pacific Studies, Waseda University. Her work takes a multidisciplinary perspective involving law, history and politics.

US INTERNATIONAL LAWYERS IN THE INTERWAR YEARS

A forgotten crusade

HATSUE SHINOHARA

CAMBRIDGE
UNIVERSITY PRESS

CAMBRIDGE UNIVERSITY PRESS
Cambridge, New York, Melbourne, Madrid, Cape Town,
Singapore, São Paulo, Delhi, Mexico City

Cambridge University Press
The Edinburgh Building, Cambridge CB2 8RU, UK

Published in the United States of America by Cambridge University Press, New York

www.cambridge.org
Information on this title: www.cambridge.org/9781107016439

First published 2012

Printed and bound in the United Kingdom by the MPG Books Group

A catalogue record for this publication is available from the British Library

Library of Congress Cataloging in Publication data
Shinohara, Hatsue.
US international lawyers in the interwar years : a forgotten crusade / Hatsue Shinohara.
p.   cm.
Includes bibliographical references and index.
ISBN 978-1-107-01643-9 (hardback)
1. Lawyers – United States – History.   2. Practice of law – United States –History.
3. International law – United States – History.   I. Title.   II. Title: United States
international lawyers in the interwar years.
KF297.S43   2012
341.023′73–dc23   2012016082

ISBN 978-1-107-01643-9 Hardback

In Memory:
Robert William Adams
(1960–2000)

"What a fine mind, and truly original good character you have."

CONTENTS

ACKNOWLEDGMENTS

This work has had a long trajectory. My first encounter with Quincy Wright took place in spring 1983, when I entered the MA program of the School of Law, Waseda University, in Tokyo. The first text for our seminar that year was Wright's *A Study of War*. The interdisciplinary academic milieu of diplomatic history and international law at Waseda helped me to develop the basic academic backbone for this work. My sincere gratitude goes to Tokushiro Ohata, and my fellow students at that time.

However, I had not fully appreciated my background in legal studies – in fact I had felt it rather a burden in an academic atmosphere in which political science oriented IR was dominant – until I rediscovered Wright at the University of Chicago when I was searching for a dissertation topic in the fall of 1990. I was lucky enough to find that his manuscript collection was stored at the university's library. The first couple of days in its reading room were enough for me to decide resolutely to write about Wright and his time. Even to a young historian like me back then, the historical significance lying in his documents was compellingly obvious.

During the first stage of primary source collection, I was highly indebted to the American Society of International Law and in particular to Jill Watson, then Director of Library Services. Without her generous help in finding the Society's documents in the summer of 1991, this work could not have reached its current academic standard. She also kindly introduced me to the late Eleanor Finch, who shared with me her recollections of the period in question.

I wish to express my deepest appreciation to the great teachers I was able to study with at the University of Chicago. The late Barry D. Karl inspired me with his faith in the relevance of theories of social science for public policy, which led me to see the importance of the relationship between international law and foreign policy in the interwar years. Tetsuo Najita introduced me to the magnitude of intellectual history, where ideas have great power. And finally, my greatest intellectual debt goes to Akira Iriye, who, in particular, taught me that an important task for an international historian is to expand the field. His demand for a high academic standard taught me one should never be content with one's work, but should always strive to improve it.

For their hospitality and friendship during my stay in Chicago, I wish to express my sincere appreciation to Kate and Jim Ficke. They have helped me and supported me since the moment I first arrived at O'Hare Airport in 1984.

I am also deeply grateful to Tadashi Aruga for his valuable assistance in enabling the publication of an earlier Japanese version of this work in 2003. Without his kind help and warm sympathy, this work would have remained unpublished for good, and even worse it would have taken much longer for me to recover from a period of great loss and sorrow in my life. After its publication in Japan, to my happy surprise, it was welcomed by the international law community. I would like to express my gratitude to Shinya Murase and Akira Kotera for giving me the opportunity to expand my research on this topic, and also to Anthony Carty, who read the whole original English thesis version and gave me encouraging comments.

My special thanks go to Yasuaki Onuma. Not only did he support my interest and orientation, but also his commitment to the study of international law led me to the biannual meeting of the Asian Society of International Law held in Tokyo in the summer of 2009. There I had the fortunate opportunity to meet Martti Koskenniemi and Finola O'Sullivan, which incidentally opened the door leading to this publication. I am also indebted to Shiro Amano, who successfully recovered original digital data for me. Sayuri Guthrie-Shimizu, Bennett Richardson and Shuichi Okuda helped me in the preparatory stage of securing a contract with the publisher. I am also grateful to the anonymous reviewers and Shuichi Furuya for their valuable suggestions. Jeffrey Hall proofread, edited and improved the manuscript with his insights and thoroughness.

I have greatly benefitted from colleagues and students at Keisen Jogakuen College, Meijigakuin University and Waseda University, who have been the source of my intellectual inspiration and support as well as the basis for fulfillment in my professional life.

Throughout it all, my family and friends have supported me in numerous ways. Without their support, in particular during a very difficult time of my life, I would have given up my academic career. I am very grateful to my parents Kazutoyo and Yuko Shinohara, my sisters and their family as well as many other friends – friends such as Shoko Aoki and Sheila Hones.

Last but not least, I would like to thank my American family. My mother-in-law, Marolyn Adams, has always had faith in me. My ultimate debt, however, goes to my late husband, Bob Adams, who was the first reader of and commentator on this work. The original version of this work would never have been finished without his love and encouragement. Despite his passing, I could still sense his invisible guidance leading me to the completion of this work. Perhaps I am in part fulfilling his dream of having his own work published. To his memory I sincerely dedicate this book.

An initial version of Chapter 1 appeared in the *Japanese Journal of American Studies* 5 (1993–4), and that of Chapter 2 in the *Keisen Jogakuen College Bulletin* 6 (1994), while an earlier full version in Japanese, *Senso no Ho kara Heiwa no Ho he* [From the Law for War to the Law for Peace], was published by the University of Tokyo Press (2003).

Introduction

In July 1934, American ambassador to Japan Joseph C. Grew wrote to James Brown Scott, "The Journal [the *American Journal of International Law*] is to me invaluable, and always has been since it started in 1907." Scott was president of the American Society of International Law (hereafter ASIL) and was widely accepted as the dean of international law. This letter was written upon the suggestion of Stanley K. Hornbeck, chief of the Division of Far Eastern Affairs at the State Department. Grew explained, "Having recently had occasion to send to Dr. Hornbeck some pages of my diary, he particularly noticed in them a reference to the *American Journal of International Law* [hereafter *AJIL*], and he has suggested that the paragraph mentioned would be of interest to you." Grew went on to say that the journal "took up some three or four shelves in my library," and that he looked on them "with great pride, having had the annual issues handsomely bound in black leather." He then mentioned how helpful the journal was to his diplomatic service.[1]

The letter and Hornbeck's advice indicated that there existed a link between scholars of international law and policy makers, a relationship that may have been enhanced by the close proximity of their offices. At the time the ASIL was located across the street from the State Department. Officials of the State Department and members of the ASIL used to lend documents to each other and occasionally had lunch together.[2] Scott had once worked for the State Department as a solicitor. For experts in international law, it was not unusual to pursue careers both in academia and government.

---

[1] Joseph Grew to James Brown Scott, July 27, 1934, Papers of the American Society of International Law (hereafter ASIL Papers), American Society of International Law, Washington, DC.

[2] Interview with Eleanor H. Finch, July 13, 1991. She is a daughter of George A. Finch, who had worked for the ASIL from its foundation as Scott's indispensable assistant. Eleanor Finch also worked for the ASIL from 1929 to 1972. See R. R. Baxter, "The Retirement of Miss Eleanor H. Finch as an Assistant Editor of the *Journal*," *American Journal of International Law* (hereafter *AJIL*) 66 (1972), 815–816.

In 1951, George F. Kennan's famous book, *American Diplomacy 1900–1950*, contended that the moralistic and legalistic approach had failed American foreign policy, and in the years since, that approach has often been labeled negative, dogmatic and futile. Because of Kennan's criticism of what he perceived to be the unrealistic and illusory bases of legalism, later works tended to downplay and neglect the judicial aspects of international relations.[3] A typical example of this neglect can be seen in Robert Ferrel's account of the Kellogg–Briand Pact (the Pact of Paris). His *Peace in Their Time* argues that the Kellogg Pact was an illusion and that policy makers were taken in by a mistaken notion of peace.[4]

General disregard for the legalistic approach in the study of American foreign relations can be attributed not only to the emergence of realism that claimed the notion of power and interests should be primary to study international relations (IR), but also to a change in the position that the study of international law occupied in American academia before and after World War II. The establishment of international relations as an independent academic discipline and its separation from the discipline of international law (IL) is important in explaining the declining interest in the legal aspects of American foreign policy. Before World War II, the distinction between international law and international relations was not clearly established both institutionally and intellectually. In the postwar years, however, international relations – particularly in the United States – integrated more fully with political science, while international law was dropped from the curriculum of many colleges and universities and came to be taught primarily at law schools.[5] Hence, with a decrease in knowledge of international law among diplomatic historians, historical investigation in foreign affairs became less associated with legal approaches.[6]

The time is ripe for reconsidering and reevaluating "legalism" in American foreign policy. More than sixty years have passed since Kennan's book was published in 1951, at a time when Cold War thinking began to

---

[3] George F. Kennan, *American Diplomacy 1900–1950* (University of Chicago Press, 1951), p. 95.
[4] Robert Ferrel, *Peace in Their Time* (New Haven: Yale University Press, 1952). In contrast, Harold Josephson gives a more positive account on the Pact. See Josephson, "Outlawing War: Internationalism and the Pact of Paris," *Diplomatic History* 3 (1979), 377–390.
[5] See Ole Wæver, "The Sociology of a Not So International Discipline: American and European Developments in International Relations," *International Organization* 52 (1998), 687–727.
[6] Cf. Dorothy Ross briefly touched on the drift of some political scientists into the field of international law after World War I, but did not discuss why it happened. Dorothy Ross, *The Origins of American Social Science* (Cambridge University Press, 1991), p. 281.

overshadow the historiography of American foreign relations. Under the dominant current of realism, scholars have taken it for granted that such notions as power, interest and military strategy are the most appropriate concepts for discussing international affairs, and dependence on law and organization has been seen as naive. It is hard, however, to imagine that international society could exist without common rules or institutions. It is true that the Kellogg–Briand Pact could not prevent World War II, but by making war illegal it took away the legitimacy of waging war. It would be possible to assume that if it had not been for the Pact there would have been more wars, because the waging of war would have remained legal. In fact, contemporary academics who focus on the compound field between international relations and international law argue that the Pact "carries considerable normative weight" even though aggressive wars by fascist states violated it.[7] Hence, the legalistic approach should be given a more positive evaluation in the longer historical perspective. International law during that period played an important role in the formation of foreign policy and it was held to have more relevance than how it is viewed today. Kennan himself wrote about the preponderance of some "of the more ambitious American concepts of the role of international law," indicating that there indeed existed such a strong current.[8]

What influence did international law have on its contemporaries? What made international law more influential then? Was the dominance of international law evident in other countries as well? In answering these questions, I propose to address the ideas of international lawyers[9] and their activities by examining them *historically*. I will highlight the doctrine, theory, aspiration and effort of international lawyers. More specifically, the narrative is underpinned by three analytical themes. Firstly, it carefully and elaborately examines the discussions and activities of important international lawyers. Secondly, it scrutinizes the implications of their doctrinal arguments for foreign policy and state practices that formed an important basis for the establishment of international law, illuminating the role of international lawyers as social engineers. And finally,

---

[7] David Armstrong, Theo Farrell and Hélène Lambert, *International Law and International Relations* (Cambridge University Press, 2007), p. 118.

[8] Kennan, *American Diplomacy*, p. 95.

[9] A brief explanation of the term "international lawyer" might be necessary. Most of the international lawyers in my study were professors and not practicing lawyers. But, following the usage in previous historical works, I use the term broadly to include those who were engaged in the discussion of international law. Other descriptions such as "theorists," "scholars," "experts" and "professors of international law" are also used as synonymous with "international lawyers."

it will take a comparative perspective that contrasts American, European and Japanese discussions, and will examine whether the differences in academic discussions among countries had an impact on diplomatic relations. Each chapter will follow events and topics in a chronological order, covering the period roughly from the establishment of the ASIL in 1906 and the Second Hague Conference in 1907 to the immediate post-World War II period, and the three themes will serve as the framework through which the investigation is organized.

In tracing the development of these themes, I focus on the debates and exchanges of opinion that took place at the meetings of the ASIL,[10] at the Conference of Teachers of International Law and Related Subjects[11] and at the International Law Association as well as on books and articles published in academic journals and non-academic magazines. Additionally, unpublished materials – correspondences, memoirs and official documents – will help to reconstruct the time and space in which the international lawyers carried out their mission.

This book demonstrates that there was a group of international lawyers, mostly American but also some European and Japanese scholars, who worked to reform international law. This group began advocating a change in the focus of international law in the early 1910s, and their ideas began to gain currency after the experience of World War I. Progressive scholars, most notably Quincy Wright of the University of Chicago and Manley O. Hudson of Harvard Law School, regarded themselves as reformers and took a leading role in this movement by publishing their views, engaging in debates, writing letters to policy makers and major newspapers, and giving lectures to the public. These reformers attempted to establish a "new" international law, because they saw the traditional one, based on the premises of the nineteenth century, as irrelevant to the twentieth century. On the other hand, traditionalists found no fault with the old legal framework and instead noted the danger of carelessly transforming international law. This split emerged around World War I and continued to grow afterwards. Insofar as this study attempts to delineate their doctrinal discussions, it also provides an intellectual history of the ideas of war and peace, as epitomized in the discourse of one academic discipline.

---

[10] For the entire history of the ASIL, see Frederic L. Kirgis' meticulously researched account. Kirgis, *The American Society of International Law's First Century 1906–2006* (Leiden: Martinus Nijhoff Publishers, 2006).

[11] This conference was held in 1914, 1925, 1928, 1929, 1933, 1938, 1941 and 1946.

These ideas, however, did not remain closeted in academia, for the international lawyers discussed in this work were not content to merely analyze legal cases. They sought to mold their views into actual policies, for their theories, they thought, could contribute to establishing a peaceful world order. The ASIL was a good channel for that purpose since eminent public figures served as its presidents. Elihu Root (1906–24), Charles Evans Hughes (1924–9), James Brown Scott (1929–39) and Cordell Hull (1939–42) successively occupied the post of president.[12] While this study concentrates on the initiatives of the scholars toward policy making, a further investigation of how policy makers appreciated and accepted the theories may also be necessary to judge the actual influence. In particular, Henry L. Stimson and Hull were supporters of *new* international law, and their foreign policies occasionally utilized extracts of theoretical arguments.

The lawyers' intellectual engagement in the work in turn will shed light on theoretical discussions concerning the role of lawyers and their scholarship in presenting and disseminating a new norm in international law. This work will suggest that international lawyers can function as social agents, as demonstrated by the fact that they successfully promoted the Kellogg–Briand Pact, although that is not its primary and explicit theme.

Nor is it possible to assess the role of international lawyers properly without a comparative perspective, because international law does not exist in a single national context. The term comparative international law may sound contradictory, because "international" connotes a sense of universality and the establishment of universal principles in the relations among nations. However, I think a comparative perspective is necessary to analyze the real meaning of the term "international." If the attitude toward law in one country is different from that in another country, the understanding of international law becomes problematic. As Guillaume Sacriste and Antonie Vauchez maintained that international lawyers in the 1920s formed an "epistemic community," transnational understanding would be important for developing its normative basis.[13] The

---

[12] The American Society of International Law also had the offices of honorary president and honorary vice-president. Almost all ex-secretaries of state became either president, honorary president or honorary vice-president in prewar years. For the year 1928–9, the honorary president was Elihu Root, the president was Charles Evans Hughes, and the vice-presidents were William Taft, Frank Kellogg and Robert Lansing.

[13] Guillaume Sacriste and Antonie Vauchez, "The Force of International Law: Lawyers' Diplomacy on the International Scene in the 1920s," *Law and Social Inquiry* 32 (2007), 83–107.

relevance and feasibility of academic discussions on the establishment of rules among nations must be tested by determining whether other countries accept them.

In essence, this work narrates the story of a group of international lawyers who sought to reorient international law and ultimately reconstruct a new international order. A successful academic inquiry on this theme necessarily requires a multi- and inter-disciplinary approach that encompasses such academic fields as legal theory and history, diplomatic history, and law and politics in international relations.[14] Accordingly, it would be appropriate to divide the review of major previous works into four categories: works on respective lawyers, legalism and American foreign policy, intellectual-legal history, and lawyers as social engineers.

Although international lawyers seem to have been assigned a marginal position in postwar historiography on American foreign relations, there are several good works concerning them and the study of international law in the early twentieth century, particularly with regard to the implications of international law for American foreign policy and the American peace movement. Warren Kuehl's authoritative account of the development of internationalism up to the end of World War I touches upon the ideals of international law at the time,[15] while Roland Marchand describes the role of lawyers in the peace movement.[16] Calvin DeArmond Davis' books on the Hague Peace Conferences of 1899 and 1907 demonstrate clearly that the study of international law served as the theoretical underpinning of the two conferences.[17] Sondra Herman discusses the views of Elihu Root and Nicholas Butler.[18]

There is, however, a dearth of historical works dealing with a younger generation of international lawyers who were emerging at the time. This group included Wright, Hudson, Charles G. Fenwick and Edwin M. Borchard. They were not only professors of international law, but also

---

[14] See Anne-Marie Slaughter, Andrew S. Tulumello and Stepan Wood, "International Law and International Relations Theory: A New Generation of Interdisciplinary Scholarship," *AJIL* 92 (1998), 367–397; Armstrong *et al.*, *International Law and International Relations*.

[15] Warren Kuehl, *Seeking World Order* (Nashville: Vanderbilt University Press, 1969).

[16] Roland Marchand, *The American Peace Movement and Social Reform 1898–1918* (Princeton University Press, 1972), pp. 42–51.

[17] Calvin DeArmond Davis, *The United States and the First Hague Peace Conference* (Ithaca: Cornell University Press, 1962); *The United States and the Second Hague Peace Conference: American Diplomacy and International Organization 1899–1914* (Durham, NC: Duke University Press, 1975).

[18] Sondra R. Herman, *Eleven Against War* (Stanford: Hoover Institution Press, 1969).

activists who gave lectures before the public, testified before congressional hearings, and cultivated relationships with those in government. Their works and activities have cursorily been mentioned in some studies dealing with that era,[19] but in other studies they have been rather neglected.[20]

Significantly though, more works on the main figure of this study, Quincy Wright, have appeared. The *Journal of Conflict Resolution*, on his passing in 1970, dedicated a whole issue to Wright and his works, discussing a wide range of issues from his contribution to international law to his theory in international relations.[21] However, as the journal frankly acknowledged, this memorial issue handled the legal side of his contribution in a light fashion, presumably because the *AJIL* was reportedly planning a similar volume with more attention on the legal side. Yet, the *AJIL* never published that volume, while an obituary section in the *AJIL* was nothing more than normal coverage.[22] This may reflect how legal scholars in the 1970s evaluated his scholarship and contribution. Interestingly, recent scholars have rediscovered him as a source of academic inspiration and some works on Wright have been published. But in doing so, they have highlighted Wright's later scholarship with particular focus on his

---

[19] Robert Divine dealt with the discussions on neutrality among international lawyers. Divine, *The Illusion of Neutrality* (University of Chicago Press, 1962). He mentions that international lawyers were working on changing the conception of neutrality, but he does not fully explore the implications of this. Robert Schulzinger's *Making the Diplomatic Mind* (Middletown: Wesleyan University Press, 1975) refers to the importance of international law in training and for conduct of the foreign service. Manfred Lachs' *The Teacher in International Law* (The Hague: Martinus Nijhoff Publishers, 1982) has a brief survey of American as well as European professors of international law. As for individual international lawyers, there are some monographs. See James T. Kenny, "The Contributions of Manley O. Hudson to Modern International Law and Organization," unpublished Ph.D. thesis, University of Denver (1976). Wright has been treated as an heir to Wilsonianism in Loyd E. Ambrosius, *Woodrow Wilson and American Diplomatic Tradition* (Cambridge University Press, 1987), p. 8. For a published recollection of Wright's life and work, see John N. Hazard, "Quincy Wright," in Edward Shils, ed., *Remembering the University of Chicago* (University of Chicago Press, 1991), pp. 558–567.

[20] For example, Justus D. Doenecke's work on American opinion-makers and the Manchurian Incident, which covers such intellectuals as John Dewey and Walter Lippmann as well as religious and labor groups, hardly mentions international lawyers. Justus D. Doenecke, *When the Wicked Rise: American Opinion-Makers and the Manchurian Crisis of 1931–33* (Lewisburg: Bucknell University Press, 1984).

[21] In total, fifteen articles appeared in the memorial issue of the *Journal of Conflict Resolution*, including Inis L. Clude, Jr., "The Heritage of Quincy Wright," 461–464; Karl W. Deutsch, "Quincy Wrights's Contribution to the Study of War," 473–478; Kenneth W. Thompson, "Policy and Theory in Quincy Wright's International Relations," 479–486. See *Journal of Conflict Resolution* 14 (1970), 443–554.

[22] Eleanor H. Finch, "Quincy Wright," *AJIL* 65 (1971), 130–131.

accomplishment in postwar international relations. His thoughts and activities in the prewar period have yet to be fully investigated.[23]

Concerning the importance of legal thinking and legalism for American foreign policy, Jonathan Zasloff's recent works share the basic premise that my work originates from.[24] Zasloff was essentially right in pointing out that postwar historiography in diplomatic history has neglected the legal approach and that this was mostly due to the fact that diplomatic historians were rarely trained in legal history.[25]

Fortunately, I had had academic training in jurisprudence when I embarked upon this project in 1990, holding LLB and LLM. In Japan in general, and particularly so at the university I graduated from, diplomatic history was taught in the law schools. My favorite subjects as an undergraduate were such subjects as *Rechtsphilosphie* or Roman Law rather than positive law. As far as the legal training prerequisite for this subject is concerned, it is possible to claim that I have fulfilled the condition set by Zasloff.

Turning to Zasloff's main argument that classical legal thought influenced those "lawyer-diplomats" – Elihu Root, Charles Evans Hughes and Francis Kellogg, the major figures of my study – younger scholars – do not seem to easily fit into this school of thought. Rather, as will unfold in the following pages, they were determined to challenge their peers' legal theory and authority.

Scholars in the field of legal history, international relations and American diplomatic history have noted the existence of different schools among American international lawyers during the interwar years. David J. Bederman's work in the centennial volume of the *AJIL* argued that the

[23] Steven J. Bucklin, "Quincy Wright's Blueprint for a Durable Peace," *Mid-America* 76 (1994), 227–240; Robert J. Beck, "A Study of War and an Agenda for Peace: Reflections on the Contemporary Relevance of Quincy Wright's Plan for 'New International Order'," *Review of International Studies* 22 (1996), 119–147; Christopher Mark Davis, "War and Peace in a Multipolar World: A Critique of Quincy Wright's Institutional Analysis of the Interwar International System," *Journal of Strategic Studies* 19 (1996), 31–73; Robert P. Hillmann, "Quincy Wright and the Commission to Study the Organization of Peace," *Global Governance* 4 (1998), 485–499; Emily Hill Griggs, "A Realist Before 'Realism': Quincy Wright and the Study of International Politics between Two World Wars," *Journal of Strategic Studies* 24 (2001), 71–103.

[24] Jonathan Zasloff, "Law and the Shaping of American Foreign Policy: From the Gilded Age to the New Era," *New York University Law Review* 78 (2003), 239–373; "Law and the Shaping of American Foreign Policy: The Twenty Years' Crisis," *California Law Review* 77 (2003–4), 583–682; Richard H. Steinberg and Jonathan Zasloff, "Power and International Law," *AJIL* 100 (2006), 64–87.

[25] Zasloff, "Law and the Shaping: The Twenty Years' Crisis," 586.

interwar period enjoyed an "intense intellectual ferment in international law." He took an intellectual history approach to cover the main legal discussions held in the journal. The topics, legal arguments and personalities in his work in part overlap with the important lawyers and debates in my project. That in turn demonstrates that the leading actors in my work – Wright, Fenwick and Hudson – were neither insignificant nor obscure figures. For instance, he argued the Kellogg–Briand Pact and the Stimson Doctrine (Non-Recognition Doctrine) aroused debates among lawyers. However, Bederman does not distinguish these reformers from the earlier generation, either, and seems to argue that Scott and Wright belonged to the same school of thought.[26]

David Kennedy also traced the scholarly discourse among international lawyers in the United States, examining the significance of scholarly debates in the study of international law. He maintained that there were debates between different groups of scholars, and that some leading scholars emerged as central figures in presenting new ideas and principles. But his passages regarding the interwar years were short and general, and he did not discuss specific projects such as the Pact or the outlawry of war. He argued that there existed two schools in the interwar period – "positivists" as the mainstream and "naturalists" as their counterpoint. Yet, since he did not name any particular scholars, it is not clear that Kennedy's categories match the traditionalist–reformer dichotomy presented in this book. His argument that naturalists faded away after disappointment with the League of Nations and the Permanent Court of International Justice (PCIJ) does not seem to apply to Wright and his colleagues.[27] Mark Weston Janis' book also traces the American experience in international law, referring to Root, Scott and Woodrow Wilson and covering the topics on the League, but it does not give any particular mention to reformers.[28]

A diplomatic historian, David Schulzinger, also refers to the division among lawyers. James W. Garner and Hudson are described as idealists who argued for ethical international law, while John Bassett Moore

[26] David J. Bederman, "Appraising a Century of Scholarship in the *American Journal of International Law*," *AJIL* 100 (2006), 20–63, 59.

[27] David Kennedy, "When Renewal Repeats: Thinking Against the Box," *New York University Journal of International Law and Politics* 32 (2000), 403, 377–379.

[28] Mark Weston Janis, *America and the Law of Nations 1776–1939* (Oxford University Press, 2010), pp. 144–175, 194–220. See also, Janis, *The American Tradition of International Law* (Oxford University Press, 2004), pp. 134–154; Heiko Meiertöns, *The Doctrines of US Security Policy: An Evaluation under International Law* (Cambridge University Press, 2010), pp. 89–99.

and Ellery Stowell are described as realists. I believe, however, that these descriptions do not express the full content of these international lawyers' arguments.[29] On the other hand, Hidemi Suganami, a UK-based scholar of international relations, examined thinkers of international relations from the perspective of "domestic analogy." Although he did not specifically deal with American lawyers, Suganami touched upon figures such as Lassa Oppenheim, Thomas Baty and Borchard.[30] In Japanese academia, Yasuaki Onuma traced the gradual formation of the legal concept of *Senso Sekinin* [war responsibility] by examining the official state practices and academic discussions of the time and argued that the development itself was the manifestation of ideology supported by the Western powers.[31]

In short, this work will describe interwar American international lawyers in a somewhat different and more meticulous constellation of personalities, classifying and sorting out the debates and scholarship in the discipline. The reformer-traditionalist framework, which is in fact based upon the groups' self-identifications, will add a new dimension to the previously mentioned classifications of interwar lawyers' scholarship.

The final category of previous literature is concerned with the role of lawyers in developing international law, or in other words lawyers as social engineers in facilitating causes and norms for international law.[32] In this vein, my work follows the tradition of Martti Koskenniemi's widely acclaimed work, *Gentle Civilizer of Nations*.[33] In part, my work shares his interest in probing the ideas of modern legal thinkers. However, American scholars of the interwar period are not fully covered in the volume, while Koskenniemi deals with their contemporaries such as Hersch Lauterpacht, Karl Schmitt and Hans Morgenthau. It should also be noted that the international lawyers in my book are more than "gentle civilizers" because they were consciously and willfully committed to reform international law. They did not constitute an "invisible college" as Oscar

---

[29] Schulzinger, *Making*, pp. 35–37, 94.

[30] Hidemi Suganami, *The Domestic Analogy and World Order Proposals* (Cambridge University Press, 1989).

[31] Yasuaki Onuma, *Senso Sekinin-ron Jyosetu* [A Study on the Concept of War Responsibility] (University of Tokyo Press, 1975).

[32] Hedley Bull in his famous book has a short but independent section entitled "The Role of International Lawyer," in which he argued lawyers can play a role in strengthening international law. Bull, *The Anarchical Society: A Study of Order in World Politics* (New York: Columbia University Press, 2002), pp. 152–155.

[33] Martti Koskenniemi, *The Gentle Civilizer of Nations* (Cambridge University Press, 2001).

Schachter once argued, either, claiming that international lawyers could function as social engineers in formulating legal norms and facilitating the causes for international law.[34] The lawyers in this book formed a vocal and active group that believed the study of international law can and should contribute to building a more peaceful world. They were committed and dedicated activists.

Wilhelm Georg Grewe, in turn, discussed in his authoritative account on the history of international law the role that interwar international lawyers played in facilitating the cause for outlawry of war. According to his analysis, the interwar years formed a transitional period when Anglo-American influence in international affairs increased. Grewe argued that Anglo-American lawyers effectively developed the Covenant of the League, the Pact and the notion of aggression into the legal system on preventing and prohibiting war, specifically referring to the works by Wright, Arnold D. McNair and John Fischer Williams.[35] My work will provide a more expanded and lively version of this.

Thus, the following chapters will narrate and shed light on the crusading efforts and spirit of reform-minded scholars who have not fully been explored and appreciated so far.

---

[34] Oscar Schachter, "The Invisible College of International Lawyers," *Northwestern University Law Review* 72 (1977–8), 217–226.

[35] Wilhelm Georg Grewe, translated and revised by Michael Byers, *The Epochs of International Law* (Berlin and New York: Walter de Gruyter, 2000), pp. 585–598, 601, 620–624.

1

The rise of a new international law

The origins of the "new" international law can be traced to the period before World War I. It is impossible to specify exactly when it came to be formulated, but it had already emerged in the early years of the twentieth century.

One possible turning point was the Second Hague Conference of 1907. James Brown Scott, a representative traditionalist, wrote that the lawyers should not be disappointed with the alleged failure of the conference but look at the progress achieved and prepare for the next conference.[1] Paul S. Reinsch, on the other hand, was disturbed by the imperfect nature of the conference,[2] and afterwards some international lawyers began raising questions concerning the conventional approach to international law. The skeptical view became more popular after World War I started, with other younger international lawyers joining their forerunners.

The war was a decisive moment in the reconsideration of the relevance of existing international law. For younger lawyers, the failure of traditional international law appeared obvious because it had not prevented the war, while older, more established lawyers maintained their belief in the importance of the traditional approach. After the war, opinions about the future of international law were divided along these lines, and the division persisted throughout the interwar years.

Root, Scott and the American Society of International Law

The ASIL was established on January 12, 1906, with about 500 members.[3] It increased its membership to almost 1,000 by 1930 and included not only

---

[1] James Brown Scott, "The Work of the Second Hague Conference," *AJIL* 2 (1908), 1.
[2] Paul S. Reinsch, "Failure and Successes at the Second Hague Conference," *American Political Science Review* 2 (1908), 216.
[3] For the formative years of the ASIL, see Kirgis, *The American Society*, pp. 1–18; Carl Landauer, "The Ambivalence of Power: Launching the *American Journal of International*

scholars but also diplomats and others practicing international law. By far the most important contributors to its initial development were Elihu Root and Scott. Not only were they instrumental in laying the foundation for the Society, but their ideas played a central role during the first decade of the ASIL's existence.

Some knowledge of the initial stages of the organization is necessary to understand the vision shared by the founding members. The Society's origins can be traced to the May 1905 Lake Mohonk Conference, where, starting in 1895, people interested in promoting peace had gathered. At the time, arbitration was considered the most effective means of solving international disputes. The success of arbitration in settling the so-called Alabama claims between the United States and Great Britain in 1871 had sealed its popularity, and this success led to the First Hague Peace Conference, through which the Permanent Court of Arbitration was established. Because of the acclaim given to arbitration, which required a professional knowledge of law, many participants at the Lake Mohonk Conferences were lawyers. Their desire for deeper discussions provided the impetus to establish an independent professional organization concerned specifically with international law.[4] A motion to set up such a professional society was proposed by three participants: Scott; George Kirchway, Dean of the Columbia University Law School; and Robert Lansing, Associate Counsel on the Bering Sea Claims Commission.[5]

At the first meeting of the Society, Oscar Straus, who at the time was Secretary of Commerce and Labor, stressed the need to popularize international law. He remarked that the Society should be composed of specialists, but that discussions and papers should seek to create broad public interest. He cautioned that if the Society limited its outreach, it would "fail of its *raison d'être*, namely, to popularize and develop international law."[6] Straus' insistence on popularization helps to explain why Article 2 of the ASIL's constitution reads: "The object of this Society is to foster the study of international law and promote the establishment of international relations upon the basis of law and justice."[7] It is worth noting that the phrase "law and justice" had a special significance for the ASIL,

Law in an Era of Empire and Globalization," *Leiden Journal of International Law* 20 (2007), 325–358.

[4] Marchand, *The American Peace Movement and Social Reform*, pp. 42–51.

[5] "History of the Organization of the American Society of International Law," *Proceedings of the American Society of International Law* (hereafter *Proceedings, ASIL*) (1907), 23.

[6] *Ibid.*, 28.   [7] *Ibid.*, 1.

as shown by the fact that it is a translation of the Society's Latin motto. Although the first part of Article 2 – to enhance the study of international law – was a natural goal for an organization comprised of academics, the second part was political, reflecting a desire for law to serve as the guideline for international relations. This dual aim would influence how the ASIL developed.

Reflecting the high positions that the lawyers occupied in public service and the Society's inclination to influence public policy, many notable public figures were among the original members of the ASIL. The first president was Root, who had served as Secretary of the War Department (1899–1904) and of the State Department (1905–9) under President Theodore Roosevelt. Root remained president of the ASIL until 1924, and throughout his tenure he was one of the most vocal and indispensable figures in the development of international law. Other distinguished figures, such as Chief Justice Melvin W. Fuller of the United States Supreme Court, Andrew Carnegie and Judge George Gray also served as vice-presidents of the Society.

No less important for the ASIL than Root was Scott, who served as its secretary (1906–24), vice–president (1924–9), and then president (1929–39). Because of his devotion to the development of international law, he later came to be known as the "dean" of international law. Scott played a significant role in the publication of the Society's journal, which was based upon a plan that he had presented at the Lake Mohonk Conference. Due to a shortage of funds, Scott personally paid the expenses for the first two volumes, but the ASIL subsequently reimbursed him.[8] He then became a solicitor at the State Department (1906–11) under Root and joined the so-called "Root cult."[9] The close cooperation between Scott and Root was crucial to the development of the ASIL.

Before examining their ideas on international law it is important to observe that 1907, the year in which the ASIL held its first annual meeting and the *American Journal of International Law* (*AJIL*) was first published, was also the year of the Second Hague Conference. The two Hague Conferences served as important background to the early history of the ASIL. The First Hague Conference (1899) had adopted two principles to promote peace. One involved codifying the conduct of war to lessen

[8] George A. Finch, "The American Society of International Law 1906–1956," *AJIL* 50 (1956), 296. See also Bederman, "Appraising a Century," 21.
[9] For the relationship between Root and Scott, see Ralph Dingmann Nurnberger, "James Brown Scott, Peace through Justice," unpublished Ph.D. thesis, Georgetown University, (1975), pp. 139–142. See also Janis, *America and the Law of Nations*, pp. 144–157.

the scale of the calamity; the other pertained to settling international disputes judicially. The Permanent Court of Arbitration was established by the First Hague Conference, but it contained no provision for compulsory arbitration, a failing which supporters of the arbitration movement hoped to fix at the Second Hague Conference.

Root was Secretary of State at the time of the Second Hague Conference, and he appointed Scott as technical advisor to the US delegation. Scott was in charge of drafting the provision for the court proposal.[10] Although the Second Hague Conference also failed to approve a court with obligatory arbitration, the results of the conference were welcomed by advocates of arbitration and deemed to be a step toward a Third Hague Conference. In 1910 Scott founded a separate organization dedicated to promoting the cause of the judicial court – the American Society for the Judicial Settlement of International Disputes. The ASIL included other supporters of or delegates to the Hague Conferences, such as David Jayne Hill, an American delegate to both conferences, and Lansing, an ardent supporter of arbitration. The support of several advocates of the cause of settling international disputes judicially would become a crucial factor in the development of the ASIL.

Historians have labeled the positions of Root and Scott on international law "conservative."[11] An elitist view of law and society, an atomistic view of international society, and a judicial approach to international relations have been mentioned as the elements of their conservatism. Root's views derived from his political and social position. More specifically, Jonathan M. Zasloff argued that Root's thinking was colored by the ideology of "classical legal thought," which was based upon the premise that law as a neutral force could be separated from the political realm, and that law was the expression of community customs and could grow through a voluntary process.[12]

In "The Need of Popular Understanding of International Law," the lead article of the first issue of the *AJIL*, Root stressed that an understanding of international law among the public was important for carrying out successful foreign policies. With an increase of democratic control in foreign policy, statesmen and diplomats would have to consult the public to

[10] Davis, *The United States and the Second Hague Peace Conference*, pp. 251–276; Zasloff, "Law and the Shaping: From the Gilded Age," 286–368.

[11] Charles DeBenedetti, *Origins of the Modern American Peace Movement* (Millwood: KTO Press, 1978), p. 45; Herman, *Eleven Against War*, pp. 22–54.

[12] Steinberg and Zasloff, "Power and International Law," 65–66; Zasloff, "Law and the Shaping: From the Gilded Age," 255–257, 283–284.

receive approval of their policies.[13] He thought that if the public had sufficient knowledge and understood the rights and duties of their country
and of other countries, they would more deeply appreciate the results of
foreign policy.

Scott on his part advocated using the case method of instruction, which
he thought was "scientific and practical" because it probed the principles of law in real situations. In 1902, while Scott was at the University of
Illinois, he revised and published a casebook on international law, which
became so popular that it was reprinted the following year.[14] In a paper
stressing the need for the case method, Scott compared legal education
to the study of medicine. He argued that just as students of medicine
learned the functions of the body by studying anatomy "students of law
must take up the concrete case, examine it, discuss it, and decide it in the
light of theory." He contrasted this method with the boredom created by
lectures, where the student "listens and looks at the clock, and falls asleep
betimes."[15] Case-method instruction did not, however, become as widespread in international law as it did in other areas of jurisprudence.

Scott's view of the nature of international law can be seen more clearly
in his 1907 study entitled "The Legal Nature of International Law," in
which he refuted the position of John Austin, a famous scholar of jurisprudence who denied the legal standing of international law. Austin had
argued that law needed to be administered by a commonalty superior to
its subjects, but because international society was composed of independent states having no superior authority, the observation of international
law depended on the cooperation of each state. Even if a common court
were to be established, submission or withdrawal of cases would depend
upon the will of each state. Scott criticized this position as being too rigor-
ous. He cited the existence of common laws that developed out of accepted
customs and which were observed without sanction by a higher authority.
Eventually, some of these customs came to be accepted by courts and were
thus elevated to the position of common law. Because international law
had likewise been accepted by municipal courts, Scott concluded that it
qualified as law in the same sense that common law did.[16]

Scott's emphasis on the case method and on judicial process formed the
theoretical basis for his advocacy of an international court. If application

[13] Elihu Root, "The Need of Popular Understanding of International Law," *AJIL* 1 (1907),
1–4.
[14] Nurnberger, "James Brown Scott," p. 41.
[15] James Brown Scott, "The Study of Law," *American Law School Review* 2 (1906–7), 3–4.
[16] James Brown Scott, "The Legal Nature of International Law," *AJIL* 1 (1907), 834–850.

of international law by municipal courts sanctioned international law, then worldwide acceptance by international courts would be even better.

New and different views: Reinsch, Borchard and Fenwick

Although the views of Root and Scoot were prevalent among academics, there existed other views that caught the attention of other audiences. In particular, a younger generation of international lawyers with innovative ideas was beginning to emerge. Among them were Reinsch, Edwin M. Borchard and Charles G. Fenwick.

Reinsch, a professor at the University of Wisconsin, was labeled a progressive intellectual because of his desire to refute unrestrained individualism and laissez-faire economics and to see the restoration of values in society.[17] He compared the individual in domestic society to the sovereign state in international relations, and just as he argued for the need to control individualism in domestic society, he predicted that a time of interdependence was coming which would "gradually make national sovereignty obsolete." For Reinsch, the main principle of international law was upholding the "community of interests upon which the law must be based if it is to be respected."[18] He considered the nineteenth century a period of nationalism and saw the world moving toward internationalism, with bonds based upon internationalism already manifest in the growing number of international unions, such as postal unions, and other administrative agreements.[19]

Deploring the incompleteness of the Second Hague Conference, Reinsch described it as a product of nationalism. To overcome the atomistic nature of international relations and to enforce judicial decisions effectively, he stressed the need for international organization. "If the idea of legality is no longer dependent upon universal and specific recognition by every individual state, but may be determined by an international organ, then it is clear that we have entered upon a new stage in the development of international law."[20]

Borchard, law librarian at the Library of Congress (1911–13 and 1914–16), a solicitor for the Department of State (1913–14) and later a professor

[17] Noel Pugach, *Paul S. Reinsch, Open Door Diplomat in Action* (Millwood: KTO Press, 1979), p. 31.
[18] Paul S. Reinsch, "International Administrative Law and National Sovereignty," *AJIL* 3 (1909), 1–12.
[19] Paul S. Reinsch, "International Unions and their Administration," *AJIL* 1 (1907), 579.
[20] Reinsch, "Failure and Successes at the Second Hague Conference," 216.

at Yale Law School, sided with Reinsch's optimistic view of international progress. He wrote in 1911 that "this present century is to be one of international development" as demonstrated by the increase in commercial and industrial transactions among nations and by the growing solidity of international organizations.[21] Stressing the need to reject individualism and to revalue social collectivity, Borchard wrote that the "early nineteenth century's individualistic notions of liberty, contract and property had to yield to new interpretations impelled by the new conception of social solidarity."[22] In the realm of international law, such concepts as independence, sovereignty and territorial jurisdiction, which Borchard described as having a strongly "individualistic flavor," needed to be tempered by the "recognition of limitations created by the interests of other states and peoples." He was critical of the static nature of the positivistic approach to the study of law because its reliance on precedents limited the understanding of current problems. He wrote that "the traditional attitude of common law toward legislation indeed has often proved a serious obstacle to social progress."[23] Borchard thought Americans should follow the German example, which had successfully solved various social problems and which emphasized what law should be, rather than merely analyzing the current situation.

Fenwick, a lecturer at Washington College of Law, also published a critique of the dominance of the positivistic approach. In "The Authority of Vattel," published in the *American Political Science Review*, he called for a reappraisal of natural law. Early in the history of international law, Hugo Grotius, a seventeenth century jurist widely regarded as the father of international law, had stressed the balance between the natural and voluntary laws of nations, the latter representing positive law. In the nineteenth century, English and American writers departed from the Grotian school and formed the analytical positivist school, which focused on studying law as it then existed. Fenwick decried the state of the discipline, writing that "international law has now come to be regarded as consisting of the rules actually observed by nations, whether or not those rules embody the principles of justice which have come to be generally recognized."[24]

[21] Edwin M. Borchard, "The Legal Evolution of Peace," *American Law Review* 45 (1911), 712.
[22] Edwin M. Borchard, "Recent Developments in International and Municipal Law," *Law Library Journal* 10 (1917), 22.
[23] Edwin M. Borchard, ed., *Guide to Law and Legal Literature of Germany* (Washington, DC: GPO, 1912), p. 11.
[24] Charles G. Fenwick, "The Authority of Vattel," *American Political Science Review* 7 (1913), 405.

In 1914 Fenwick further elaborated his argument in "Two Representatives of the Grotian School" in which he dealt with two recent French treatises that emphasized Grotius' principle of the balance between the natural and voluntary laws of nations. Henry Bonfils and Frantz Despagnet had both stressed the need to test actual and positive international law to determine if it conforms with principles. Fenwick approved of their position because "They are not both content with merely stating the law but are ready to criticize it when it appears to them to be based upon principles not consistent with international morality." Fenwick called for a balance between rules actually in force and those that should be in force. He recommended translating the two works into English because they would be "a valuable addition to English and American textbooks, which are generally more concerned with practice than with theory."[25]

Taking into account these two views, the positivistic represented by Scott and the theoretical represented by Fenwick, what can be said about the general situation of the study of international law at that time? In 1913 a nationwide survey of colleges and universities in the United States was conducted by the Carnegie Endowment for International Peace to obtain information on how international law was being taught.[26] It asked about the departments in which the subject was taught, whether it was required or elective, who taught it, how many course-hours were offered, and what textbooks were used. The published report included lists of colleges and universities that taught and did not teach international law as well as of the instructors. Of the 613 institutions that responded to the survey, 244 claimed to offer courses in the subject.[27] Still, there was no agreement about whether international law should be taught as an independent discipline. At some universities it was confused with private international law or the conflict of laws, while at other universities it was often confused with the study of law in general, political science, or comparative constitutional law. Departments where international law was taught also varied and included those of history, political science, and law.

In regard to teaching methods, the report did not state a preference for the case method but only said that "it is fundamental that international law be considered as a system of jurisprudence, that its principles be treated as legal principles, and that their nature, application, and

---

[25] Charles G. Fenwick, "Two Representatives of the Grotian School," *AJIL* 8 (1914), 39–44.
[26] Carnegie Endowment for International Peace, *Report on the Teaching of International Law in the Educational Institutions of the United States* (n.p., 1913), p. 1.
[27] *Ibid.*, p. 2.

development be clearly shown." It also did not cite a preference for any particular textbooks, noting that any textbook might be used if it was ample and clear enough "to give the student an adequate idea of the origin, nature, and importance of international law."[28]

Despite indicating no preferences concerning methods and textbooks, the report concluded that it was necessary to improve the study of international law at institutions of higher education. It stated that in spite of the favorable impression given by the survey, a closer examination of the tables made it clear that "a relatively small number of students actually take the courses offered." At universities and colleges, those who did comprised only 3.9 percent of all students, while at law schools the figure was 15.5 percent.[29] The report offered several recommendations for enhancing the study of international law.

Following recommendations found in the Carnegie report, the ASIL sponsored the Conference of American Teachers of International Law in April 1914 to "increase and broaden instruction of international law." Invitations were distributed and about forty professors from all over the country participated, including not only such distinguished scholars as Scott and George G. Wilson of Harvard, but also young scholars, such as Stanley K. Hornbeck from the University of Wisconsin, who later became chief of the Far Eastern Division in the Department of State. The conference was divided into seven committees, with each committee discussing a different set of issues, such as how to increase interest in the study of international law or the desirability of adding a section on international law in state bar exams.[30]

Perhaps the most important topic discussed was "the placing of instruction in international law on a more uniform and scientific basis," which necessarily involved setting general guidelines for the study. The subcommittee that discussed this subject presented a resolution stating that "In the teaching of international law emphasis should be laid upon the *positive* [italics added] nature of the subject and the definiteness of the rules" and that the "widest possible use should be made of *cases* [italics added] and concrete facts." It therefore explicitly supported the case method and the positivist approach. Although not an official delegate, Fenwick was given permission to speak during the general discussion. He argued that a distinction should be made between law

[28] *Ibid.*, pp. 32–33.   [29] *Ibid.*, p. 29.
[30] For a list of the participants at this conference, see *Conference of American Teachers of International Law* (Washington, DC: Byron S. Adams, 1914), pp. 8–9.

schools and political science departments and that it would be a mistake to place too much emphasis on the case method in the courses taught in departments of political science because "a large part of international law never comes before the court"[31] and because students would not receive an adequate breadth of knowledge if they were only taught by the case method.

Despite Fenwick's opposition, the resolution was adopted without any changes and the Conference ended with a declaration of the importance of the case method and of the positivist approach. The resolution manifested the prevalence of the positivist school and showed disregard for theoretical approaches, but it was doomed to be cast aside. In Fenwick's words, "a rude awakening came with the month of August 1914," and, a mere three months after the Conference closed, international law faced "a crisis in its development."[32] War had started in Europe.

World War I and division

The outbreak of war in Europe was a shock to many international lawyers. In April 1915 at the annual meeting of the ASIL, Root remarked that the entire structure of international law had been "rudely shaken." The fundamentals on which the laws of war were based had been destroyed by an escalation in the destructiveness of warfare and by the introduction of new technology. Root even remarked that a "nation will observe law only when national interest prevails." He was pessimistic about the future of international law, saying that the civilized world would have to determine "whether what we call international law is to be continued as a mere code of etiquette, or is to be a real body of laws imposing obligations much more definite and inevitable than they have been heretofore."[33]

This sense of crisis was shared by many members of the ASIL and led to vigorous discussion about international law at the annual meetings of 1916 and 1917. As the war in Europe dragged on, numerous violations of international law were reported, and since the United States had increased its trade with the Allies, the idea of American neutrality was called into question. Under these circumstances, views emerged that were skeptical of the old rules of international law.

---

[31] *Ibid.*, pp. 23, 41–42.
[32] Charles G. Fenwick, "The Sources of International Law," *Michigan Law Review* 16 (1918), 393.
[33] Elihu Root, "The Outlook for International Law," *Proceedings, ASIL* (1915), 2.

During the discussion at the annual meeting in 1916, both of the assigned speakers were critical of the traditional concept of neutrality, according to which neutral countries were entitled to continue selling arms and munitions to belligerents. James Wilford Garner of the University of Illinois raised questions about the ethics of this practice. He charged that the United States was "a party to the war across the ocean" because it was furnishing arms. He noted the contradiction in the attitude of most Americans, who went to church to pray for peace on Sundays while they produced arms to export on weekdays. He concluded by asking why "a double standard of conduct" was maintained.[34]

Professor Philip Marshall Brown of Princeton University, on the other hand, remarked that the system of neutrality contradicted the view which regarded the world as one body. "Under modern conditions of easy intercommunication," he argued, "no great nation can affect a selfish indifference to the interests of other nations, whether in times of peace or times of war." Rather than sticking to the old view of neutrality, he recommended the principles enunciated by a newly established organization, the League to Enforce Peace, which supported the collective use of force against aggressors. Brown described this as "a frank abandonment of the idea of neutrality" and stressed that neutral nations were obliged to judge which nation was the aggressor and then to unite against it.[35]

Brown's paper completely rejected the idea of neutrality and argued strongly that all countries had an interest in any war. This viewpoint was debated again at the next meeting held in 1917. That meeting opened three weeks after the United States declared war against Germany, and it was natural that US entry into the war would lead the way to discussions about the future possibilities of international organization. Fenwick, Scott and William C. Dennis presented papers on this topic. While Fenwick and Dennis lent their support to a new international organization, Scott vehemently defended his opposition to the establishment of any such organization.

Although the topic assigned to Fenwick was "International Organization: Judicial," he emphasized administrative issues. Stating that a league of nations would be indispensable for securing peace in the world, he argued that it should be more expansive than the Second Hague

---

[34] James Wilford Garner, "Some True and False Conceptions Regarding the Duty of Neutrals in Respect to the Sale and Exportation of Arms and Munitions to Belligerents," *Proceedings, ASIL* (1916), 19–31.

[35] Philip Marshall Brown, "Munitions and Neutrality," *Proceedings, ASIL* (1916), 33–42.

Conference. He also saw the need for intimate connections between an international judicial organization and an international executive body, because the latter should "compel the parties to come before the court, and see to the execution of the award when rendered."[36]

Dennis favored allowing the envisioned international organization to use force when necessary, and quoted Lord Balfour of England: "If existing treaties are no more than scraps of paper, can fresh treaties help us? ... Law is not enough; behind law there must be power." Dennis was an ardent supporter of the League to Enforce Peace, an internationalist organization established in 1915 as a first step toward establishing a world organization, and he too held that any war was of concern to every nation: "It is no longer a mere figure of speech to say that no nation can break the peace without endangering the peace of every other nation."[37]

In rebuttal, Scott launched an attack on the idea of establishing any international organization that would be based on the proposals of the League to Enforce Peace. He began by stating that his "purpose is not to quarrel with the League to Enforce Peace," but to enunciate complete opposition to it. He doubted whether a unity of mind or an agreement among all nations was possible, arguing that "nations have insisted on living up to agreements when in harmony with their interests, and they have not lived up to them when they have not been to their interest." The reason, for example, that Great Britain went to war for Belgium but not for Serbia was that there was "an interest which appealed to Great Britain" in helping the former. He believed that national interest was in the long run the primary concern of all nations.[38]

Scott returned to his favorite theme – the importance of education. The solution to international problems was not "to draw the sword, but a process of education." He admitted that this would take time, "winning over one generation, winning over another generation, and another generation ... until justice shall be the great interest of the world." The abolition of war would depend upon the power of reason over force: "Little by little, the powers of reason have won over the powers of darkness, the cause of justice has triumphed over physical force." By justice he meant the act of

---

[36] Charles G. Fenwick, "International Organization, Judicial," *Proceedings, ASIL* (1917), 64–75.

[37] William C. Dennis, "International Organization, Executive and Administrative," *Proceedings, ASIL* (1917), 92–101.

[38] James Brown Scott, "International Organization, Executive and Administrative," *Proceedings, ASIL* (1917), 104.

being judged by a court, and he went so far as to write that "the judgment of a court of justice is almost self-executing."[39]

Scott's paper was not received favorably, and many opinions against it were aired in the ensuing discussion. C. D. Pugsley pointed out a contradiction in the reasoning. Scott had said that the decisions of an international court would be self-executing and that countries would observe those decisions. At the same time, however, he had argued that nations acted only out of self-interest and cited examples from history. Pugsley argued that since the world was experiencing a period of nationalism, it would take a while to establish a common ideal through education, and that a league with some joint force to enforce its decisions would be necessary for the time being.[40] Hornbeck concurred, stating that the threat of sanctions would be required: "Force behind the law will make the law effective, but I cannot conceive that mere instruction will cause all peoples to be law-abiding."[41] Scott responded by pointing out the need to establish a general standard. He noted that there had been a change in the standards of humankind and added that "if that public opinion is not created, treaties are scraps of paper, judged by the history of the past."[42]

The criticism of Scott's views at the 1917 meeting might have been one of the factors that led to the canceling of the next three annual meetings.[43] From 1918 to 1920, the ASIL held only executive council meetings. Discussions on international affairs were conducted and published in the form of proceedings to inform other members of the executive council's ideas about the international situation. With only Root, Scott and other senior members present, these discussions reflected a conservative attitude toward international organization and the prospects for the postwar years.

By this time a division clearly existed between supporters and opponents of the League to Enforce Peace. The opponents were mostly advocates of the Hague Conferences and, not surprisingly, given their long adherence to the Hague system of an international court, Root and Scott were among the leading critics. Scott, in fact, was considered to be the biggest obstacle for the League to Enforce Peace.[44] Robert Lansing, then Secretary of State under President Woodrow Wilson and an active member of the ASIL from its inception, was another conspicuous advocate

---

[39] *Ibid.*, 106.   [40] C. D. Pugsley, "Discussion," *Proceedings, ASIL* (1917), 118.
[41] Stanley K. Hornbeck, "Discussion," *Proceedings, ASIL* (1917), 123–124.
[42] *Ibid.*, 122.   [43] See also Kirgis, *The American Society*, pp. 55–58.
[44] Martin Dubin, "The Carnegie Endowment for International Peace and the Advocacy of a League of Nations 1914–1918," *Proceedings of the American Philosophical Society* 123 (1979), 349, 364.

of the Hague system. He had appointed Scott as technical advisor to the American delegation at the Paris Peace Conference, where Scott drafted a peace treaty under his direction that incorporated the ideas of the Hague Conferences.[45] President Wilson, however, endorsed using military or economic force against law breakers and constantly opposed judicial procedures to settle international disputes. Wilson more than once deleted the section on judicial organization from the draft.[46]

The record of the ASIL executive council meeting held on April 19, 1919, vividly reflects the frustration among the participants concerning the plans for peace. Root took the lead by expressing his opposition to the League of Nations. He said that "international law was mentioned in the preamble and never mentioned again. Apparently the whole Hague system was treated as scrapped." John H. Latené deplored the neglect of the Hague Conferences and referred to the opinion of a friend, who told him that "the Hague Conferences had been a complete failure, because the Hague system could not avoid the outbreak of war" and that "accordingly, reference to international law and to the Hague Court had been purposely omitted." David Jayne Hill pointed out the implications of establishing the League while ignoring the tradition of the Hague Conferences, saying that to scrap them was "to repudiate the whole conception of international law." According to Hill, "there was nothing binding at all in the Covenant," and the League would not make law but "just crystallize policies." Root mentioned two proposed amendments to the Covenant of the League of Nations that he had cabled to Lansing in Paris.[47] The first provided that "the high contracting powers agree to refer to the existing Permanent Court of Arbitration at the Hague," and the other called for a convention of the powers to deal with the status of international law.[48]

But while the leaders of the ASIL were hoping to maintain the tradition of the Hague system and were critical of the League of Nations, other scholars of international law were striving to promote the League to Enforce Peace and the League of Nations. World War I served to crystallize emerging philosophical differences. Moreover, developments after the war that led to the establishment of an international organization forced each member to clarify his position.

[45] *Ibid.*, 367; David Hunter Miller, *The Drafting of the Covenant*, vol. 1 (New York: G. P. Putnam's Sons, 1928), pp. 32–33.
[46] For the differences between the two groups at the conference, see Davis, *The United States and the Second*, pp. 330–368; Dubin, "The Carnegie Endowment," 359, 367.
[47] "Minutes of the Meeting of the Executive Council," *Proceedings, ASIL* (1919), 45–62.
[48] Miller, *Drafting*, vol. 1, pp. 377–382.

Rising stars from the war era: Garner and Wright

Garner had been critical of neutrality at the ASIL meeting in 1916 and had established himself during the course of the war as the most notable opponent of current international law. Although Garner had been a distinguished political scientist, he was a relative newcomer to the study of international law. Before the war broke out, his main interests had not been in international affairs. His specialty was comparative government, with a particular interest in the government of France, but the war changed the course of his studies and he gave all his materials on comparative government to a colleague. From that time on he devoted himself to writing, teaching and speaking about international law. In the 1920s and 1930s he traveled extensively – including to Europe, China and Japan – to speak about the cause of peace and international law.[49]

Garner sided with the League to Enforce Peace and authored a leaflet for its Illinois branch, in which he stressed the importance of the United States accepting its share of responsibility in world affairs. Among the duties of great nations, he said, was serving as "the trustees of our common civilization and the guardians of the general peace," and hence Americans should not "withdraw into their shells and maintain an attitude of indifference." He also contended that the Covenant of the League of Nations did not contradict American adherence to the Monroe Doctrine.[50]

In 1920 Garner published a two-volume study entitled *International Law and World War*, which was hailed as a monumental contribution to the field. Favorable reviews appeared not only in American and British journals, but also in French and German ones, and the work sold so well it was reprinted and its price was reduced from $25 to $15. In it he detailed the applications and violations of international law and concluded that "the whole system of international law itself has been rudely shaken to its very foundations" because many of the rules of war were "inadequate, illogical, or inapplicable."[51] Garner cited the need for an obligatory international court at some time in the future, but he also stated that it was important to have an international organization for enforcement.

---

[49] John A. Fairlie, "Studies in Government and International Law by James Wilford Garner," Papers of James Wilford Garner (hereafter Garner Papers), University Archives, University of Illinois, Urbana, Illinois.

[50] James Wilford Garner, *The League of Nations and the Monroe Doctrine* (Chicago: League to Enforce Peace, Illinois Branch, n.d.), 4, Garner Papers.

[51] James Wilford Garner, *International Law and the World War* (London: Longmans, Green, 1920), p. 452.

More importantly, he emphasized changing attitudes toward international conflict. He wrote that although the traditional tendency among countries not engaged in a conflict was to remain neutral, every nation should be concerned with violations of law. He asserted that "the making of war, except in case of self-defense, should be declared illegal and the disputants should be restrained by the joint action of the body of States from attacking each other and thereby disturbing the general peace."[52] This position would develop into support for the idea of the "outlawry of war," which would become significant later in the 1920s, and for the idea of "collective security."

Garner trained many students in the study of international law, but perhaps most notable among them was Quincy Wright. When the war in Europe started, Wright was working on his doctoral dissertation, "The Enforcement of International Law through Municipal Law in the United States," which was completed in 1915 and described by Garner as "one of the most thorough and scholarly works."[53] Analyzing the history of how international law had been enforced by municipal law, Wright went beyond mere case analysis and tried to clarify the relationship between the two types of law.

Wright asked Scott about the possibility of publishing his dissertation through an arrangement with the Carnegie Endowment, but Scott suggested that publishing the entire work would be difficult, and instead offered to publish one chapter in the *AJIL*.[54] Thus "The Legal Nature of Treaties" was published in November 1916 as the first of 515 articles that Wright published during his lifetime.[55] In it he asserted that there existed a contradiction between the power to ratify treaties and the power to put them into effect, which was caused not only by the American constitutional system of government, with its division of powers between executive and legislative branches, but also by changes in the nature of treaties themselves. Treaties had formerly only specified the conduct of states – for example, cession of territories – but with the development of communications and increase in transactions involving peoples and goods, treaties had gradually come to deal also with the rights of individuals. Such new treaties required administrative, legislative and judicial enforcement.[56]

---

[52] *Ibid.*, p. 466.
[53] Garner to Wright, March 22, 1916, Papers of Quincy Wright (hereafter Wright Papers), Joseph Regenstein Library, University of Chicago, Chicago, Box 18, Folder 4.
[54] Scott to Wright, July 10, 1916, Wright Papers, Box 18, Folder 5.
[55] Lachs, *The Teacher in International Law*, p. 119.
[56] Quincy Wright, "The Legal Nature of Treaties," *AJIL* 10 (1916), 706–736.

From 1916 to 1919, Wright was an instructor of international law at Harvard University, the president of which, Abbott Lawrence Lowell, had been one of the founders of the League to Enforce Peace. Wright culti- vated an acquaintanceship with Lowell and came to support the cause. In particular, he defended Article 10 of the League of Nations Covenant, which specified the territorial integrity and political independence of states. In April 1919, as debate about the Covenant intensified in the press, he criticized the *New Republic*'s stand against the League in a letter to a friend, noting that its "condemnation of Art. 10 has got my goat." In the same letter, he also referred to Walter Lippmann's critique of Article 10, saying, "I am unable to see how a guarantee against 'external aggression' can be read as a guarantee of the territorial *status quo*."[57]

In 1919 Wright began to teach at the University of Minnesota, and dur- ing his stay there he wrote prolifically. His interests focused on two topics. One was the new awareness of international law that had emerged dur- ing and after World War I, including issues such as how to interpret the League of Nations and the effect of war on international law. In 1919 he published an article entitled "Effects of the League of Nations Covenant" in which he praised the Covenant because it indicated that "a shifting of emphasis from rights of state to responsibilities of state is the fundamen- tal change of international law."[58] In another paper on the effect of war, he repeatedly used phrases such as the "interest of the family of nations," and he emphasized the need for a change in international law from laws governing war to laws governing peace.[59]

Wright's contention that the world was becoming integrated into a family of nations led naturally to his other primary concern: how to ensure domestic enforcement of international agreements. This had been a theme of his dissertation, and during the winter of 1920, when the Treaty of Versailles had still not been ratified by the Senate, the question of whether the American system was appropriate for control- ling foreign relations was at "the forefront of everyone's mind." Wright forged his ideas on this into a paper presented to the American Political Science Association in February 1920 and later published in the *American Political Science Review*. His expanded treatise was awarded the Henry

---

[57] Wright to Pittman Potter, April 13, 1919, Wright Papers, Box 18, Folder 8.
[58] Quincy Wright, "Effects of the League of Nations Covenant," *American Political Science Review* 13 (1919), 558.
[59] Quincy Wright, "The Effect of the War on International Law," *Minnesota Law Review* 5 (May 1921), 457, (June 1921), 517.

M. Phillips Prize by the American Philosophical Society in April 1921 and published as *Control of American Foreign Policy* the next year. Wright sought to find a way to avoid friction with Congress and concluded that "under present conditions we must frankly recognize executive leadership in foreign affairs," but only "after the most careful consideration possible." As concrete proposals, he suggested that the departments concerned with foreign policy deepen their understanding and that Congress declare permanent policies.[60]

Introduced to the field of international law during World War I, Garner and Wright flourished in the interwar period as they elaborated a theory that aimed to prevent war and organize the world into a collective framework.

Reconstruction or departure: the Committee for the Advancement of International Law

After the war, the members of the ASIL became settled in their different views of international law. A conflict developed over the question of whether international law should continue to be taught using some method based on the Hague system or whether that system should be discarded altogether and fresh approaches tried. Discussion was focused in the Committee for the Advancement of International Law, which was the product of an initiative of the League of Nations.

Although the Covenant of the League of Nations did not mention anything about the Hague Conferences, Article 14 provided that "the Council shall formulate and submit to the Members of the League for adoption plans for the establishment of a Permanent Court of International Justice." Based on this article, the Council of the League of Nations issued an invitation in February 1920 to international jurists from various countries to discuss plans for a Permanent Court of International Justice (hereafter PCIJ). Root was invited,[61] and in the summer of 1920 the committee met in The Hague. Generally referred to as the Committee of Jurists, it adopted a report on establishing a permanent court of international justice and passed a resolution calling for periodic conferences for the advancement of international law. The resolution provided that "a new conference of the

---

[60] Quincy Wright, *The Control of American Foreign Relations* (New York: Macmillan, 1922), pp. ix, 370.
[61] Root to Eric Drummond, March 11, 1920, [C]. 20/4/46. [V], Document of the League of Nations, microfilm edition (hereafter DLN).

nations in continuation of the first two conferences at The Hague be held as soon as practicable."[62]

In the fall of 1920, Scott, who had returned from Paris, began working to resume the annual meetings of the ASIL. When preparing for the meeting of the Executive Council that same fall, he informed Root of his preference for topics and wrote that the members of the Executive Council should discuss "various international events, particularly the project for the International Court of Justice and the services which periodic conferences in continuation of The Hague Peace Conferences might render."[63]

A meeting of the Executive Council was held on November 13. Root explained the activities of the Committee of Jurists at The Hague and support was given to the idea of resuming the Hague Conferences. Lansing, who had declared that "the maintenance of individualism among nations was the very life blood of modern civilization" at a meeting of the American Bar Association in early September that year, was completely against the League. He stressed that the project recommended by the Committee of Jurists had "nothing to do with the League of Nations" and was rather a separate conference that was "entirely distinct ... entirely in line with the ancient order of the Hague Peace Conference." Admiral Stockton expressed his relief by saying, "It seems to me a very happy thought in this resolution that its recommendation is rather in the nature of a continuation of the consideration of the first two conferences at The Hague."[64]

Scott began to prepare for the next annual meeting of the ASIL based on the recommendations of the Committee of Jurists by attempting to convince members of the importance of establishing the PCIJ. When asking Root to contribute the lead article for the January 1921 issue of the *AJIL*, Scott wrote with typical but somewhat excessive eloquence:

> Nothing would be, nothing could be, more timely than an article on the Permanent Court of International Justice. It would be peculiarly appropriate, as you know, from the pen of the statesman who directed and planned for such an institution to be laid before the Second Peace Conference at The Hague and who, thirteen years later, was privileged to put the finishing touches to the project drafted at a conference in pursuance of his instructions. More I cannot say; less would not be the truth.[65]

---

[62] "Resumption of Annual Meeting of Society," *Proceedings, ASIL* (1920), 15.
[63] Scott to Root, October 20, 1920, ASIL Papers.
[64] *Proceedings, ASIL* (1920), 15–35.
[65] Scott to Root, November 19, 1920, ASIL Papers.

Scott organized the participants of the committee into four groups and chose chairmen to lead discussions about the different topics in the resolution: restating the old rules, amending and adding to established rules, reconciling divergent views, and new regulations in international law. Each member was to submit his ideas before the meeting, and each committee would discuss its final conclusion at the ASIL meeting. The chairmen were Reinsch, ex-minister to China; Charles Noble Gregory, formerly dean of the Department of Law at George Washington University; Harry Pratt Judson, the president of the University of Chicago; and Simeon E. Baldwin, a former governor of Connecticut.[66]

Root gave the opening address at the 1921 meeting, stressing the importance of establishing the PCIJ and of codifying international law.[67] The Committee for the Advancement of International Law was organized according to Scott's guidelines, but it was not particularly successful because of the difficulty of dealing with such diverse problems in strictly divided groups. Worse yet, some members expressed their doubts about the rationale behind the project itself. Reinsch candidly stated that in his committee "a strong feeling was expressed that it would not be desirable for the emphasis of the action of the Society to be placed entirely or even primarily on the rules of war or laws of war." A similar opinion was expressed by Judson who declared "I confess I feel not to be very much interested after all to amend the rules of international law," and Fenwick remarked that "We have not discussed at this meeting the question of international organization. The process of extending international law by judicial decision is very slow." Fenwick also admitted to entertaining "disappointment which has already been expressed by others that so many of our papers have dealt with the reform of the laws of war."[68]

Despite the complaints about the general orientation of the Committee for the Advancement of International Law, however, the following year's program was also designed to deal exclusively with the laws of war. When Albert Bushnell Hart of Harvard University saw the program in late March, a month before the meeting, he complained in a letter to Scott that "I am not the only one who feels that the Society is too much personally conducted and that its Proceedings are too much confined to long

---

[66] See Scott to Paul Reinsch, March 24, 1921, March 31, 1921; Scott to Harry Pratt Judson, April 1, 1921, ASIL Papers. See also Kirgis, *The American Society*, pp. 59–66.

[67] Elihu Root, "Opening Address," *Proceedings, ASIL* (1921), 1–13. See also Kirgis, *The American Society*, pp. 61–62.

[68] "Meetings of the Committee for the Advancement of International Law," *ASIL, Proceedings* (1921), 89, 95.

and often very juiceless papers." Hart had also expressed the opinion that
"most of the papers seem to me to hark back to a stage of the world in
which we no longer live," and he had complained about the extravagant
cost, $7, of the yearly banquet and about the attitude of the lawyers in the
Society.[69] Scott invited him in a telegram to "Come, give us juice and eat
with us,"[70] but Hart replied "I confess that Advancement of International
Law does not seem to me likely to be reached by committee meetings or
reports."[71] Hart's premonition was destined to be fulfilled.

At the beginning of the 1922 meeting of the Committee, Root restated
his belief in the importance of the project. Although the League had, for
the moment, declined to act on the proposal for a conference on international law, preparations by the Society were necessary, he said, because
"The Hague Conference would not have been able to do anything if the
work had not been done beforehand."[72] The topics that the Committee
was to deal with concerned the laws of war: "Visit, Search and Capture,"
"Status of Government Vessels," "Problems of Maritime Warfare" and
"Offenses Which May Be Characterized as International Crimes and
Procedures for Their Prevention."

Not surprisingly, the discussion proceeded exactly the same way it had
the previous year. Again, but this time more assertively and vehemently,
Fenwick attacked the topics. He remarked, "We have discussed war, war,
war, war, under each subheading," and he argued that the topics were
scarcely "worth discussion" because, as shown by the experience of World
War I and clearly demonstrated by Garner's book, the Hague Conference
had tried to legislate rules of war but "it absolutely failed." Fenwick reiterated his position by saying "I feel that our attention should be devoted to
the constructive side of international law. The most vital problem before
the world today is the problem of international organization." Jackson H.
Ralston then indicated the fundamental problem in the general orientation of the study of international law, which was that "we stumble about
what is practice." Many scholars had discussed, for instance, the conditions of contraband, but they had never questioned whether contraband
itself was legal. Referring to the example of prisoners of war, Ralston indicated the inherently contradictory nature of the laws of war: "You cannot kill wounded prisoners. How utterly absurd! One instant you have a

<hr />

[69]   Albert Bushnell Hart to Scott, March 28, 1922, ASIL Papers.
[70]   Scott to Hart, March 3, 1922, ASIL Papers.
[71]   Hart to Scott, April 5, 1922, ASIL Papers.
[72]   "Meeting of the Committee for the Advancement of International Law," *Proceedings,
ASIL* (1922), 38.

right to wound a man, you have a right to kill him, and the next instant, he being wounded and you capturing him, you have no right to kill him, perfectly absurd. "[73]

Hill, a veteran of the Hague Conferences, replied to these criticisms by stressing that chaos and anarchy were conspicuous in international society and that "war has existed, may exist, probably will exist, if it is not averted." He noted that until human beings abolished war, there was "no hope of international organization," and that because war in the future was inevitable, "we should discuss the belligerents' rights." Hill argued for the benefits of the type of neutrality that the United States had practiced previously and which involved preserving trading interests with belligerents without getting involved in their wars. Fenwick countered by stressing the growing perception of common interests among nations and said that "the common interests of the nations are bigger than their mutual differences."[74]

At the end of the session, Arthur Kuhn, once a legal specialist for the Paris representatives of the League to Enforce Peace, suggested in a resolution that the Committee consider "the feasibility of some international organization as a means of conducting the international relations of states, in which the United States may properly cooperate." Scott, however, requested that this not be adopted because it "appealed to the political power of the government." It was the last time that Scott would be able to resist the Fenwick group.[75]

In April 1923 the triumph of Fenwick and his supporters was unmistakably manifested in the list of speakers for the session on the orientation of international law. The title of the session itself was changed to "The Existing State of International Law, its Bases, its Scope, and its Practical Effectiveness, Together with Constructive Suggestions for its Extension into New Fields." The first speaker was Fenwick, followed by Manley O. Hudson and Borchard.

In his presentation, Fenwick mentioned that for the last two years the laws of war had been stressed but "no adequate study has been given to the laws of peace." He hoped to correct that deficiency by suggesting possibilities for future development in international law: the need of collective responsibility among the states, the necessity of an international legislature, and the codification of laws. Above all, he emphasized that international law should also take into consideration international

---

[73] "Consideration of Reports of the Subcommittees," *Proceedings, ASIL* (1922), 85, 88.
[74] *Ibid.*, 89.   [75] *Ibid.*, 92.

economic relations. He argued in favor of widening its scope, stating that "the history of international law in the past shows the gradual widening of its scope to include questions which were at one time regarded as purely political."[76]

Hudson, a professor of international law at Harvard Law School, had been a member of the inquiry under Colonel Edward House and a legal advisor to the American delegation to the Paris Peace Conference. Hudson became an advocate of the PCIJ in the following decades, though he did not regard it merely as a continuation of the Hague Conferences but as one of many international organizations to support peace. He also stressed the need for a change in focus to keep up with the development of international conventions – for example, the International Air Navigation Convention – and said that they needed a "new philosophy" in order "to catch up with what is going on."[77]

Borchard, who even before the war had argued that sociological factors were important in international jurisprudence, gave the final paper of the session. While siding with Fenwick in recognizing the importance of economics, he was not as favorable toward a complete shift in focus in international law from war to peace. He cautioned against an easy disposal of neutrality and argued the merits of the traditional approach to neutrality. After lamenting the apathy of many toward restructuring international law after the war, he raised the fear that a complete abolition of neutrality would only increase the rights of belligerents while forfeiting those of neutrals. Without rights for neutral parties, it might become possible for belligerents to starve entire enemy populations, which would be suicidal for human civilization. He thus stressed the importance of practical compromise rather than mere logic. He also noted that legally regulating economic affairs was important because of the "legal vacuum of international unfair economic competition," something which could not be found in municipal law where there were safeguards such as the Interstate Commerce Act and the Anti-Trust Law. A "true operative force for war," Borchard concluded, lay in unfair economic competition.[78]

The 1923 meeting adopted a resolution calling for the establishment of "a committee of five to study and report upon the existing state of

---

[76] Charles G. Fenwick, "An Outline of the Problems Presented in the Further Development of International Law," *Proceedings*, ASIL (1923), 47–52.

[77] Kenny, "The Contributions of Manley O. Hudson," pp. 44–66; Manley O. Hudson, "International Legislation," *Proceedings*, ASIL (1923), 52–55.

[78] Edwin M. Borchard, "The Resurrection of International Law," *Proceedings*, ASIL (1923), 61–70.

international law, and the further extension of the substantive body of international law." With the adoption of this resolution, the Committee for the Advancement of International Law ceased to exist. Scott's letter to Root reporting this change was filled with quiet resignation: the "three most active members of this committee were, as you will no doubt recall, Messrs. Fenwick, Borchard, and Hudson. Their appointment would be in the nature of a continuation."[79] He also suggested the addition of Wright and mentioned Jesse R. Reeves, professor at the University of Michigan, as a possible chairman. Borchard, Fenwick, Hudson and Wright would become the most active and influential international lawyers in the following decades.

After receiving the letter from Scott, Root expressed his intention to retire from the presidency of the ASIL. He wrote that "the Society ought to have a new president with a new mind and a new experience and fresh initiative."[80] The year 1923 was the last of Root's presidency, and with his resignation and the appointment of the four younger scholars to investigate the problems of international law, the ASIL entered a new era in its history.

The generation represented by Root and Scott favored judicial approaches to international relations. They thought that an international court based on unified codes of law would be able to solve international disputes, and they believed that the American example should serve as a model for international relations. Scott revered the Supreme Court of the United States and thought the world should learn from the experience of American federalism. For lawyers of his generation, the basic unit of international relations was the sovereign state, and they did not hold a positive view of universalistic concepts like internationalism or the community of nations. As their emphasis on the laws of war indicates, they did not think it was likely that human beings would be able to abolish war.

Those who supported change in the study of international law were a generation younger. Fenwick was born in 1880, Borchard in 1884, Hudson in 1886, and Wright in 1890, while Root was born in 1845, Scott in 1866, and most of the architects of the Hague Conference in the 1860s and 1870s. The contrast between these two generations highlights a shift from a sovereign state centered consciousness to one inclined toward international society.

[79] Scott to Root, May 8, 1923, ASIL Papers.
[80] Root to Scott, May 11, 1923, ASIL Papers.

Another feature of this younger generation was their background in political science. Among the four members of the new committee to investigate international law, only Hudson had a doctoral degree in law; Borchard, Fenwick and Wright held PhD degrees. The possible introduction of scholarship from political science into the study of international law may have resulted in a declining interest in juridical approaches to international problems.[81] Not content with merely analyzing cases, the younger scholars broadened the perspective of international law to include policy making and the political implications of international law. The topic presented by Fenwick's committee during the 1924 meeting was "The Distinction between Legal and Political Questions."

In the larger picture of American history, the new approach to international law was a part of the general trend toward internationalism. Root and Scott did not envisage the world as a single body or a "family of nations," but as divided into separate, sovereign states. As a last resort, war between sovereign states was permissible, and thus they did not feel the need to shift the emphasis of law from war to peace. Theirs was an international law in the age of nationalism and imperialism. Reinsch, Fenwick, Borchard, Garner and Wright, however, viewed the world as a single society. Wright, for example, often used such terms as "community of nations" or "family of nations." These international legal theorists saw the world as having entered a stage of cooperation. Because the world was deemed to be one collective body, they favored the view that war between any of its members was a concern for all, and they believed that preventing war was necessary. These supporters of the new vision of international law regarded the world as entering a new, civilized stage of development, and they would continue to work for the cause of peace during the following decades.

---

[81] See Ross, *The Origins of American Social Science*, p. 281.

2

Toward a more ambitious international law

The group of younger scholars in the United States, whose presence became distinctive during World War I, threw its efforts into reorienting the discipline of international law. Armed with the newly developed concept of a "family of nations," which stressed collective existence, these scholars turned their attention to formulating a new notion of "law." If the meaning of "international" was changing from relations between atomistic states to the world seen as a single community, this was the next logical step. What notion of "law" would suit the emerging world order? This was the question they strove to answer.

Before entering the American discussion, however, I will briefly discuss the condition of international law in Europe and Japan for the purpose of comparison. The American discussion was not isolated.

The worldwide configuration

Lassa Francis Oppenheim (1858–1919) was influential in establishing the new current of international law. He was originally from Germany, where he taught at the University of Freiburg (1885–91) and the University of Basel (1891–5). He then moved to England and became a lecturer at the London School of Economics (1898–1908) and ultimately a professor at Cambridge University (1908–19). His most well-known book, *International Law: A Treatise*, was first published in 1905 and went through eight editions. It became popularly known as "Oppenheim's *International Law*." Oppenheim's great contribution was to combine the Anglo-Saxon tradition of case-law with the German theoretical approach to jurisprudence.[1]

---

[1] For recent works on Oppenheim, see, for instance, Mathias Schmoeckel, "The Internationalist as a Scientist and Herald: Lassa Oppenheim," *European Journal of International Law* (hereafter *EJIL*) 11 (2000), 699–712; Benedict Kingsbury, "Legal Positivism as Normative Politics: International Society, Balance of Power and Lassa Oppenheim's Positive International Law," *EJIL* 13 (2002), 401–436.

Even before World War I, Oppenheim was concerned about the weakness of international law. In 1911 he published a short book in German, *Die Zukunft des Völkerrecht* [The Future of International Law], in which he stressed the importance of the concept of "the family of nations."[2] The book was translated into English, had been typeset, and was about to be printed when World War I postponed its publication.

With the outbreak of the war, Oppenheim's concern turned to international organization, and after the war he zealously promoted his views supporting the League of Nations in *The League of Nations and its Problems*. Identifying the League with the historical growth of international society, he emphasized its continuity. "You believe no doubt ... that the conception of a League of Nations is something quite new." Yet, he argued, this was not the case; the conception was very old, "as old as modern international law, namely about four hundred years." Oppenheim equated the concept underlying the League of Nations with that of the organized body of nations, upon which international law rested. This point was further elaborated in the third edition of his *International Law* (1920), the last edition that he revised. He wrote, "the League of Nations is intended to take the place of what hitherto used to be called the Family of Nations, namely the community of civilized States." Therefore, "the Covenant of the League is an attempt to organize the hitherto unorganized community of States by a written constitution."[3]

As a basis for enhancing the idea of the family of nations, Oppenheim frankly and explicitly argued for the importance of internationalism. World War I had destroyed "the so-called internationalism," but because the war had led to the establishment of the League, war had done "more for it [internationalism] than many years of peace could have done."[4] Oppenheim endorsed an important legal concept based on internationalism: the concept of a "law-making treaty." Its origin can be found in the nineteenth century, when "it became apparent that customs and usages were not sufficient ... New rules were created through law-making treaties being concluded which laid down rules for future international conduct." In other words, law-making treaties had the possibility of serving as legal standards. Previously, treaties had only been binding on the parties

[2] Lassa Francis Oppenheim, *Die Zukunft des Völkerrechts* [The Future of International Law] (Leipzig: W. Engelmann, 1911).
[3] L. F. Oppenheim, *The League of Nations and its Problems* (London: Longmans, Green and Co., 1919), p. 6; *International Law*, 3rd edn. (London: Longmans, Green and Co., 1920), p. 296.
[4] Oppenheim, *The League of Nations*, p. 12.

concerned. But law-making treaties contained "a tendency to become universal because such States as hitherto did not consent to it will in the future either expressly give their consent or recognize the rules concerned tacitly through custom." Oppenheim cited particular examples of such "pure" law-making treaties: the Geneva Convention of August 22, 1864; the Final Act of the Hague Peace Conference of July 29, 1899; and the Final Act of the Second Hague Conference of October 18, 1907.[5]

In Great Britain, the notion of a "law-making treaty" had also been discussed by other scholars. Sir Frederic Pollock (1845–1937), a well-known scholar of jurisprudence who introduced a new approach into English law by emphasizing principles, had already mentioned the significance of these treaties in 1902. He described them as "agreement[s] made not by two or three states but by a considerable proportion in number and power, of civilized states at large, for the regulations of matters of general and permanent interest." And he noted that "it is hardly too much to say that declarations of this kind may be expected to become part of the universally received law of nations within a moderate time."[6] Not all English lawyers supported this progressive approach, however.

At the other extreme was the positivist W. E. Hall. He wrote that "the existing rules are the sole standard of conduct or law of present authority." He did not believe that law could change easily, writing that "changes and improvements in those rules can only be effected through the same means by which they were originally formed, namely, by growth in harmony with changes in the sentiments and external conditions of the states." As for the treaties, he held the traditionalist view that treaties were binding only for signatories and refuted the call to enhance the legal effectiveness of law-making treaties. He contended that "in spite of the largeness of the support" that treaties received, "there can be no hesitation in dismissing it at once as essentially unsound."[7] Before the war some law professors in the United States used Hall's *A Treatise on International Law* as a textbook,[8]

---

[5] Oppenheim, *International Law*, 3rd. edn, pp. 16, 22.

[6] Frederick Pollock, "The Sources of International Law," *Columbia Law Review* 2 (1902), 512. See also Pollock, "Cosmopolitan Custom and International Law," *Harvard Law Review* 29 (1916), 565–581; "The Work of the League of Nations," *Law Quarterly Review* 138 (1919), 193–198; "Methods of International Arbitration," *Law Quarterly Review* 140 (1919), 320–333.

[7] W. E. Hall, *A Treatise on International Law*, 3rd edn. (Oxford: Clarendon Press, 1892), pp. 2, 7.

[8] See Appendix B, "Professors and Instructors of International Law (1911–1912)," *Teaching of International law at the Educational Institutions in the United States* (n.p., April 18, 1913), pp. 43–46.

but in the 1920s Charles Fenwick and Manley O. Hudson, opponents of legal positivism, criticized him and his approach harshly. Fenwick criticized his work "for its utter lack of a critical attitude toward international law" and remarked that "Mr. Hall is no critic of the existing conceptions of international law."[9]

In Japan, on the other hand, Hall's views were widely accepted. His *A Treatise on International Law* was published in English in Tokyo,[10] and Sakutaro Tachi, a professor of international law at Tokyo Imperial University who had close connections with the Japanese Foreign Ministry, later translated it into Japanese. Tachi acknowledged the significance of Oppenheim's *International Law* and recommended the book to his students as the best book on international law in English, but he did not endorse Oppenheim's views of the League or of internationalism.[11] In an article entitled "Essential Characteristics of the League of Nations," Tachi wrote that the League was a federation of sovereign states and that it was impossible to regard the League as equivalent to a family of nations because there existed non-member states such as the United States.[12]

During the war, the Japanese Foreign Ministry hired a British scholar, Thomas Baty, as an advisor on international law.[13] He came to Japan in 1916, succeeding Henry Willard Denison, who had died in 1914. Baty had not been the first choice, but after aborted efforts to find a suitable person both in the United States and Britain, the Japanese government decided to invite Baty, who had himself offered to take up the post. Baty was born in Britain in 1869 and studied international law both at Oxford and Cambridge. He was a specialist in prize law, a branch of the law of war dealing with the issue of goods captured at sea in time of war. He had had experience serving in a prize court.[14]

[9] *Proceedings of the Second Conference of Teachers of International Law and Related Subjects* (Washington, DC: Carnegie Endowment for International Peace, 1926), 67. (This series is hereafter cited as *Proceedings, Second Teachers*.)

[10] Hall's second edition (1884) was published by Igirisu Horitsu Gakko in 1889. The fourth edition (1895) was published by Sanseido in 1896.

[11] Sakutaro Tachi, "Oppenheim kyoju to sono chosho kokusaiho" [Professor Oppenheim and his Work *International Law*], *Kokusaiho Gaiko Zasshi* 20 (1921), 241.

[12] Tachi, "Kokusai Renmei no honshitu ni kanshite" [Essential Characteristics of the League of Nations], *Kokusaiho Gaiko Zasshi* 20 (1921), 520–524.

[13] For Baty's life and the list of his works, see Shinya Murase, "Thomas Baty in Japan: Seeing through the Twilight," *British Year Book of International Law 2002* 73 (2003), 315–342.

[14] *Gaimusho no hyakunen* [A Hundred Years of Japanese Foreign Ministry], vol. 2 (Tokyo: Harashobo, 1969), pp. 1347–1353; Masao Ichimata, *Nihon no kokusai hogaku o kizuita hitobito* [The Scholars who Established the Study of International Law in Japan]

Baty was known in Great Britain and the United States as a supporter of the traditional approach to international law. As early as 1911, Paul S. Reinsch had criticized him in an article that argued in favor of the World Court. Reinsch cited Baty as an opponent of the progressive view regarding the judicial settlement of international disputes. According to Reinsch, Baty thought that "the application of the concept of legality in international arbitration is inopportune and dangerous, as it involves the subjection of the flexible life of the state to the rigid criteria of legal reasoning."[15] Baty was not only against the formation of the court, but he also warned against the growing current of internationalism. He noted that authors "imbued by a genuine spirit of cosmopolitanism" cease to "regard the various nations as living in separate compartments."[16] When Reinsch reviewed Baty's book *International Law* published in 1909, he was critical, writing that "the author gives no attention to the world-wide organization of numerous economic and scientific interests which are now going on through the formation of unions."[17] When Reinsch wrote this review in 1911, he was a professor at the University of Wisconsin and Baty was in Britain. It is interesting, however, that a few years later both Reinsch and Baty would be stationed in the Far East: Reinsch, a progressive and liberal international lawyer, in China as the US minister; and Baty, who cherished the nineteenth-century notion of international law, in Japan.

In Germany there were some pacifist-internationalist scholars of international law.[18] Even before World War I there was a conspicuous movement supporting the cause of peace through international law. Scholars such as Otfried Nippold (1864–1938), Hans Wehberg (1885–1962) and Walther Schücking (1875–1935) strove to advance international law by founding the Verband für Internationale Verständigung (Association for International Conciliation).[19] Their efforts came to naught before the

---

(Tokyo: Nihon Kokusai Mondai Kenkyujo, 1973), pp. 172–176; Thomas Baty, "Neglected Fundamentals of Prize Law," *Yale Law Journal* 30 (1920), 34–47.

[15] Paul S. Reinsch, "The Concept of Legality in International Arbitration," *AJIL* 5 (1911), 610.

[16] Thomas Baty, "A Modern Jus Gentium," *Juridical Review* 20 (1908–9), 110.

[17] Paul S. Reinsch, Review of *International Law*, by Thomas Baty, in *AJIL* 5 (January 1911), 270.

[18] See also Koskenniemi, *Gentle Civilizer*, pp. 192–195, 215–222.

[19] Roger Chickering, *Imperial Germany and a World without War: The Peace Movement and German Society 1892–1914* (Princeton University Press, 1975), pp. 150–178. For Walther Schücking, see Mónica García-Salmones, "Walther Schücking and the Pacifist Traditions of International Law," *EJIL* 22 (2011), 755–782, Christian J. Tams, "Re-Introducing Walther Schücking," *EJIL* 22 (2011), 725–739; Frank Bodendiek, "Walther Schücking

war, but their ideas survived. Even in 1917, Nippold – originally from Switzerland – had written "The true international law, which aspires to the dominance of law and nothing else, is in its nature actually democratic. It proceeds from the idea of the equality of states, small as well as large, and has no place for imperialistic aspirations. It places right above might and therefore opposes militarism."[20] Nippold coupled the idea of international law with democracy, writing, "democracy and international law are two conceptions that must be complementary to each other ... for the international idea can only prosper fully in the soil of democracy."[21] As soon as the war ended, German liberal scholars started elaborating theories on international law. In the interwar period, both Schücking and Wehberg endorsed the League of Nations, and throughout the 1920s and 1930s they contributed to the study of international law and to the cause of peace.[22] Schücking became a judge on the PCIJ in 1930, while Wehberg became a professor at the Geneva Institute of International Relations and remained there until 1959.

Nicolas Politis (1872–1942) of Greece also contended that international law had entered a new stage in its development. Before the war he had been teaching at the University of Paris (1910–14), but with the outbreak of war he went back to his country and assumed the position of Foreign Minister (1916–20). After the League was established he served as a Greek delegate to the organization, playing a significant role in its development. He wrote in his book, which was based upon a lecture he had delivered in 1926, that "the general conviction is, however, that international law has already entered, or is about to enter, on a new phase of its evolution." The new development, he argued, resulted from the growth of an international society in which the concept of state sovereignty was to be questioned. On the issue of sovereignty, he wrote that especially in the United States there had appeared numerous notable works, citing the

and the Idea of 'International Organization'," *EJIL* 22 (2011), 741–754; Ole Spiermann, "Professor Walther Schücking at the Permanent Court of International Justice," *EJIL* 22 (2011), 783–799; Jost Delbrück, "Law's Frontier – Walther Schücking and the Quest for the *Lex Ferenda*," *EJIL* 22 (2011), 801–808.

[20] Otfried Nippold, *The Development of International Law after the World War* (Oxford: Clarendon Press, 1923), p. 104.

[21] *Ibid.*, p. 188. Regarding the quotation I cited, Nippold wrote, "I wish to note *expressly* that the above was written before America entered the war," see footnote 1, *ibid.* The original German version of this book was written in 1917.

[22] Walter Schücking and Hans Wehberg, *Die Satzung des Völkerbundes* (Berlin: Franz Vahlen, 1921); Hans Wehberg, *The Limitation of Armaments* (Washington, DC: Carnegie Endowment, 1921).

names of James Garner and Manley O. Hudson as representative scholars on the subject.[23]

American international lawyers, in particular the younger group, were
associated with the works of Oppenheim, Pollock and Wehberg even
before the war. Oppenheim's *Zukunft des Völkerrecht* and Nippold's book
were translated from German into English immediately after the war, and
published under the auspices of the Carnegie Endowment. Politis also
referred to the works by Garner and Hudson, a development that demonstrated how American scholarly discussion had been also acknowledged
and appreciated by progressive European scholars.

The Covenant of the League of Nations and the Washington Conference

After World War I, American scholars of international law faced the
question of how to interpret and evaluate the postwar machinery of
international relations, such as the Covenant of the League of Nations
and the treaties and agreements signed at the Washington Conference
of 1921–2. For those who held a traditional view, this machinery signified a departure from the established positivistic system of international
law. On the other hand, the junior group of scholars agreed with the
postwar system, but they were not yet equipped with the legal theory
necessary to support it. Therefore, the junior group focused on establishing the new system's theoretical foundations. These two groups presented sharply contrasting views on how to define the scope of law as
adopted in the Covenant and other treaties signed at the Washington
Conference.

Elihu Root and the supporters of the old judicial approach emphasized
the importance of the international court and criticized the Covenant of
the League of Nations. Root's critique was based on the premise that the
Covenant was a political document and not a legal one. Regarding Articles
10 through 16 and 19, the heart of the collective framework against military action, he remarked that "these provisions are well devised and should
be regarded as free from any just objections, insofar as they relate to the
settlement of the political questions." But they were defective, because
the scheme abandoned "all efforts to promote or maintain anything like

---

[23] Nicolas Politis, *The New Aspects of International Law* (Washington, DC: Carnegie
Endowment for International Peace, 1928), pp. 2–6. For Politis, see also Koskenniemi,
Gentle Civilizer, pp. 305–309.

a system of international law or a system of arbitration." For Root, the positive, specific rules of international law were central, but provisions specifying general guidelines, like Article 10, did not qualify as legal. In his mind, political and legal questions were distinct and not reconcilable: "This [the Covenant] is a method very admirable for dealing with political questions; but it is wholly unsuited to the determination of questions of right under the law of nations."[24]

More specific criticism of the preamble to the Covenant came from Philip Marshall Brown, professor at Princeton University, who drew attention to the phrase "understandings of international law." The preamble stated that international peace should be promoted "by the firm establishment of understandings of international law as the actual rule of conduct among nations." According to Brown, international law was "to be regarded first as not having been clearly understood." "Understandings" was too vague a word and did not mean anything concrete in legal terms. And since this was the only reference to international law in the Covenant, Brown argued that "by implication the great system of law that has been laboriously built up by judicial action and by firmly established custom and positive consent is seriously slighted in the preamble." Brown deplored the inclusion of this phrase as "a feeble reference" to the true standing of international law, and wrote, "it affronts especially our Anglo-Saxon conceptions of a solid system of law that has grown up by custom and consent."[25]

Quincy Wright challenged Brown's interpretation of the phrase with an "illuminating article" in the *AJIL*.[26] According to Wright, the term "understandings" was the crux of the Covenant. Citing President Wilson's usage of the term in the 1908 edition of his book *Congressional Government*, he argued that "apparently this phraseology was the work of President Wilson." He pointed out that Wilson preferred the term and noted that in the index of the 1908 edition "understandings" was made "a special subject, followed by twenty-one page references." Wright disclosed that the term "understandings" had not been used in the earlier edition and suggested that its later inclusion reflected the influence of

---

[24] Elihu Root, "Letter of Honorable Root to Honorable Will H. Hays, March 29, 1919," *AJIL* 13 (July 1919), 586–587. See also, Zasloff, "Law and the Shaping: From Gilded Age," 342–356; Kirgis, *The American Society*, p. 59.

[25] Philip Marshall Brown, "The 'Understandings' of International Law," *AJIL* 13 (1919), pp. 738, 739, 741.

[26] James W. Garner, *Recent Developments in International Law* (University of Calcutta, 1925), p. 402, footnote 1.

A. V. Dicey's *Introduction to the Study of the Law of the Constitution*,[27] which had been published just after Wilson's first edition. Dicey used the term "understandings" in his explication of the US Constitution to distinguish two meanings of the notion of law: "judge-made law, in strict sense law, enforced by courts," and "constitutional morality," represented by the concept of "understandings." Thus, Dicey argued that the Constitution embodied a dual notion of law, including both specific legal rules and rules associated with morality.[28]

Wright proceeded to argue that both Wilson and Dicey agreed that "the essence of an understanding is its origin in agreement or assent and its flexibility." Understanding should be distinguished, "on the one hand, from commands of superior authority and on the other from formal and inflexible rules and principles." Wright found the essence of understanding in its flexibility but did recognize the danger of such flexibility in law, which could easily lead to misunderstandings. Since international society was in the process of being organized, however, rules relating to international organization were not yet ready for codification. Many found a "flexible constitution better than rigid constitutions," and Wright contended that the drafters of the Covenant had "wisely" seen that the organization of the League could only be prescribed "in the bare outlines." He wrote that "understandings" were the key to the dual nature of the Covenant: "the constitution of the League of Nations is to be built up of understanding in the twilight zone of law and morality, enjoying the regularity of obedience of one and the flexibility of the other, infinitely tenacious yet capable of indefinite adaptations."[29]

Although Brown questioned Wright's assertion about President Wilson's influence on the wording of the preamble, on the whole, he accepted the analysis. Brown agreed with Wright's interpretation of "understanding of international law" as "the portion of international law not embodied yet in formal principles of justice, but sanctioned by general assent and dealing especially with the organization of international society."[30] While acknowledging the importance of this notion in the Covenant, Brown nevertheless asked what had become of the rules of international law that had been established before the Covenant. He complained that the drafters of the Covenant "ignored in the main, the

---

[27] A. V. Dicey, *Introduction to the Study of the Law of the Constitution* (London: Macmillan, 1889).
[28] Quincy Wright, "The Understandings of International Law," *AJIL* 14 (1920), 572–574.
[29] *Ibid.*, 575–580.   [30] *Ibid.*, 569.

great problem of the firm establishment and orderly development of the existing body of international law." Stating that this issue was not only one of "terminology" but involved the grave danger that "the established principle of international law would be obscured," he warned that "in building up an international organization the vastly more important task of laying its foundation on the bedrock of law would be neglected." Brown concluded that "this is no mere verbal quibble: the issue is fundamental," thereby challenging the basis of judicial development.[31]

Another post-World War I framework was the Washington Conference of 1921–2, originally convened because of the need to limit naval armaments among the Powers. Root attended the Conference as an official delegate and James Brown Scott as a technical advisor. Beforehand, Scott wrote that the reason for calling the Conference was to address issues concerning arms limitations, China and the Pacific. For the questions regarding the Pacific and Far East there were several precedents, while "for the conference of the nations on the limitation of armament there is but one precedent, the first of the two Hague Conferences was called in 1898 for this purpose." Scott hoped the conference would yield a continuation of the Hague Conferences: "the temple of peace is still in the distance; and the approach to it runs through conferences like the two which have already assembled at The Hague."[32]

The Conference at least partly fulfilled Scott's expectations. He was reassured by the question of submarines being put on the agenda for discussion. While during the war there had been a growing sentiment against the laws of war, the Washington Conference took up the topics in the laws of war, such as the issue concerning the legal regulation of submarines. But in the end the Powers failed to reach agreement about submarines during the Conference. Great Britain insisted that they should be regulated and suggested their total abolition. The French argued that submarines were essential to preserving their independence, and Italy and Japan stressed that submarines were effective defensive weapons.[33] The Conference, however, did produce a "Resolution Establishing

---

[31] Philip Marshall Brown, "The Understandings of International Law," *AJIL* 15 (1921), 69–70.

[32] James Brown Scott, "Conference on the Limitation of Armament and Problems of the Pacific," *AJIL* 15 (1921), 504–505, 510.

[33] *Conference on the Limitation of Armament, Washington, November 12, 1921– February 6, 1922* (Washington, DC: GPO, 1922), pp. 474–592; "Conference on the Limitation of Armament, Report of the American Delegation, Senate Document, No.125, 67th Cong., 2nd Sess.," *AJIL* 16 (1922), 185–189.

a Commission of Jurists to Consider Amendment of the Laws of War," which was adopted by the United States, the British Empire, France, Italy and Japan.[34] This resolution called for the establishment of a committee to discuss whether the existing rules of international law adequately covered new methods of warfare that had emerged since the Hague Conference of 1907. The resolution reflected a desire to discuss the laws of war within the framework dominant prior to World War I.

The discussion on submarine warfare and the resolution to form a committee of jurists were only a minor part of the Conference. The major achievements included a treaty to limit naval expansion and the treaty concerning China. Root entitled his opening address for the ASIL meeting of 1922 "International Law at the Arms Conference." In it, he remarked that the main business of the Washington Conference had been the limitation of armaments and that this was undertaken to "reach agreement which would bind the parties by contractual obligation," but not by "obligation imposed by law." He did not think that the obligations prescribed in the naval treaties and the Nine Power Treaty on China were legally binding. The Washington Conference had not been designed to make new laws, but "it did, naturally and effectively as incidental to giving effects to its policy of limiting armament, take quite important steps in the direction of developing and strengthening international law."[35]

The two guest speakers at the 1922 session were Westel W. Willoughby and Frederick Moore, who were officially affiliated with the Chinese and Japanese governments respectively. Willoughby, who was a professor of political science[36] at Johns Hopkins University, served as a legal advisor to the Chinese government between 1916 and 1919, and accompanied the Chinese delegation to the Washington Conference. Willoughby had once been critical of Scott's view that the legal status of international law lay in its application in municipal courts.[37] He, like Garner, favored dealing with international law in terms of theory rather than cases, and he mentioned at the outset of the ASIL meeting that he intended to present the issues in terms of "abstract principles of international law and of international

---

[34] "Resolutions Establishing a Commission of Jurists to Consider Amendment of the Laws of War," *Conference on the Limitation of Armament*, p. 1640.

[35] Elihu Root, "International Law at the Arms Conference," *Proceedings, ASIL* (1922), 1–12.

[36] For a brief account of Willoughby's position in the study of political science, see Ross, *The Origins of American Social Science*, pp. 280–281.

[37] Westel Willoughby, "Legal Nature of International Law," *AJIL* 2 (1908), 365.

right." The main principle involved in the Chinese case was mutual cooperation, and the primary issue was the validity of the Twenty-One Demands, which had been signed under threat of force. According to Willoughby, this coercion contradicted the fundamental principle of international law, because "the essential purpose of international law was to maintain international peace and cooperation." In other words, Japan's forcing China to sign contradicted the principle of mutual cooperation. Willoughby also mentioned the right to set tariffs independently and to station troops in another country, pointing out that in these matters China was not being dealt with fairly.[38] In the end, however, he thought that the Nine Power Treaty was a "great victory" for China because the principles such as promoting cooperation among countries were laid down "in a formal treaty to which all other Powers with Far Eastern interests are asked to adhere."[39]

The presentation by Frederick Moore, Foreign Councilor to the Japanese Foreign Ministry, reflected a quite different perspective. Claiming that "much has been said against the Japanese unfairly with regard to their position in the Far East," he proceeded to defend the Japanese position. Whereas Willoughby spoke in terms of the abstract principles of international law, Moore presented the "simple facts" of the situation in China and of Japan's interests in that country. He referred to the situation in China as peculiar and stressed the importance of China for Japan. He mentioned Japan's population problem and the need for raw materials and markets for her products. He even remarked that "the so-called infringements of China's sovereignty have not always been detrimental to China's interests ... Indeed, without the British it is doubtful if China proper would be intact today."[40]

Perhaps Willoughby had put too much stress on principles without clarifying what the principles were about. Harold Quigley of the University of Minnesota similarly dealt with the question of principles

---

[38] Westel Willoughby, "Principles of International Law and Justice raised by China at the Washington Conference," *Proceedings, ASIL* (1922), 19–24.

[39] Westel Willoughby, *China at the Conference* (Baltimore: Johns Hopkins Press, 1922), pp. 336, 342–343.

[40] Frederick Moore, "The Far Eastern Settlement of the Conference of Washington," *Proceedings, ASIL* (1922), 26–36. Moore also presented a paper on Japanese policy at the Conference on China held in September 1925 at Johns Hopkins University. See *American Relations with China, a Report of the Conference held at Johns Hopkins University, September 17–20, 1925* (Baltimore: Johns Hopkins Press, 1925). Also present at this conference were Willoughby and Sao-ke Alfred Sze, a Chinese Minister to the United States.

but with a different emphasis. After examining many works on the issue of treaty validity, including those by John Bassett Moore and W. E. Hall, Quigley reached the conclusion that the Twenty-One Demands were binding because "the practical unanimity of these authorities is sufficient warrant for rejecting the argument from *force majeure* on legal, however strong it may be on moral grounds." He was aware that the validity of a treaty signed under threat of force could not be morally defended and wrote that "the degree to which Japanese activities in Shantung have been found legally justifiable is an indication of a gap that still separates law and ethics, revealed when a strong power deals with a weak one."[41] Quigley, therefore, recognized that there was a gap between ethical values and international law. Both Willoughby and Quigley argued that when international law allowed treaties to be imposed by force it was incompatible with moral and ethical principles.

Wright's paper on the Washington Conference focused neither on the legal aspect of treaties nor on the realities of the situation in the Far East. Rather, he simply noted the Conference's implications for international relations and that it was successful in assigning a historical role to the event. He argued that there were two types of international conference, one of which was held to "consider general principles or methods for conducting international relations." Of this character were the Geneva Conferences on the Red Cross (1864, 1904) and the Hague Peace Conferences (1899, 1907). The second type were conferences called to settle particular political problems or controversies. These usually took place after wars, as was the case with the Congress of Vienna (1815) and of Versailles (1919). But the Washington Conference combined both types. The five-power negotiations on the limitation of armaments were of the first type, while the nine-power negotiations and the debate on the Pacific questions were of the second type.[42]

With regard to the situation in the Far East, Wright argued that Chinese sovereignty had suffered "progressive impairments." He judged the Nine Power Treaty positively, writing that "the more important Chinese treaty begins by reiteration of *general principles* [italics added] in respect to China formulated by Mr. Root and resembling the Hay Statements." Wright did not explain fully why these "general principles" were so important. He emphasized that the specific resolutions, such as

[41] Harold Scott Quigley, "Legal Phases of the Shantung Question," *Minnesota Law Review* 6 (1922), 380–394.
[42] Quincy Wright, "The Washington Conference," *Minnesota Law Review* 6 (1922), 291.

the abolition of extraterritoriality in China, were formulated within the framework of the Nine Power Treaty.[43]

More importantly, Wright found in the Washington Conference implications for the development of international organization. Entitling one section of his paper "Association of Nations," he argued that "the problem of an association of nations, though not on the agenda, lay in the background of the conference." The problem was emphasized because disagreement in the United States over the League of Nations had led to the United States declining to become a member. According to Wright, President Harding hoped that the conference to limit armaments might provide a precedent for future conferences, thus creating a loose association of nations that would serve as equivalent to the League. At the Washington Conference, it was decided to set up commissions and hold periodic conferences, though not in connection with any permanent organizations. "Thus," Wright wrote, "the Washington Conference has brought both the United States and Europe to an increased understanding of the value and necessity of international organization."[44]

A distinction between political and legal questions?

While discussion of the Covenant and of the Washington Conference revealed a low regard for moral principles in international law, another issue, the relationship between politics and law, was brought to light at the 1924 meeting of the ASIL by Charles Fenwick of Bryn Mawr College. Through this issue, Fenwick pointed out another deficiency in the prevailing notion of international law. He selected the topic "The Distinction between Political and Legal Questions" for his report to the Committee for the Extension of International Law, which had been established in 1923 to consider the future direction of international law. Describing his reasons for addressing this topic, he argued that it was one of the questions "which lay at the threshold of any study of the future development of international law."[45]

Before turning to the discussion in Fenwick's committee, it should be noted that the ASIL had a new president in 1924. After serving as president for sixteen years, Root stepped down and Charles Evans Hughes, Secretary of State from 1920 to 1924 assumed the office.[46] While the selection of Hughes was Scott's idea, Fenwick opposed the choice because he

---

[43] Ibid., 294.   [44] Ibid., 295–298.   [45] Proceedings, ASIL (1924), 43.
[46] See also Kirgis, The American Society, pp. 85–86.

thought that the president should be selected on the basis of academic merit rather than political position. He wrote to Scott, "The Secretary of State has done practically no scientific work in the field of international law, such as should be the ground for selecting a man for the president of the Society."[47] Scott, however, thought that the Society needed an authoritative figure and replied, "There are, as our French friends would say, 'titles,' and for your own information he is not only willing, but will be pleased to accept."[48] Although Scott's opinion prevailed, in Fenwick's session Scott for the first time showed an inclination toward Fenwick's view of international law.

At the session Fenwick, Wright, Edwin Borchard and Manley Hudson presented papers.[49] Fenwick began with the premise that legal questions had become more important than before, saying that the "history of international relations during the past two centuries shows a gradual enlargement of the field of legal questions and a corresponding narrowing of the field of political questions." The fact remained, however, that in many cases countries avoided submitting issues to international arbitration on the ground that they were "political questions." He then analyzed the limitations of existing international law and organization and how these encouraged the tendency among states to phrase issues as political questions and bypass legal solutions. First of all, international law was based upon customary laws, but some of the leading principles – for example, the equality of states and territorial independence – were still not established as law. Legal principles did not cover all aspects of international relations. Secondly, legal solutions were shunned due to "defective organization of the society of nations"; current international society lacked a sense of collective responsibility and in the end states had to defend their interests. Finally, each state was the "ultimate arbiter" of its own domestic questions. For example, the admission of immigrants had been regarded as a domestic issue, in spite of the fact that it affected the welfare of other states. In sum, there were many problems that were "not yet ripe for settlement by the adoption of a common rule of international statutory law."[50]

Borchard, a professor at Yale Law School, dealt with the issue differently. Instead of looking for deficiencies in institutions or laws, he

---

[47] Fenwick to Scott, February 16, 1924, ASIL Papers.
[48] Scott to Fenwick, March 3, 1924, ASIL Papers.
[49] See also Kirgis, *The American Society*, pp. 504–505.
[50] Charles G. Fenwick, "The Distinction between Legal and Political Questions," *Proceedings, ASIL* (1924), 44–50.

emphasized the willingness (or unwillingness) of states to treat problems as legal questions. He wrote:

> Does it [the answer] not lie less in the fundamental nature of the question than in the willingness of the nation to submit it to judicial determination? ... What is known as a political question becomes a legal question solely because there is a willingness, induced by any one of many considerations counseling self-restraint, to have it peaceably settled.

Only when a state was convinced that it had "more to lose by war than by a peaceful solution" would it seek a legal solution. Borchard pointed out that it was impossible to make every international question into a legal one, however well established laws and institutions might be.[51]

Wright was closer to Fenwick than to Borchard in his emphasis on law rather than on the intentions of states. He opened his talk by referring to Roscoe Pound, a scholar of jurisprudence at Harvard. Pound was known for his idea of "sociological jurisprudence," which held that law should respond to social needs and not merely be a reflection of abstract principles. In a similar vein, Wright advocated flexibility in law and argued for the need for an "engineering interpretation of law." He remarked that "principles and standards devised by men" should permit "a greater satisfaction of human and social wants." He called for the further development of law, because there were still many fields not sufficiently covered – for example, communications, transportation, and the suppression of contraband such as opium. With an increase in international activity, law needed to change in response to the needs of society.[52]

The last speaker, Hudson of Harvard Law School, went even further and denied the practical possibility of distinguishing between political and legal issues. He cited the example of the Corfu Crisis of 1923, in which three Italians had been killed near the Greek frontier. Italy judged that the killing had been carried out by Greeks and demanded indemnity. Hudson asked, "Is there any rule in international law which can decide the amount of indemnity?" He contended that there existed an "interconnection of legal and political phases" and concluded that it would not be easy to separate them. Discussing problems with the PCIJ, he remarked, "I find it very difficult to find any legal principles or any legal standards according

---

[51] Edwin M. Borchard, "The Distinction between Legal and Political Questions," *Proceedings, ASIL* (1924), 50–57.
[52] Quincy Wright, "The Distinction between Legal and Political Questions with Especial Reference to the Monroe Doctrine," *Proceedings, ASIL* (1924), 57–67.

to which the PCIJ might have proceeded to determine the amount of the indemnity payable by Greece or Italy."[53]

During the discussion that followed, Admiral William Rodgers pointed out the futility of law itself, saying, "Against national interests of great states, municipal and international law are alike powerless." Most comments, however, were not so pessimistic about the role of law. Garner and Wright supported Hudson's position. Garner said that "it is quite futile to attempt to define or classify legal and political differences," while Wright remarked, "I should go further and say that perhaps there is no line at all."[54]

The effectiveness of the PCIJ was repeatedly questioned during the discussion. Those who favored the traditional notion of law held that the PCIJ would be strengthened by the further development of international law. Brown argued that "you cannot agree to submit to an international court a question for which there is no rule of law." Refuting this notion, Howard Kingsbury, a practicing lawyer, mentioned the utility of the Permanent Court of Arbitration, which had been established at the First Hague Conference in 1899. The PCIJ was intended to advance a step further by applying the rule of law to international questions. Yet, because of a deficiency in international codes and the difficulty of judging the legal issues, Kingsbury suggested that the Court of Arbitration served better in resolving actual conflicts than the PCIJ. Hudson showed interest in this opinion, and surprisingly even Scott, who had been the most vocal advocate of the establishment of an international court, supported it. He remarked, "Mr. Hudson will not tax me with attacking the PCIJ ... for a court of international justice has been for many years one of the reasons for my existence." Scott hoped that there would be many ventures for settling problems and looked for a separation of functions between them, believing that "the greater the number of remedies we have, the fewer the disputes we are likely to have outstanding." Scott's remarks were significant, especially insofar as he admitted that an international court could not be omnipotent as he had once thought.[55]

Wright criticized Brown's definition of law as being too narrow, noting that the sources of international law should not be confined to treaties, codes or other written documents. "It seems to me," Wright proposed,

---

[53] Manley O. Hudson, "The Distinction between Legal and Political Questions," *Proceedings, ASIL* (1924), 126–132.

[54] "Discussion," *Proceedings, ASIL* (1924), 72–74, 141.

[55] *Ibid.*, 79, 134–135, 138–139.

"that we can resort to general principles so long as we apply them with a legal spirit." Hudson's concluding remarks also made this point: "We are using the same word, law, but we mean very different things by it." Echoing Wright, he argued for the flexibility and enlargement of international law. While words like "pure justice" and "strict law" had been used in the past, he did not think that international law should be conceived of as "something that is handed down to us, full-grown and full-blown, so that its content is never to be varied or changed as we face our varying problems." He concluded, "Let us not limit ourselves to an application of strict law. Let us view our task as that of making an intelligent and effective use of the materials that have been handed on to us, in the interest of the society which we serve."[56] Hudson presented a bold position in which international lawyers can and should take a leading role in defining the scope of "law" as long as it would ultimately contribute to the welfare of international society, even though it might entail the risk of flexible legal interpretation.

On the whole, the general trend at the ASIL this time supported the denial of a distinction between political and legal questions. This inevitably led to the disapproval of a strict notion of law in favor of expanding the law – that is, its principles and standards – in order to serve social needs better.

The ASIL had discussed the relationship between politics and law in terms of legal theory, but the issue also came up at the 1925 Conference of Teachers of International Law and Related Subjects.[57] The initiative to resume this Conference, which had been held once in 1914 and then discontinued, came from the American Political Science Association (APSA) and not from the ASIL, but many active members of the ASIL were also members of the APSA. At the Round Table on International Affairs held at the December 1924 meeting of the APSA, the suggestion was offered and enthusiastically received to "have a conference of teachers of international law and related subjects in Washington in connection with the next annual meeting of the ASIL." This motion was supported by twenty-one professors, including Borchard, Fenwick, Garner and Wright.[58]

At one session of the Teachers' Conference, some scholars mentioned the difficulty of separating international law from other related subjects. Quigley noted that, from his experience, it was hard to distinguish law from policy. When he taught specific rules of international law, he also

---

[56] *Ibid.*, 141, 145.   [57] See also Kirgis, *The American Society*, pp. 97–100.
[58] Edward Dickinson to George A. Finch, January 5, 1925, ASIL Papers.

had to explain American foreign policy.[59] In the discussion following Quigley's presentation, Pittman Potter of the University of Michigan counseled to "keep them distinct," while Hudson reaffirmed his position by discounting the need to distinguish sharply between law and politics. He stated, "I find myself tending in the opposite direction, to say that the thing that has been needed in our international law has been emphasis on its very relation to policy." He proposed the creation of an "international social science" that would integrate subjects relating to international affairs. One participant from a small college also noted that it was difficult to separate international law from other related subjects, especially at institutions that did not offer a great variety of courses on international subjects.[60]

Opinions on the case method were also expressed. Garner said that too much reliance on the case method had the "danger of giving the student a one-sided, national view of what international law is." Hudson likewise remarked, "I cannot bring myself to impress upon my students the definiteness and positive character of the rules of international law ... Rather, it is principles and standards to which we resort." The definiteness and positive character of international law had been stressed at the 1914 Conference. Eleven years later, opinions against the case method constituted the majority and, as Hudson stated, principles and standards were regarded as more important for teaching international law.[61]

Several resolutions designed to enhance the study of international law were adopted at the 1925 Conference. One concerned the special desirability of providing more comprehensive instruction. A part of this resolution noted that "the Conference favors the development of undergraduate courses in international relations including the trade and economic relations as well as in international organizations." This reflected the opinion that instruction at universities and colleges should not be limited to international law but that general courses on international relations should also be offered. On the other hand, Resolution 4 proclaimed the desirability of instruction in international law for advanced degrees in political science and history. It was recommended that at graduate institutions the subject be taught even to students who were not law majors. Both

[59] Harold Scott Quigley, "The Scope, Organization and Aim of Courses in International Law in Relation to Other Courses in International Subjects," *Proceedings, Second Teachers*, pp. 9–11.
[60] *Proceedings, Second Teachers*, pp. 12–13.   [61] *Ibid.*, pp. 32, 39.

resolutions called for an expansion of the curriculum in international law at universities and colleges.[62]

Nevertheless, there was heated debate over whether the Conference of Teachers of international law should take concrete steps to popularize international law. When a proposal was made to set up the administrative machinery and provide the necessary funds by which professors could be sent to institutions offering no courses in international law, Hudson voiced vehement opposition: "I wish we as teachers of international law could get rid of the desire to vulgarize our subject." He did not think that "Tom, Dick, and Harry ought to be taught international law," but he did think it necessary for "Tom, Dick, and Harry to have some ideas about international relations," because "knowledge of a little international law is much more dangerous." Ellery Stowell of the American University responded that it was important to widen the base of the study of international law, but in the end the resolution was dropped, and a resolution supporting the desirability of teaching international law at summer school was adopted in its place. As Wright explained, "summer school is the home of the high school teacher." While Hudson considered popularizing international law tantamount to pandering to the peace movement and wanted the study of international law to be a science, Wright and Stowell embraced the idea that the teaching of international law would in itself enlighten the public.[63]

A happy synthesis: from theory to practice

While vigorous discussions on the definition of law were taking place at the ASIL and the Conference of Teachers of International Law, scholars were beginning to produce some progressive theories. One had to do with the limitation of sovereignty. Borchard contributed an article entitled "Political Theory and International Law" to a book edited by Charles Merriam.[64] Borchard's premise was that while in the social sciences theory most often followed practice this was not true for the scientific development of international law – particularly in the case of national sovereignty, where "the supporting theory lagged behind." He pointed out

---

[62] "Resolutions and Recommendations of the Conference," *Proceedings, Second Teachers*, pp. x–xi.
[63] "Discussion of Resolutions and Recommendations of the Conference," *Proceedings, Second Teachers*, pp. 142, 143, 148.
[64] Charles E. Merriam, ed., *A History of Political Theories, Recent Times* (New York: Macmillan, 1924).

that national sovereignty was detrimental to international law, writing, "the theory of sovereignty ... proved one of the most severe handicaps and dangers to the growth of a rational system of international relations." There was a gap between the theory of the seventeenth century and the reality of the twentieth century. In the twentieth century, with its international organization and tendency toward internationalism, national sovereignty had become an obstacle to the sound development of international law.[65]

Garner also chose the issue of sovereignty for his Presidential Address to the APSA on December 29, 1924. In line with Borchard, yet more explicitly, Garner argued that the notion of sovereignty was effective only within national boundaries and that its power ended "at the frontier." When a state tries to enforce its will outside its borders, "it is limited by the rights of other states and of their nationals, to say nothing of the rights of the society of states as a whole." This limitation was enforced "through the principle of international responsibility," one of the foundations of international law, which governed how all civilized states act in their relations with one another. Thus the notion of sovereignty was criticized because it "no longer corresponds with the facts of international life or practice, and indeed [was] incompatible with the existence of a society of states." Garner noted that the conduct of nations was in fact already limited by the existence of many multilateral conventions, and claimed that "in the place of an 'anarchy of sovereignty' we have a society of interdependent states, bound by law and possessing a highly-developed solidarity of interests."[66]

Around this time, Fenwick and Garner began publishing their ideas on international law. Fenwick's ambitious views were laid out in the preface of his 1924 book *International Law*. Pointing to the law's current impotence, he wrote that while international law had successfully addressed a large number of the less important national interests it had failed to address the most acute problems of the international community. In the future, however, "the existing rules of international law may be tested by the general conceptions of justice prevailing within individual states, and conclusions may thus be drawn for the constructive amendment or *enlargement of law* [italics added]."[67] As for the Covenant of the League of Nations, he

[65] Edwin M. Borchard, "Political Theory and International Law," in Merriam, *A History of Political Theories*, pp. 120–139.
[66] James W. Garner, "Limitations on National Sovereignty in International Relations," *American Political Science Review* 19 (1925), 2, 3, 6, 16–18.
[67] Charles G. Fenwick, *International Law* (New York: The Century Co., 1924), pp. vi–vii.

believed that "the system of the balance of power was impliedly, if not formally, repudiated in the collective responsibility assumed by all the members of the League for the future peace of the world." Yet he was cautious about the effects of the Covenant, explaining that "it is difficult if not impossible to determine at the present moment how far the fundamental character of international law as it existed in 1919 has been changed by the establishment of the League of Nations."[68]

Garner went even further in his bold interpretation of the Covenant in *Recent Developments in International Law*, a book based on lectures he had given at the University of Calcutta in 1922.[69] He wrote that "the effect of the Covenant has been to alter some of the fundamental bases on which international law has heretofore rested." The Covenant established a new conception of international duty, "shifted emphasis more and more from the right of states to obligations and responsibilities," and exalted "the idea of interdependence and solidarity at the expense of nationalism and independence." He also noted that many of the stipulations of the Covenant of the League "fall within the category of what Oppenheim calls 'law-making' treaties."[70] In particular, Articles 11 and 16 introduced the new principle of collective responsibility, which was "reinforced by the application of physical sanctions." More importantly, he wrote, "under Article 10 the so-called right of conquest would seem to be abolished" because the League condemned "external aggression" against the territorial integrity and political independence of all members.[71] With regard to the Covenant's binding force on non-signatory countries, Garner was optimistic. Although admitting that the new principles were "of course principles which only the members of the League of Nations have agreed to recognize" he argued that "since the membership of the League now embraces more than fifty states ... they may almost be said to constitute a part of the public law of the world." From a strictly positivist view, his use of phrases like "almost said" and "seem to be abolished" was too casual and was certain to cause problems. In addition to his frequent usage of the term "principle"

---

[68] *Ibid.*, pp. 30, 46, 56.
[69] Garner was elected to the Tagore Professorship of Law at the University of Calcutta. He was the first American to receive the appointment. See miscellaneous newspaper clippings in Garner Papers.
[70] Law-making treaties are treaties that have the possibility of serving as legal standards. Lasa Francis Oppenheim emphasized this notion. See Oppenheim, *International Law*, 3rd edn., pp. 16–22.
[71] Garner, *Recent Developments in International Law*, pp. ix, 397–398.

and his bold statements about the legal effects of the Covenant, he used the terms "international law" and "policy" almost as synonyms. For instance, when he wrote that "other new principles of international law or of policy which may be said to find recognition in the Covenant," he seems not to have distinguished between the two.[72]

In the meantime, Hudson was emerging as a spokesman for new international law by presenting numerous papers on new developments in international law.[73] He also made the effort of writing to influential officials. On one occasion in 1926 Hudson wrote to Eric Drummond, Secretary General of the League of Nations, that the League secretariat should receive the visit of the American scholars cordially and carefully, because "professors will write a great deal more about the League."[74] In addition, like Garner, he visited the University of Calcutta in 1927, and his lecture there was published as a book, *Current International Co-Operation*. He did not hesitate to urge a limited role for the PCIJ: "we must see the role of courts as it is, and the truth seems to be that the serious international differences cannot be pressed into legal questions." Therefore, it was important that besides the court, "the international community should have other agencies to deal with the disputes which only lend themselves to political adjustment."[75] He stressed the significance of conferences, newly established as a practice of the League of Nations, and "numerous international conventions" such as the International Labor Conventions.[76] Hudson was aware that these multilateral agreements had not been "ratified by all states, not even by all members of the League of Nations, but they might serve as the guideline, as exemplified by the Declaration of Paris of 1856." He continued, "It would be improper to treat all multipartite conventions as having the same value as law-making

---

[72] *Ibid.*, pp. 401–402, p. 401, footnote 2.

[73] In addition to the address "The Contemporary Development of International Law" at the Second Conference of Teachers of International Law, April 25, 1925, Hudson spoke before the American Branch of International Law Association at its annual dinner January 9, 1925; before the Cornell University College of Law, March 30 and 31, 1925; and before the Bar Association of the City of New York, February 16, 1928. The latter addresses were published as, respectively, "The Outlook for the Development of International Law," *American Bar Association Journal* 11 (1925), 102–107; "The Prospect for International Law in the Twentieth Century," *The Cornell Law Quarterly* 10 (1925), 419–459; "The Development of International Law since the War," *AJIL* 22 (1928), 330–350.

[74] Manley O. Hudson to Eric Drummond, January 30, 1926, Papers of the League of Nations, League of Nations Archives, Geneva, Box 1340, Folder 36451.

[75] Manley Hudson, *Current International Co-operation* (University of Calcutta, 1927), p. 95.

[76] *Ibid.*, p. 125; "The Development of International Law since the War," 339–341.

measures; but it would be equally improper to deny them any value as such."[77] Here again Hudson echoed Garner's observations.

Criticism of Garner, Fenwick and Hudson came from John Bassett Moore,[78] a positivist and the compiler of the *Digest of International Law*, an eight-volume collection of cases and statutes. In his review of *A Handbook of Public International Law* by T. J. Lawrence, Moore argued that some writers had overemphasized the effect of law-making treaties. Lawrence, a British scholar whose opinions resembled those of Oppenheim, had died in 1915 but his book continued to be published. Moore was critical of a recent edition of the book that dealt with instruments like the Peace Treaty of Versailles and the Washington Treaties of 1922 for including the limitation of naval armaments in the category of law-making treaties.[79] In Moore's opinion, they were not universally binding because the number of signatories was limited. The *Handbook* contained the following passage: "We may speak of Law-Making Treaties as forming a statute-book of the laws of nations. Most of them are very recent, and none go back beyond modern times. The existence of such *corpus juris* is a new and most significant development in the evolution of an organized society of nations."[80] Moore did not support this view and contended that writers on international law should be as careful as writers on municipal law "to keep within the range of legal ideas and legal terminology." And he concluded, "If international law is to be restored to the legal position which it formerly enjoyed, those who essay to expound it must keep within the realm of legal conceptions."[81]

Moore's criticism was that of a legal positivist who wanted to keep the range of law narrow. A different criticism came from Nicholas Spykman of Yale University, a realist from the field of international relations who would, in the 1930s, become known as an advocate of geopolitics. At the 1927 meeting of the ASIL, Spykman pointed out the confusion between reality and ideals in the discussions presented by the advocates of new international law. He remarked:

> I want to plead with you to be a little more theoretical when you are practical and to be a little more practical when you are theoretical ... For ten

---

[77] Hudson, *International Co-operation*, p. 128.
[78] See also Janis, *America and the Law*, pp. 204–206.
[79] John Bassett Moore, "Post-War International Law," *Columbia Law Review* 27 (1927), 406–407.
[80] T. J. Lawrence, *A Handbook of Public International Law*, 10th edn., by Percy H. Winfield (London: Macmillan, 1925), p. 32.
[81] Moore, "Post-War International Law," 411.

minutes I was sure we were discussing what the rules are, and the next
ten minutes I was lost because we were discussing what the rules ought
to be.[82]

The members were not unmindful of this kind of criticism. At the
Conference of Teachers of International Law of 1925, Carl Christol of the
University of South Dakota posed the question of "whether the teachers
of international law should limit their discussions strictly to the law as it
is pretty generally recognized or should go beyond that and consider the
question as to what law ought to be." He stated his preference for the latter
view because "international law was still formulating" and he felt teachers
should participate in its formulation.[83]

An opportunity for scholars of international law to have a role in the
actual process of forming international law came from the League of
Nations in 1925, when it began a program of codifying international law
and asked societies of international law all over the world for their technical assistance. The Director of the Legal Section of the League sent a
letter to the ASIL asking for its collaboration.[84] The ASIL was requested
to consider what the problems of international law were and what kind of
agreements would seem to be most desirable. The ASIL appointed a special committee to consider the problem, consisting of Borchard, Brown,
Fenwick, Stowell, Wright, Jesse S. Reeves and Arthur K. Kuhn.

At the 1926 meeting of the ASIL, the issue of codification was discussed.
Garner stated that "the progress of international law has lagged behind the
development of international relations" and that codification was the most
important and practical means for it to catch up. Hudson again suggested
that in some questions codification should be "loose" – for example, with
regard to the difference between domestic and international problems. He
remarked, "for my part, I should depreciate any attempt to put that difference into cold language that would perpetuate itself." It was better to leave
them "undetermined," so that future progress could deal with it better.
While the League had suggested such concrete topics as nationality, territorial waters, and so on, Fenwick argued that "it is the general principles of
codification that we most need to discuss." He wanted to codify such general principles as the equality of states and international comity.[85]

---

[82] "Discussion," *Proceedings, ASIL* (1927), 71.
[83] "Discussion of Resolutions and Recommendations of the Conference," *Proceedings, Second Teachers*, p. 142.
[84] Van Hamel to the Chairman of the ASIL, April 1, 1925, ASIL Papers.
[85] "The Function and Scope of Codification in International Law," *Proceedings, ASIL* (1926), 28; "General Discussion," *Proceedings, ASIL* (1926), 41, 55–56.

The League's request for professional help in effect authorized scholars to discuss what they thought international law ought to be. Without a definite concept of law, any future codification would be nothing more than a recollection of customs and old rules, the positivistic strategy that many scholars had been fighting against. Since the war, theorists had argued for changes in international law, and they saw codification as their chance to effect actual change. This was also a time of new international legislation such as that controlling air traffic and regulation of the opium trade, most of which came under the auspices of the League. The scholars' hopes for further progress in international law were inspired by the successful promulgation of such legislation. Under these circumstances, scholars of international law felt that they were entitled to discuss what international law ought to be. Rather than indulging in purely abstract discussions, they had good reason to expect that their discussions and writings would yield concrete results. It was a time when international society was setting rules, and intellectual and professional help was expressly called for.

That the younger international lawyers were not content with ideas of pure justice or the mere judicial settlement of international problems is reflected in their evaluation of the role of the PCIJ. Even though its creation had been a long-standing dream of scholars of an earlier generation, the members of the ASIL who were active in the 1920s believed that the Court could play only a limited role. Even Scott came to accept this and noted that the PCIJ could fulfill one function in international society.

Although the phrase "enlargement of law" was frequently used in discussions and writings, even its advocates did not clearly explain what it meant. The enlargement of law had several dimensions. First of all, it was associated with "law-making" treaties. These were not new, but the drafting of multilateral conventions in various fields after World War I confirmed the soundness of the concept. If a majority of states agreed on, for example, the abolition of the slave trade, then this agreement would certainly affect the rest of the world.

Secondly, progressive international lawyers accepted the Covenant of the League of Nations as the constitution of international society, one which not only prescribed concrete legal rules but also contained a code of morality. Encouraged by this view and probably helped by their critical attitude toward positivism, some international lawyers, notably Garner and Willoughby, sought to promote the "enlargement of law" by defining the principles of international law. Their definitions were not precise, and sometimes included ethical and moral rules, or referred to international comity and responsibility. No matter how vague the content of the principles might be, this group of lawyers regarded them as practically applicable in foreign relations. This was the case in their discussions of the 1924 prohibition of Japanese immigration to the United States. Garner asserted that the Japanese government could "invoke the doctrine of equality of states ... as a principle of international law."[86]

Particularly notable in Hudson and Wright's arguments were an emphasis on flexibility and a readiness to adapt to changes. The frequent references to Roscoe Pound indicated that they were influenced by his theory of "sociological jurisprudence."[87] Echoing Pound's premise that law should respond to social needs, Hudson and Wright argued that international law, too, should adapt to the needs of a changing world.

And finally, the enlargement of law led to the question of whether a distinction between political and legal issues, between policies and international law, was necessary or even possible. The general discussions at the ASIL favored the view that any clear distinction between the two was futile. When collaboration with the League on the matter of codification was discussed, a question was posed about the danger of getting involved in the League's political activities. Fenwick answered: "Get into the politics of the League. Every effort to codify international law leads you inevitably into the political activities of the world."[88] Fenwick and his supporters came to realize that law-making was not isolated from policy making and they were willing to play a role in the political world.

What kind of international law did these scholars hope to achieve? Not just a judge-made law, certainly. Nor an international law that merely reflected the policies of one country. Wright, Fenwick, Garner, Hudson and others who supported the progressive view of international law wanted something much more comprehensive. They were aiming to establish an international order, through which the welfare of international society could be achieved. They wanted a framework for fair, peaceful and prosperous relations among nations.

---

[86] "Discussion," *Proceedings, ASIL* (1924), 74.
[87] Hudson and Wright referred to Pound's articles, particularly, "Philosophical Theory and International Law," *Bibliotheca Visseriana* 1 (1923), 71–90. See, for instance, Hudson, "The Prospect for International Law in the Twentieth Century," 421; Wright, *Proceedings, Second Teachers*, p. 95.
[88] "General Discussion," *Proceedings, ASIL* (1926), 55–56.

3

Can international law master war?

Humankind would not survive another world war. This was the premise that underlay the new trend in international law after World War I. The invention of new technologies that increased casualties fueled the fear of war, and an earnest desire to prevent war became a general concern in Europe and the United States. Even before the war, the study of international law had shown signs of change, and calls had been heard for interpretive renovations to construct a family of nations, as opposed to the existing system of atomistic states. Reformers advocated a more ambitious law. But even with aspirations for peace and for a more ambitious international law, how did scholars deal with the issues surrounding war? What was their intellectual contribution to the regulation of war?

Intellectual discussions on the legal limitations of war

Among the reformers, it was Quincy Wright who took up the issue of war most prolifically and forthrightly. In his 1924 article entitled "Changes in the Conception of War," he attempted to answer the question of whether existing international law considered war "lawful" or not. His conclusion was that war had never been legal in the positive sense. Within the limits of the laws of war, and only through the certain procedures such as a declaration of war, had war become "extra-legal." The fact that war was characterized by its status as an emergency deprived lawyers of the opportunity to judge any given war's appropriateness. Wright stressed the point that war was not a normal or regular event but that it was given an exceptional position in the scheme of international law. He stated, "war is not a lawful institution, but an event, an unfortunate event" that makes "the operation of normal law impossible and makes application of emergency law of war and neutrality *a pis-aller*."[1]

---

[1] Quincy Wright, "Changes in the Conception of War," *AJIL* 18 (1924), 761.

Wright was critical of the attitudes of earlier legal theorists, who had given up discussing "the responsibility for and the justice of wars." With the increase of its destructiveness, demand for the abolishment of war increased and scholars could no longer evade the problem. Referring to Roscoe Pound's "sociological jurisprudence," which stressed legal function as an agency for progress, Wright argued for a legal development capable of regulating war. Specifically, he mentioned the need to devise criteria of responsibility for beginning war, criteria for determining justifiable self-defense, and adequate agencies that could adequately enforce the legal will of the international community.[2]

In an article published the following year, Wright sought to elaborate these three issues. The first issue involved the search for a precise legal means for determining who had started war. He strove to find it in existing obligations and treaties. Wright noted that Professor Charles de Visscher of Ghent University had recently pointed out that while the neutralization of frontiers might not be regarded as an effective guarantee against invasion, "it may still serve a useful purpose by providing a means for judging the legality of certain acts of war," because a state that violated such an agreement could be deemed as committing an irresponsible act. He believed that the legal regulation of war based on definite space and time would be possible, contending, "the initiation of war has been outlawed in certain places, at certain times, for certain objects by an increasing number."[3]

The determination of what constituted rightful self-defense was meant to provide legal criteria for distinguishing between what was justifiable and non-justifiable. Wright analyzed the circumstances under which international law recognized the invocation of the right of self-defense and cited five criteria: (1) when there existed an instant and overwhelming need to defend territory or citizens; (2) to seek redress for properly validated legal claims; (3) to prevent flagrant violations of international law; (4) to fulfill privileges expressly granted by treaty; and (5) to enforce law that fell within the state's own jurisdiction. Only in these cases, Wright concluded, could military action with the claim of self-defense be justified.[4]

In addition to setting up the legal criteria for both the beginning of war and self-defense, Wright argued for the need for enforcement. He was well aware of the fact that legal criteria would remain ineffective,

[2] *Ibid.*, 767.   [3] Quincy Wright, "The Outlawry of War," *AJIL* 19 (1925), 86, 103.
[4] *Ibid.*, 94.

unless they were backed up by the threat of sanction. The very nature of an international society devoid of a central authority made it even more necessary to have the guarantee backed by power. Although this was still a new idea, Wright concluded that Articles 10 and 16 of the Covenant of the League of Nations signified important progress toward its implementation.[5]

The ASIL itself devoted a session at its 1925 meeting to "Legal Limitations upon the Initiation of Military Action." David Jayne Hill pointed out that the prevention of war through laws essentially involved resolving the conflict between the "practical limitation of war powers" and the "freedom and independence of sovereign states." At present, it was impossible for international law "to go so far as to deny the right of a free and independent nation to levy war." Yet, he was not totally pessimistic. The experience of history had witnessed "progressive renunciation of the idea that war powers are absolute." He cited as examples the proposals for the reduction of armaments and for the amelioration of the use of war. More specifically, Article 1 of the Second Convention of the Second Hague Conference determined that states should not "have recourse to armed force for the recovery of contract debts." Hill argued that in the course of history the limitation of military action had been advanced through treaties and conventions.[6]

The second speaker, Thomas Raeburn White of the Philadelphia Bar, focused on the development of international law in the last hundred years and noted that the use of arbitration and judicial procedure to settle international claims had made significant progress. These methods had been used as alternatives to war. At the same time, the Covenant of the League of Nations and the Geneva Protocol defined wars of aggression and thus limited the scope of legal wars.[7] The optimism evidenced in both papers resulted from the same belief in the gradual, historical development toward the regulation and abolition of war.

Despite the optimistic tone of the two papers, however, Albert Bushnell Hart of Harvard University was skeptical about the possibility of enforcing legal limitations on war. He stressed that the theorists should take into account "the actual status and condition of the world." According to Hart, these actual conditions could be defined in terms of

[5] Ibid., 96–101.
[6] David Jayne Hill, "Legal Limitations upon the Initiation of Military Action," Proceedings, ASIL (1925), 95, 98, 100.
[7] Thomas Raeburn White, "Limitations upon the Initiation of War," Proceedings, ASIL (1925), 102–111.

three observations. First of all, it was not wise to compare domestic and international societies, because the world is not made up of equal units. Secondly, he doubted that judicial methods could resolve international conflicts, citing the examples that neither Russia nor Japan in 1904, nor any of the Balkan states, had resorted to such methods. Hart's third observation concerned the dominance of the great powers. In his words, "The greater nations of the world, especially the eight or ten most populous, possess the greater part of the wealth and the power." Charles G. Fenwick responded by arguing that scholars should look at the interests common among the states instead of emphasizing "the things that separate us."[8] Those who were optimistic about the abolition of war shared the historical view that international law had progressively developed toward the regulation of war, but they did not go beyond the realm of analysis, nor did they pay much attention to actual policy.

Another important issue concerning war was how to deal with the laws of war, such as those governing contraband, neutrality and prisoners. These topics had occupied a significant place in the traditional approach to international law, because in the older interpretations the rationality of going to war, a right of sovereign states, had not been questioned. However, during World War I some scholars became skeptical about the laws of war. After the war this tendency became stronger,[9] as epitomized by the remark, "the preoccupation of writers and statesmen with the laws of war has been a real obstacle to the progress of international law."[10] Opponents argued that the emphasis had to be shifted to the laws of peace, because maintenance of the laws of war would in effect justify the legality of war. Some even expressed the radical opinion that the laws of war were totally useless and should be stricken from the textbooks of international law.[11]

Although James W. Garner and Fenwick were among the reformers, they did not seek to overly restrict the task of the laws of war. Responding to the above attacks, Garner admitted that there was an "urgent need for revision of the whole body of the laws of war," but he did not desire their total abolishment. In his book concerning new currents in international

---

[8] *Proceedings, ASIL* (1925), 112, 114.

[9] Kendal C. Brynes, "The Status of the Rules of War in International Law," unpublished Ph.D. thesis, University of Chicago (1952), p. 96.

[10] "The League of Nations and the Laws of War," *British Year Book of International Law* 1 (1920–1), 116.

[11] Jackson H. Ralston, review of *International Law and the World War*, by James Wilford Garner, *AJIL* 15 (1921), 621; see also Jackson H. Ralston, "How Fundamental International Law is to be Discovered," *American Law Review* 56 (1922), 236–249.

law, he analyzed which laws of war had been violated during World War I and which had been observed. He concluded that "the deliberate violations of the law, numerous as they were, have been greatly exaggerated." The effort to regulate the conduct of war did not have to be abandoned in order to lessen the destructiveness and inhumanity of future wars. At the same time, however, Garner acknowledged that the priorities of the study should be redefined, writing that "the true function of international law should be not the regulation of war but the regulation and promotion of pacific relations between states."[12]

Fenwick published his book *International Law* at about the same time. He assigned nearly a quarter of its 600 pages to the treatment of the laws of war, including such topics as "the laws of land warfare," "the laws of maritime warfare" and "neutral duties." Explaining the reason why a substantial portion of the book dealt with the laws of war, he asserted that statesmen and publicists were "unwilling or unable to deny to states at variance the rights to maintain their claims by force" and instead relied on the development of the laws of war to remedy war. In this, Fenwick sounded somewhat apologetic and ambivalent. It was common for modern international law to be divided into the two branches of peace and war, but they were clearly different because the former was constructive and the latter procedural. Fenwick did not try to clarify the relation between them.[13]

A review critical of Fenwick's book appeared in the *AJIL*. Jackson Ralston wrote that Fenwick seemed to want to present a new view but the book was filled with old premises. Because Fenwick attached "an entirely secondary importance to the so-called laws of war," he treated them "as if today they approached the dignity of a science." In addition, Ralston was critical that Fenwick did not "condemn but tentatively accepts the validity and legality of war as instrumentality." Fenwick's analysis was based on an analogy between international and domestic society, in which the purpose of law was to safeguard peace and equality. The abolishment of war must be the primary aim, Ralston stated, for "insofar as war exists between nations at all, it demonstrates the failure of international law." The attitude of theorists toward the issue of war mattered, and Ralston suggested that dealing with war as a legal institution might not "inspire enthusiasm."[14]

---

[12] Garner, *Recent Developments in International Law*, pp. 805–808.
[13] Fenwick, *International Law*, pp. 429–430.
[14] Jackson H. Ralston, review of *International Law*, by Charles G. Fenwick, *AJIL* 18 (1924), 853–855.

Responding to the review, Fenwick, in a letter to Wright, claimed that Ralston omitted "all discussion of the major portion of the volume and condemns the whole because it gives the laws of war in a general system." Fenwick asked Wright to contribute a brief editorial review on "the place of the laws of war in a scientific survey of the laws of war."[15] Wright declined the offer, but voiced his understanding. He thought that Ralston was wrong in holding that "the best way to get rid of war is to pretend it doesn't exist." At that moment, Wright was more realistic in admitting the ubiquitous nature of war than he would later be, saying that "As long as it does exist in fact it is better to regulate it as far as possible."[16]

At the 1925 Conference of Teachers of International Law and Related Subjects, the issue of the laws of war was brought up and opinions were exchanged. Fenwick, chairman of the session, started the discussion by referring to several reviews that were critical of his book because one-quarter of it dealt with the laws of war. After stating that there was a great amount of confusion in the present study of the laws of war, he lamented, "I have a strong feeling that the laws of war are on the wane." Manley O. Hudson spoke up, acknowledging that he might be among those who criticized Fenwick's book because it dealt "too extensively with the so-called laws of war." Hudson argued that if a student of international law were to go into practice he would have little chance of encountering the laws of war. Replying to the question of whether future textbooks should include sections on the laws of war, Hudson declared "my advice is, leave it out." Wright said that he was sympathetic to Hudson's concerns, but that he did not support the view that the laws of war should not be taught at all. While he did not agree with the rationale of the laws of war, he emphasized that it was important to give students all the possible sources of law and acquaint them with judicial decisions "even in such a marginal case as war."[17]

In the face of widespread ambivalence to the decline of the laws of war and their importance, Edwin M. Borchard stood up to defend them. He referred to Thomas Baty's recent article in the *Yale Law Journal* as an example of strong opposition to the new trend. In the article, Baty had argued that the present attack on international law was not unheard of; after the Napoleonic wars the same claim of the demise of international law had been made. He stressed the significance of maintaining both the

---

[15] Fenwick to Wright, November 20, 1924, Wright Papers, Box 5, Folder 6.
[16] Wright to Fenwick, December 1, 1924, Wright Papers, Box 5, Folder 6.
[17] *Proceedings, Second Teachers* (1925), pp. 68, 80, 81.

distinction between belligerents and neutrals and the systematic integrity of the laws of war.[18] Supporting Baty's argument, Borchard enunciated his own belief that it would be impossible to completely abolish war. He stated that "wars for this coming generation or two are very likely to occur." With that in mind, he counseled, "I think it a mistake to minimize the importance of the laws of war."[19]

Three years later, in 1928, the Third Conference of Teachers of International Law focused again on the laws of war. This time the issue took up an entire session entitled, "The Distribution of International Law among the Laws of Peace, War, and Neutrality, and the Relative Emphasis Upon Each in College, Graduate, and Law School Course." Most of the discussion focused on whether or how the laws of war should be taught at colleges and law schools.

Garner related how his opinion had changed. He stated that he had become skeptical about teaching the laws of war. In teaching this subject, instructors explained to students about each type of conduct in war, for example, whether the shooting of a spy was legal or not. Garner wondered, however, whether these kinds of detailed rules were qualified to be called "law" at a time when the focus of international law had shifted from regulating war itself to the peaceful settlement of conflicts. Professor Norman MacKenzie of Toronto University also stated his opposition. MacKenzie argued that teachers of international law were assisting in the "perpetuation of war," because "the laws of war have been used and can be used by nations as a means of furthering their own interest." Hudson stressed that while at graduate schools the laws of war had to be taught for the facilitation of research, there was no need to teach them at colleges or law schools.[20]

Pittman Potter of the University of Wisconsin described himself as a "pessimist" and pointed out the false assumption – that war would never happen again – cherished by those "optimistic" scholars. He held instead that war was not obsolete and would happen again. Professor Royal B. Way of Beloit College held an opinion similar to Potter's. He argued that "teaching the laws of peace will not establish peace in the world; nor will the exclusion of the laws of war from our classroom discussions have the effect of staying conflict." He stressed the danger in neglecting the laws of war: "We all realize that the last war was a terrible one; so terrible that we

[18] Thomas Baty, "Danger Signals in International Law," *Yale Law Journal* 34 (1925), 468.
[19] *Proceedings, Second Teachers* (1925), 78–81.
[20] *Proceedings, Third Teachers* (1928), 105–106, 108, 110.

do not want it repeated. But there is one thing more terrible; and that is totally unregulated warfare."[21]

The debate over the status of the laws of war did not produce any definite conclusions. The division between the reformers and the traditionalists was reflected most distinctively in their views on the legal feasibility of abolishing war. Or, put another way, behind their optimism and pessimism lay their attitudes toward war. While reformers thought that the abolition of war was possible and worked toward that end, traditionalists regarded war as inevitable.

This disagreement led to a relative decrease in the number of works published concerning the laws of war. Hudson wrote that no progress had been made since the war on "restating, clarifying, or improving our international law concerning the conduct of war."[22] In 1930 Wright himself completed a report for the Social Science Research Council on the status of international law. He saw the increased interest in the elimination of war as one of the characteristics of the field and cautioned that "detailed discussion of the rules of war and neutrality have received little attention." He candidly stated that the dominant opinion gave only the "insignificant importance" to the rules of war.[23] During the interwar years, although Garner, Baty and scholars from the older generation in general continued their research on the rules of war, there was a relative decline in interest in the subject.

The Geneva Protocol

While theorists had been debating the regulation of war by law, the League of Nations was advancing a system to prevent war. Although the American theorists were not directly committed to the League's efforts, their efforts had significance for European scholars' arguments. In addition, Nicolas Politis, a Greek delegate to the League, who was directly involved in the process, was an advocate of the new international law.

After several years of discussions, the League's final result on the regulation of war was the Geneva Protocol of Pacific Settlement, adopted on October 2, 1924. Based on the principles of the Covenant, the Protocol reconfirmed the necessity to link security matters with methods for

---

[21] *Ibid.*, 95, 115–116.
[22] Hudson, "The Development of International Law since the War," 338.
[23] Quincy Wright, *Research in International Law since the War: A Report to the International Relations Committee of the Social Science Research Council* (Washington, DC: Carnegie Endowment for International Peace, 1930), pp. 24–25.

peaceful settlement of international conflicts. With the addition of sections concerning peaceful settlement, the system was considered comprehensive, and the report noted distinctively that "Our purpose was to make war impossible, to kill it, to annihilate it. To do this, we had to create a *system* [italics original] for the pacific settlement of all disputes which might arise." The Protocol aimed at establishing a comprehensive system that was composed of three elements: a compulsory method for pacific settlement, the achievement of disarmament, and a feasible method for levying sanctions. The significance of the Protocol lay in the fact that it showed that the abolition of war had to be dealt with systematically. Legal principles and frameworks had to be dealt with as one of the several pillars necessary for the abolition of war, not as the only one. The Protocol defined aggression as occurring when a country's actions were not approved by the League Council, or when the country refused to submit the case to the required procedure for pacific settlement.[24]

American international lawyers responded to the Protocol with mixed observations. While the reformers generally welcomed it, the traditionalists were doubtful. Garner focused on its completeness as a system and praised it wholeheartedly. He wrote that the Protocol was the biggest step yet taken toward the peaceable settlement of international controversies and the regulation of aggression. He detailed the discussions and developments leading up to the Protocol and stated, "No one can study it without being impressed by its completeness as a scheme for the accomplishment of the objects which are contemplated, by its freedom from lacunae." He also speculated on the actual effect of the Protocol, writing, "The very knowledge of the existence of such an obligation" would "serve as a powerful deterrent to acts of aggression and make actual resort to measures of repression relatively rare."[25] Wright also judged the Protocol positively, paying particular attention to its definition of aggression. The Protocol, he stated, narrowed down the permissible use of military force and presented objective and automatic criteria for determining aggression.[26]

Philip Marshall Brown, however, criticized the Protocol on four points. First of all, the definition of aggressor was "most questionable." The Protocol supposed that a nation had to wait for the Council's decision, but in some instances troops had to be dispatched without delay to

---

[24] League of Nations, "Arbitration, Security, and Reduction of Armaments," C. 708, DLN, p. 355; David Hunter Miller, *The Geneva Protocol* (New York: Macmillan, 1925), pp. 50–63.
[25] James Wilford Garner, "The Geneva Protocol for the Pacific Settlement of International Disputes," *AJIL* 19 (1925), 123, 132.
[26] Wright, "The Outlawry of War," 95.

secure the life of nationals, as was the case in China and Haiti. Secondly, the Protocol would in effect secure the status quo by prohibiting the use of force. Thirdly, if the League were equipped with the authority to forbid war, it would assume the "responsibilities of a superstate." Since the Treaty of Westphalia, the international system had been based on the "recognition of the personality of states," which deemed each state to be the highest authority. And finally, international law had developed with a common consent, but the Protocol recommended a method of compulsion through military sanction.[27]

In spite of the high valuation given to the Protocol by the reformers, they were not sure whether it would be effective. It was decided that ratification by at least thirteen members of the League, including three of the four great powers, was necessary for effectuation, and a deadline of May 1, 1925 was set. When the American Political Science Association met in December 1924, most participants were pessimistic about actual ratification. Garner frankly stated his concern that the Protocol would not be ratified and criticized as irresponsible the attitudes of the countries, saying that "most of the world wishes to obtain the great advantages without assuming the necessary correlative obligations."[28]

Hudson also anticipated difficulty in ratifying the Protocol, but he had faith in its value for the long-term progress of international law. He wrote that "its provisions are bound to affect the place which war will have in international law as it is to be developed in the future." He did not seem to care about the concrete effects, contending, "Even if no further progress were made immediately, the drafting of the Protocol is in itself a fitting celebration of the third centenary of the publication of Grotius' classic *De Jure Belli ac Pacis*."[29]

For all the significance that American theorists attached to the League's effort, the official US response was nothing short of rejection. The State Department feared that the American right to intervene in Latin America, authorized by the Monroe Doctrine, would be hampered by the Protocol. Secretary of State Charles Evans Hughes even hoped that the Protocol would die a natural death. The British government more than once inquired about American intentions toward the Protocol. Neville Chamberlain, British Foreign Minister, felt that the British government

---

[27] Philip Marshall Brown, "The Geneva Protocol," *AJIL* 19 (1925), 338, 339.
[28] Edwin D. Dickinson, "Reports of the Round Table Conferences," *American Political Science Review* 19 (1925), 375–376.
[29] Manley O. Hudson, "The Geneva Protocol," *Foreign Affairs* 3 (1924), 235.

could not accept its broad obligations because the United States was not a member.[30]

The supporters of the Protocol were not unmindful of the Protocol's possible effects on American foreign policy. The Chicago Council on Foreign Relations, an organization established for the purpose of enhancing international understanding among intellectuals, called for papers on the implications of the Protocol for the United States. Wright's submission won first prize and Garner's third. In his essay, Wright frankly stated that as far as the Monroe Doctrine implied "a right of the United States" to intervene, the Protocol seemed to oppose that right. If, following the present procedures of the Protocol, a Latin American country appealed to the League about US intervention it was possible that other nations could impose sanctions against the United States.[31] Garner wrote that the Protocol reminded the United States of the fact that she could not afford to remain aloof forever while the rest of the world steadily worked toward shaping a new international order.[32]

The Geneva Protocol was a comprehensive and theoretically elaborate system, as most scholars acknowledged. But in terms of actual international relations, it would remain nothing more than a scrap of paper unless it were ratified and went into effect. Only Czechoslovakia ratified the Protocol, however, and it never went into effect. Theorists were optimistic about the gradual development of the regulation of war, but if their theories failed to yield concrete results, there could be no significant changes in the system. The Protocol revealed a gap between theory and reality. While Wright, Garner and other reformers praised the theoretical developments, the great powers were not ready to accept "the responsibilities of organized peace" embodied in the theory.[33]

Outlawry of war and the Kellogg–Briand Pact

Whereas the League failed to adopt the Geneva Protocol in spite of its completeness as an institutional approach, in the United States a movement

---

[30] David D. Burks, "The United States and the Geneva Protocol of 1924, 'A New Holy Alliance'?" *American Historical Review* 64 (1959), 897, 901. See also *Foreign Relations of the United States* (hereafter *FRUS*) 1925, I, pp. 16–20.

[31] *Significance to America of the Geneva Protocol* (Chicago Council on Foreign Relations, n.d.), p. 10.

[32] *Ibid.*, p. 41.

[33] F. P. Walters, *A History of the League of Nations* (London: Oxford University Press, 1952), p. 277.

for the "outlawry of war" had arisen and was flourishing. The movement was initiated and promoted by Salmon O. Levinson, a wealthy corporate lawyer in Chicago. Levinson had had little interest in international affairs until the outbreak of World War I, when he had been shocked to discover that war was not illegal. From his studies, Levinson concluded that in international law war was treated as legal. Most books on international law, he found, actually detailed rules for the conduct of war rather than for preserving peace.[34] In spring of 1918, when war was still raging in Europe, Levinson published an article entitled "The Legal Status of War," in which he contended that it would be absurd to oppose war if war itself were legal. What grounds could people use, Levinson asked, to oppose war, militarism or the build up of armaments if it was legal for a nation to wage war? He decided that what was needed was a movement to make war illegal.[35]

On December 9, 1921, the American Committee for the Outlawry of War was established, and throughout the 1920s Levinson was its most vociferous supporter. He financed it out of his own pocket and had copies of the pamphlet *A Plan to Outlaw War* sent to government officials, governors, congressmen, school teachers, journalists and even farmers. Levinson was successful in enlisting two important figures of the time, the philosopher John Dewey and Senator William Borah. Professor Dewey wrote the foreword for the pamphlet and, in collaboration with Levinson, published several articles on the outlawry of war in the *New Republic* and *Foreign Affairs*.[36] Although Senator Borah's support for this movement might have been based on political calculations, his association with the cause was a great asset.[37] He was one of the so-called "irreconcilables" in the Senate, opposing US participation in the League of Nations, and became chairman of the Senate Foreign Relations Committee in 1925. Borah's introduction of resolutions in Congress in 1923 and 1926 to outlaw war gave political credibility to the movement. The American public was attracted to the simple yet eloquent catchphrase of "outlawry of war," which unlike membership in the League did not entail any form of responsibility or obligations. The outlawry

[34] John E. Stoner, *S. O. Levinson and the Pact of Paris* (University of Chicago Press, 1942), p. 28.

[35] Salmon O. Levinson, "The Legal Status of War," *New Republic* 14 (March 9, 1918), 172.

[36] Stoner, *S. O. Levinson*, pp. 68–72, 81–95,106–107. See also Levinson, *The Outlawry of War*, December 25, 1921, American Committee for the Outlawry of War.

[37] Borah arranged for Levinson's *The Outlawry of War* to be published by the US Government Printing Office. See *The Outlawry of War* (Washington, DC: GPO, 1922).

movement spread like wildfire, particularly among church groups and the women's peace movement.

The theoretical significance of the outlawry of war lay in its emphasis on the abolition of "war as an institution." Levinson explained this by virtue of an analogy between dueling and war. When dueling was still legal, there existed a set of codes regulating it. However, once dueling was abolished by law, it became equivalent to murder. Levinson argued that if human society deprived war of its legal status, it could be abolished in the same way that humankind had abolished dueling, the slave trade and piracy.[38] According to the theory behind the outlawry of war, the right of self-defense would not be prohibited. Still, although the right of self-defense was seen as an inherent right of nations, in the strict theoretical sense all types of war were to be abolished. The outlawry of war was designed to abolish "war as an institution," leaving no room for permissible war. Accordingly, differentiation between aggressive war and defensive war, or special treatment of wars for collective security, was meaningless. War in every sense would be prohibited, though if a nation launched a military action in self-defense, that action would not be called war.[39]

Criticism of the outlawry of war movement came from Walter Lippmann as early as 1923. First of all, he pointed out a contradiction that was epitomized by Borah's support for the movement. Senator Borah had opposed "every established institution for the prevention of war," such as the League of Nations and the PCIJ. If he were serious about international cooperation for world peace, Lippmann asked, why hadn't he and others in the movement supported these organizations, which some fifty nations of the world had joined? Furthermore, he suggested that a danger existed in its very scheme, the danger of overemphasizing the power of legal restrictions in dealing with conflicts among nations and thus of neglecting such political means as conference, compromise and bargaining.[40]

Wright was also critical of the movement. While Levinson counted on the overarching ethical and moral power of law, Wright favored a more elaborate notion of jurisprudence to regulate war. By setting up definite legal criteria for responsibility, aggression and sanctions, he believed that

---

[38] Levinson, "The Legal Status of War," 172; Charles Clayton Morrison, *The Outlawry of War* (Chicago: Willett, Clark, & Colby, 1927), pp. 96–98.

[39] Salmon O. Levinson, "Abolishing the Institution of War," *Christian Century* 65 (1928), 379; Levinson, "A Proposed Treaty to Outlaw War," *Christian Century* 63 (1926), 1582; Morrison, *Outlawry*, pp. 206–214; Stoner, *S. O. Levinson*, pp. 194–195.

[40] Walter Lippmann, "The Outlawry of War," *Atlantic Monthly* 132 (1923), 245–253. See also Lippmann, "The Political Equivalent of War," *Atlantic Monthly* 142 (1928), 181–187.

the regulation of war could be achieved. He argued, "To expect anything from a mere agreement on the principle, unsupported by organization seems fatuous indeed … International law, supported by adequate organization, may actually outlaw war." Simply declaring war to be illegal would not suffice.[41]

While the theorists were skeptical of legal effectiveness in outlawry of war, a new development had been taking place. In April, 1927 French Premier Aristide Briand proposed an anti-war treaty with the United States. It led to an American counterproposal for a multilateral treaty to renounce war, and the Kellogg–Briand Pact was signed in Paris on August 27, 1928.[42] In substance, the Pact turned out to reflect the premise of the outlawry of war as enunciated by Levinson. The original French proposal for a bilateral treaty contained a section dealing with the levying of sanctions against an aggressor. But as is well known, the Kellogg–Briand Pact had only two articles, which simply proclaimed that each signatory would not resort to war as a means to solve international conflicts and that war would be illegal. It embodied the idea inherent in Levinson's theory, which was independent in origin of developments in the League of Nations. It was a formula that Lippmann and Wright criticized.

Among international lawyers, the most straightforward attack against the Pact came not surprisingly from Borchard, who wrote, "it seems to me more dangerous to sign the Kellogg Pact than to enter the League."[43] He argued that the reservations and interpretations issued by other powers during the negotiations were legally effective, since they were officially made and communicated to the US government. Likewise, Borchard held that Kellogg's note of June 23 which acknowledged the American insistence on preserving the right of self-defense was legally effective. Based on this interpretation, he wrote that "the Pact of Paris is not a renunciation of war, but formal recognition of the legality of all the wars mentioned in the reservations and exceptions." He concluded that the Pact did not enhance the cause of peace, but rather created new misunderstandings. Besides, any attempts to abolish war by treaty, by a simple pledge, failed to consider the causes of war, which were "the more fundamental factors of political rivalry and unfair competition."[44]

---

[41] Wright, "The Outlawry of War," 103.
[42] As for diplomatic negotiations, see *FRUS*, 1928, I, pp. 39–56; Ferrel, *Peace in their Time*, pp. 170–191.
[43] Borchard to Finch, November 17, 1928, ASIL Papers.
[44] Edwin M. Borchard, "The Multilateral Treaty for the Renunciation of War," *AJIL* 23 (1929), 110–120. See also Bederman, "Appraising a Century," 33.

Other international lawyers were more favorable, although most of them noted weaknesses in the Pact. David Jayne Hill wrote that it required a means of enforcement but that the renunciation of war constituted "a solid foundation for inaugurating a new era in the life of mankind."[45] Fenwick found the contribution of the Pact to be the "definition of the place which war is henceforth to have in the scheme of international relations." Meanwhile, he pointed out that the most serious flaw was that the "lack of a definition of self-defense left the interpretation of the Pact extremely elastic." He also warned specifically, and somewhat prophetically, that this deficiency would become apparent when Japan launched actions in Manchuria, or Italy in the Mediterranean.[46]

Wright had been critical of the outlawry of war before and was no less critical of the Pact. He proposed the theory that in multilateral treaties the force of interpretative notes was weaker than in bilateral treaties, because multilateral treaties can be seen as analogous to statutes in the domestic law. In the case of statutes, there was a tendency to concentrate on the text itself, because statutes had a normative effect. Wright argued that although this was technically true, an exception should be made for multilateral treaties, and he acknowledged that his theory probably did not apply to the Pact, because it did not qualify as a legally perfect document. According to Wright, the Pact's real significance lay in the political effect it would have by mobilizing public opinion, not in its legal effects.[47] While Wright foresaw only political results for the Pact, Fenwick contended that "The obligations may be vague and may present numerous loopholes of escape, but such as they are being embodied in a formal international contract, they are legal."[48]

The debate over whether the Pact had any legal significance continued at the annual meeting of the ASIL in April 1929.[49] The speaker for the session entitled "The Pact of Paris for the Renunciation of War: Its Meaning and Effect in International Law" was Roland S. Morris, a professor at the University of Pennsylvania and a former ambassador of the United States to Japan. Morris, at the outset of his remarks, emphasized that he would

---

[45] David Jayne Hill, "The Multilateral Treaty for the Renunciation of War," *AJIL* 22 (1928), 823–826.

[46] Charles G. Fenwick, "War as an Instrument of National Policy," *AJIL* 22 (October 1928), 826–829.

[47] Quincy Wright, "The Interpretation of Multilateral Treaties," *AJIL* 23 (1929), 94–107. See also Bederman, "Appraising a Century," 32–33.

[48] Fenwick, "War as an Instrument," 826.

[49] For the ASIL and the Pact, see also Kirgis, *The American Society*, pp. 103–104.

confine his discussion to the "strictly limited field of international law." While recognizing that the Pact might also have significance for the fields of politics and public opinion, Morris stated that he wished to analyze "what the Pact legally means." His basic point was that broad reservations concerning the right of self-defense would nullify the legal obligations of the Pact, and he therefore argued that "the Pact is far inferior in legal effectiveness to the Locarno Treaty."[50]

An intense debate followed Morris' paper. One participant recalled the historical development of the Interstate Commerce Act of 1887, which at the time of its completion was not widely expected to have much significance for the future and suggested that the Pact held great promise and was likewise capable of exceeding expectation. Howard T. Kingsberry offered the opinion that a treaty should be considered analogous to a contract, stating "a treaty, just as any contract between individuals, must be lived up to and construed and interpreted in good faith." He also suggested that whether a war waged by a signatory was a violation of the treaty or a defensive action undertaken on reasonable grounds should be determined in an international tribunal. Arthur K. Kuhn stressed the responsibility of lawyers in formulating a concrete definition of aggression.[51]

Borchard, who shared Morris' doubts, rose to speak out once more against the Pact. He stressed that its danger lay in its unrealistic and idealistic aspects, and he asserted that the Pact would not be effective because war occurred more from unexpected and irrational causes than from tangible ones. Borchard also argued that even if all controversies were submitted to arbitration not all of them could be resolved, because the fundamental causes of war had been overlooked. He repeated the theme, familiar to pessimists among the scholars that "man is a combative animal" and concluded that an overemphasis on the Pact would run the risk of "shutting one's eyes to the obvious facts of international life."[52]

Despite Borchard's inflammatory opposition, however, the general tone of the discussion was one of optimism about the future of the Pact. After all, the question that the theorists faced and had to answer was whether to regard the Pact as legally ineffective and thus ignore it, or to support and maintain it by seeking legal elaboration. Confronted with this choice, most theorists, particularly the reformers, endorsed the latter alternative. The cause enunciated by the Pact was too magnificent and fascinating for them to dismiss completely.

[50] *Proceedings, ASIL* (1929), 89–91.
[51] *Ibid.*, 100, 103, 106.   [52] *Ibid.*, 105–106.

The discussions at the 1929 meeting had set the stage for future elaboration by identifying the key issues: first, the Pact was after all in the form of a treaty, and it was therefore legally binding; second, appropriate self-defense had to be determined by an international tribunal; and third, the need for a concrete definition of self-defense was apparent. Morris concluded the session by noting that discussion had drifted into the question of policies rather than holding to the narrow question of "the actual legal effect of the Pact," and he suggested that this indicated where its importance lay. If the lawyers wanted to strengthen and maintain the Pact, they would have to come to terms with the relationship between law and policy. Because the Pact was vague, not legally elaborated, and political, the means for its advancement and enforcement would have to be sought in concrete policies.

Another issue raised in the context of debate on the Pact was that of neutrality. The practicality of maintaining neutrality during actual war and neutrality's moral value had been called into question during World War I. The Pact provided a new impetus for reconsidering the issue. Wright was quick to discuss neutrality in the September 1928 issue of the *International Conciliation*. He noted that the Pact suggested a legal basis for the appropriateness of discriminatory actions against a violator of the anti-war treaty, pointing to a clause in the Preamble concerning release from obligation in the event that the treaty was violated.[53] However, Wright himself was by no means so sure about the legal effect of the Pact on an arms embargo. In a letter to Representative Morton Hull, a member of the House Foreign Relations Committee, he wrote that the Kellogg Pact contained "no express requirement against arms trade, as a matter of law," but added, "as a matter of policy and morality, I think the United States would be in a very embarrassing position."[54] Hull, who believed that the United States "must find a way of cooperating with the rest of the world," was preparing a report on the revision of neutrality for the American Group of Interparliamentary Union and had sought Wright's technical help. In one letter, Hull asked Wright, "does a state violate the Kellogg Pact by assisting another state which is employing war as an instrument of national policy?" Wright answered in the affirmative, because the Pact had the character of legislation and imposed duties upon each of the signatories with regard to every other signatory as if it

---

[53] Quincy Wright, "The Future of Neutrality," *International Conciliation* 242 (1928), 353–372.

[54] Wright to Morton D. Hull, January 31, 1930, Wright Papers, Box 16, Folder 6.

were a collection of bilateral agreements.[55] Wright came to the conclusion that it was the nature of the Pact as a multilateral treaty rather than the Preamble that provided a legal basis for collective action.

At the annual meeting of the ASIL in April 1930, Wright elaborated this viewpoint in a paper entitled "Neutrality and Neutral Rights Following the Pact of Paris for the Renunciation of War." On this occasion, he was more definite about the effect of the Pact on neutrality. Because the Pact took the form of a multilateral treaty, war was no longer the concern of belligerents alone but of all signatories. The assumption of collective obligation that Wright deduced from the nature of the Pact suggested that signatories should take a differential attitude toward belligerents. Since all of the signatories had pledged not to resort to war, it could be assumed that any nation resorting to military action was waging an unjust war.[56]

The other speaker at the session, Clyde Eagleton of New York University, contended that the experience of World War I had proved that the traditional concept of neutrality had not kept up with the times. Items categorized as contraband goods during that war included ostrich feathers and milk, indicating how futile it was to attempt to maintain strict neutrality. He referred to the two arms embargo bills that had been introduced in Congress: one calling for an arms embargo on all belligerents, and the other, the Capper bill, only on aggressor nations. Eagleton called the former bill irresponsible, and he stated that "the question raised by the Capper resolution is the most vital question of foreign policy before the American people today."[57]

The debate following the two papers was even more intense than that which had taken place a year before. Some international lawyers stated that they simply could not understand at all how the Pact had abolished the old concept of neutrality, even if "there might be certain ethical considerations, which might cause the United States in the future to abandon neutrality." Wright and Eagleton, opponents argued, had merely stressed the possibilities of the Pact, but in actual practice the old neutrality still existed. Even Hudson, who shared with Wright a similar view of the new direction of international law, regarded Wright's paper as "a wide interpretation of the terms of the treaty" and argued that the two papers overstated the effect of the Pact on neutrality. Against this type of opposition, supporters of the

[55] Wright to Morton D. Hull, February 14, 1930, Wright Papers, Box 16 Folder 6.
[56] Quincy Wright, "Neutrality and Neutral Rights Following the Pact of Paris for the Renunciation of War," *Proceedings, ASIL* (1930), 79–87.
[57] Clyde Eagleton, "Neutrality and Neutral Rights Following the Pact of Paris for the Renunciation of War," *Proceedings, ASIL* (1930), 87–95.

Pact rallied behind it. George Finch, Secretary of the ASIL, repeated the assertion that the Pact provided a rallying point for future action. Eagleton, defending his position, stated that "the whole purpose of my argument was to improve the Kellogg Pact and make something out of it." Eagleton and Wright had produced the broadest and most enlightening interpretations of the Pact with regard to the matter of neutrality. Professor John B. Whitton of Princeton University observed that "neutrality is doomed ... In fact we stand in this matter today between the international law of the past and the international law of the future." As this statement suggests the schism over neutrality essentially reflected a broader schism over conflicting visions for the future direction of international law.[58]

The progressive and innovative views on the laws of war, the Pact and its effect on neutrality that were held by many American theorists were also shared by some European scholars. Several distinguished international lawyers from Europe were invited to the Fourth Conference of Teachers of the International Law, held in the fall of 1929. Professor Charles de Visscher from Ghent University in Belgium noted in his paper that there had also been much discussion in Europe about "what place should still be given to the teaching of the laws of war." De Visscher argued that "this teaching should be restricted to very narrow limits and be reduced to a few fundamental ideas."[59] Professor Hans Wehberg of the Academy of International Law at The Hague offered an even stronger opinion against the laws of war, asserting "one can ... treat the law of war in connection with the history of international law, but one must ignore it when considering the recognized law."[60] Wehberg's strong affinity for the new trend in international law had been clearly apparent in his recently published book *The Outlawry of War*. Based on his lectures at The Hague in the summer of 1928, the book dealt primarily with efforts at the League to regulate and forbid aggressive war and also touched on the American movement to outlaw war. Wehberg's usage of the phrase "outlawry of war" was much broader than Levinson's and was not confined to the abolition of the institution of war. Consequently, he associated the American outlawry movement with larger currents in the world. Wehberg's contribution was to integrate the Kellogg Pact into the international and historical context of the movement to abolish war.[61]

---

[58] *Proceedings, ASIL* (1930), 95–114.
[59] *Proceedings, Fourth Teachers* (1929), 18.
[60] *Ibid.*, 23.
[61] Hans Wehberg, *The Outlawry of War* (Washington, DC: Carnegie Endowment for International Peace, 1931).

Changes in the definition of neutrality as a corollary of the Kellogg Pact were also discussed by some European theorists. At the International Law Association in 1929, Wyndham A. Bewes from Great Britain proposed a resolution to the effect that aid to a violator of the Pact "would constitute an infringement of the Laws of Nations." A discussion of Bewes' resolution was held at the annual meeting in the fall of 1930, but the proposal was abandoned and in its place a resolution stating that "adoption of a policy of non-intercourse with a Pact violator will not be deemed a violation of neutrality" was put to the members.[62] The Association failed by a close vote to adopt even this diluted resolution, but the discussion of the Pact and its interpretation eventually led to the drafting of the Budapest Articles of Interpretation in 1934, which declared the abolition of the traditional concept of neutrality.

The Pact was not the ideal legal device that lawyers had hoped for. It was simply a declaration of principles, lacking precise legal definitions and means for enforcement. The imperfect nature of the Pact was severely criticized by some, primarily the traditionalists, but most reformers were not disappointed by it. Instead they emphasized its legal significance. The Pact contradicted neither the ultimate goal of abolishing war nor the basic premises for advancing international law. It furthered the idea of a family of nations in the sense that war became the concern of all countries. At the same time, the overarching and ethical nature of the Pact was in harmony with the reformers' ambitious contention that international law had to become to international society what a constitution was to a domestic society. The Pact served as a logical cornerstone for abolishing the old concept of neutrality, a goal that had been discussed since World War I.

Testing the ideals of the Pact: diplomatic repercussions

Though the reformers would strive to buttress the Kellogg Pact with elaborate theory, its future was in the hands of diplomats and statesmen. Endorsement of the Pact under concrete circumstances would ultimately determine its value. While the Pact's general nature had enough merit to compel reluctant countries to become signatories, it was not certain how sincerely these countries would adhere to its spirit. As was later recalled,

---

[62] International Law Association, *Report of the Thirty-Sixth Conference* (1930), pp. 125, 182.

Japan's attitude toward the Pact was one of "dubious acquiescence,"[63] and that country [Japan] was the least faithful holder to its principles.

The initial response of the Japanese government to the American proposal for a treaty renouncing war was dismay, resulting from its concern over the effect of such a treaty on Japan's position in China. At a cabinet meeting on May 22, 1928, Japanese policy makers debated how to reply to the American proposal, and they decided to employ phraseology that would leave room for future Japanese actions in China.[64] On the same day, a cable was sent to the Japanese embassy in Great Britain requesting the full text of the British reply, in particular the section dealing with the right of self-defense and the reservation registered by Britain regarding areas in her special interest.[65] In a British diplomatic note to the United States on May 19, 1928, the foreign minister had written that with respect to regions in her immediate interest Britain would maintain freedom of action. Three days later, the earlier decision of the Japanese cabinet was reversed and the cabinet decided not to register any reservations other than a general reference to the right of self-defense.

The Japanese Foreign Ministry drafted a document entitled "Advantages and Disadvantages in Registering Reservations for Japanese Action in China to the Proposed Treaty." It raised three points. Firstly, if specific reservations were made for its actions in China, this might lead to mistrust of Japan by the Powers. Secondly, the notion of self-defense in international law was ambiguous and weak, and thus the right of self-defense would be "elastic enough to rationalize future Japanese actions in China." Finally, though the British reservation regarding areas in her interest was compatible with the Japanese position, it would not be favorable for Japan to make a direct reference to the British reservation. Japan had imminent and specific interests in China, while Britain could make its claim in general terms because of her position as a worldwide empire. For this reason, the other Powers would probably interpret a Japanese reference to the British reservation as a clear indication of Japan's intention to carry out further actions in the future.[66] Thus, Japan's seemingly simple reply

[63] J. V. A. MacMurray, "Opening Remarks of the Presiding Officer," *Proceedings, ASIL* (1932), 44.

[64] Tokushiro Ohata, "Fusen joyaku to Nihon" [The Kellogg–Briand Pact and Japan], *Kokusai Seiji* 28 (1965), 72–86.

[65] Tanaka to Saburi, May 22, 1928, Senso hoki ni kansuru kokusaikaigi oyobi joyaku kankei ikken [Documents Concerning the Abolition of War], Fusen joyaku kakuju kosho kankei, vol. 1, Diplomatic Archives, Tokyo (hereafter JDA).

[66] "Fusen joyaku ni kansuru taibei toan chu ni Teikoku no taishi kodo no jiyu o ryuho suru no tokushitsu" [Advantages and Disadvantages in Making Reservation for Japanese

to the United States was the product of long deliberation and represented an attempt to balance the need for international cooperation with the nation's interests in China.

Then came reassuring news from Washington. On May 31, the Japanese ambassador to the United States, Tsuneo Matsudaira, had met with Secretary of State Kellogg. In his cable to Tokyo, Matsudaira reported that during their conversation Kellogg had stated that since Japan could take necessary actions in order to protect her interests in any area, she should accept the American proposal without modification. The Japanese government naturally welcomed this. As the frequent quotation of this statement in official Japanese documents shows, the Japanese government accepted Kellogg's remark as a more or less tacit American endorsement of Japanese actions, even within the limits of the treaty to renounce war. Matsudaira also noted in the same telegram that Kellogg had stated that the significance of the treaty lay in its moral effect.[67] Taking into account the British reservation and Kellogg's remarks, the Japanese government concluded that the Pact had only spiritual and moral implications and that future actions in Manchuria and China would not be hampered.

Sakutaro Tachi of Tokyo Imperial University produced a cynical interpretation of the Pact based on two sources: the text of the Pact itself and the diplomatic notes that had been exchanged during the negotiations. He argued that the renunciation of war in the text of the Pact did not signify the absolute abolition of war, because parties were required to renounce war only as a means of national policy. Tachi wrote that "prohibiting war as a means of national policy is more limited in its scope of application than prohibiting war in general." Tachi did not realize that "war as instrument of national policy" had originally been adopted in order to leave room for war as a means of collective security, such as military sanctions sponsored by the League of Nations. The term "national" had been used as an antonym for "international." Tachi interpreted the phrase as signifying a limitation on the prohibition of war in the treaty. He used this interpretation to create a loophole, one based on the practicability of war as self-defense. Tachi cited an American diplomatic note on self-defense that asserted, "the state exercising self-defense alone is competent to decide whether circumstances require recourse to war in self-

Action in China to the Proposed Treaty], Fusen joyaku kakuju kosho kankei, vol. 3, JDA.

[67] Matsudaira to Tanaka, May 31, 1928, Fusen joyaku kakuju kosho kankei, vol. 1, JDA.

defense." From this, he concluded that "the act of self-defense is clearly not constrained by the Pact."[68]

Tachi also raised the point of immediate national interests by quoting a British note that claimed the right to reserve application of the Pact in areas in which Britain had immediate interests. Tachi called this proclamation a "New British Monroe Doctrine" and noted that it was repeated again in a British note to the United States dated July 18. He drew implications for Japanese policy from it, writing, "thus, as long as Britain maintains an exception with regard to the application of the Pact, Japan also has the right to proclaim an exception to it, for example, concerning the Manchuria-Mongolia question."[69] Tachi put his energies to work trying to reveal weaknesses in the Pact, especially those that were favorable to Japan's interests and actions in China.

Tachi was not the only Japanese intellectual to respond to the Pact in an unfavorable way. Another writer expressed the opinion that the renunciation of war was just rhetoric, behind which each country would continue to pursue its own interests.[70] In addition to this skepticism about the Pact's efficacy, some writers criticized American foreign policy in view of the Pact. Masamichi Royama, a professor at Tokyo Imperial University, argued that American diplomacy contradicted itself because while the United States supported the renunciation of war it maintained a policy based on the Monroe Doctrine.[71] Hikomatsu Kamigawa, one of the first to study international politics as an academic discipline in Japan, also pointed out a contradiction in American foreign policy, citing the fact that the United States, an advocate of the Pact, was not a member of the League of Nations, which would ensure its enforcement.[72] In contrast to these Japanese critics of the United States, some international lawyers in Britain received the Pact favorably for the very reason that "it enabled the United States to come back and assist in the maintenance of peace." They welcomed the Pact as a sign of the United States' interest in playing

---

[68] Sakutaro Tachi, "Fusen joyaku no kokusaiho-kan" [View of International Law in the Kellogg–Briand Pact], *Kokusaiho Gaiko Zasshi* 27 (1928), 925.

[69] Sakutaro Tachi, "Eikoku no shin Monro-shugi sengen oyobi Fusen joyaku no jikko" [New British Monroe Doctrine and the Effect of the Kellogg–Briand Pact], *Gaiko Jiho* 577 (1928), 945.

[70] Shinnosuke Yanagisawa, "Fusen joyaku no seiritusu to Beikoku no sekinin" [The Kellogg–Briand Pact and American Responsibility], *Gaiko Jiho* 570 (1928), 96.

[71] Masamichi Royama, "Fusen joyaku to Taiheiyo no shorai" [The Kellogg–Briand Pact and the Future of the Pacific], *Chuo Koron* 43 (October 1928), 47.

[72] Hikomatsu Kamigawa, "Fusen joyaku no kachi hihan" [Critics on the Value of the Kellogg–Briand Pact], *Gaiko Jiho* 572 (1928), 68.

a greater role in the world.[73] These positive arguments, whether for the future of the Pact or for the changes in the United States' attitude toward the international situation, were nowhere to be seen in Japan. The Japanese translation for the name of the Kellogg–Briand Pact, *Fusen Joyaku* [No War Treaty], appropriately conveyed the principle intention of the document. But they did not seem to appreciate the effect or spirit of the words as literally as the translation would suggest. The Pact's cool and cynical acceptance by Japanese was to become the source of future controversy.

A year later, in fact, Japan's presence in China raised questions about what effect the Pact would actually have on diplomacy. During that year, Henry L. Stimson, who found more political advantages in the Pact than his predecessor, had become Secretary of State. On June 24, 1929, the Chinese minister in Washington called on Secretary Stimson and raised his concerns about the Pact. He mentioned the fact that in recent discussions at the Privy Council, the Japanese government had stated that a broad interpretation of the right of self-defense allowed for the exercise of this right outside of its territory, particularly in Manchuria and Mongolia. The Chinese minister asked whether correspondence during the negotiation of the Pact contained any interpretation of the right of self-defense that supported this argument.[74] In response, a memorandum was written by an assistant chief of the Division of Far Eastern Affairs that analyzed the correspondence in detail but did not produce a clear-cut answer for the Chinese minister. It stated that the Pact neither confined the right of self-defense nor defined the nature of permissible self-defense. However, if a controversy occurred, even though the Pact imposed no explicit obligation on the signatories, it argued for "the right to expect the other powers to live up to the agreement." The assistant chief pointed out the need for long-term vision, saying that the Pact was "so new and its provisions are so simple that time must elapse before the nations can come to a common understanding in regard to its practical applications to different sets of circumstances." At the same time, however, he did mention that the situation in southern Manchuria deserved special attention due to its complexity, for Japan did have a treaty right to station troops there. In the end, the assistant chief suggested that the Chinese draw their own conclusions from the correspondence.[75]

---

[73] John C. Colombos, "The Pact of Paris, Otherwise Called the Kellogg Pact," *Transactions of the Grotius Society* 14 (1928), 100–101.

[74] *FRUS*, 1929, III, pp. 249–250.

[75] *FRUS*, 1929, III, pp. 250–253.

A chance to actually apply the Pact to "different sets of circumstances," and in particular to Manchuria, soon presented itself. The occasion was the imminent threat of a military clash between the Soviet Union and China over the Chinese Eastern Railway. On July 24, 1929, Secretary Stimson, who regarded this both as a threat to world peace and as an opportunity to test the Pact, proposed to set up a committee for conciliation composed of the Powers.[76] Japanese policy makers fiercely opposed the proposal. They held that the "internationalization" of Manchuria would be harmful to Japanese interests. The Japanese ambassador to the United States, Katsuji Debuchi, who received Stimson's proposal in person, cabled his opinion against the overture to Tokyo. Even if the sphere of interest between China and the Soviet Union changed drastically as a result of direct negotiations between them, he wrote, the effect would still be more favorable for Japan than the entanglements caused by the intervention of third powers. Japan, he concluded, should kill this proposal without seeming to block it overtly.[77] Kensuke Horiuchi, a diplomat stationed in China, also sent a message expressing his opposition to the proposal, because "Japanese interests in Manchuria are by far the most important concern, far more important than international cooperation."[78]

Stimson failed to win the endorsement of the other powers and the plan did not materialize, but this did not affect his strong commitment to the Pact. For Stimson, the Pact was important not only because it would serve as the foundation for peace in the world, but also because it would provide a cooperative framework that would give the United States a rationale for participating in world affairs. This intention was apparent in another attempt by Stimson to reinforce the Pact in early October 1929, when British Prime Minister Ramsay MacDonald visited the United States for preliminary talks on the forthcoming Naval Conference in London.[79]

During the talks, the British showed interest in reinforcing the Pact. When Stimson asked Prime Minister MacDonald whether the British would endorse the amendment if Stimson could solve the problems related to the League and assure support from the French prime minister,

---

[76] *FRUS, 1929*, II, pp. 237–239. See also Robert Ferrel, *American Diplomacy in the Great Depression* (New Haven: Yale University Press, 1957), pp. 45–67; Zasloff, "Law and the Shaping: The Twenty Years' Crisis," 648–652.

[77] Debuchi to Shidehara, July 28, 1929, To-shi tetudo kankei ikken, Shina gawa no To-shi tetsudo kyosei shuyo ni gen'in suru Ro-Shi funso mondai, kakkoku no taido, vol. 1, JDA. See also Akira Iriye, *After Imperialism* (New York: Atheneum, 1978), p. 265.

[78] Horiuchi to Shidehara, August 20, 1929, To-shi Tetsudo, Teikoku no Taido, JDA.

[79] Ferrel, *American Diplomacy*, pp. 68–86.

MacDonald answered that he would "with open arms." It was reaffirmed by both delegations that "the enactment of the Kellogg Pact created a new starting point for international negotiations for the preservation of peace," and issues concerning the Pact were discussed "at considerable length." Robert L. Craigie, chief of the American division of the British Foreign Office, also sought to strengthen the Pact. During the talks, he attempted to have the following section added to the final communiqué: "We believe that the provisions of the Pact of Peace renouncing war as an instrument of national policy would be further strengthened if the interested Powers were to undertake to consult together with a view to agreement as to the best method of preventing a threatened outbreak of war." In the end, however, it was decided not to include discussions of the Pact in the final communiqué, and in the final joint statement reference to it remained general.[80]

In late November the danger of a clash between the Soviet Union and China over the railway again became imminent. This time, Stimson, not discouraged by his experience in July, was more determined. He suggested a joint statement by the powers to China and the Soviet Union, calling attention to their obligations vis-à-vis the Pact. Japan declined his offer, citing the fact that direct negotiations between the Soviet Union and China were already taking place. France and Great Britain agreed with Stimson's proposal, but they emphasized the need for the inclusion of Japan in such a diplomatic venture in order to secure international cooperation. Stimson therefore had to settle for a unilateral US statement to China, and eventually to Russia through France, after which other powers followed suit. In a diplomatic note to other powers, Stimson put forward the view that "the efficacy of the Pact of Paris depends upon the sincerity of the governments which are party to it."[81] If we take into account the fact that Japan opposed sending any statement, we may conclude that it did not have the sincerity about the Pact that Stimson advocated.

At the end of the 1920s, there was an emerging awareness on the part of international lawyers that theories in and of themselves would not yield any results. If they were not content with indulging in theoretical argument, and if they intended to apply their intellectual ideas to actual situations, lawyers needed to be aware of the feasibility of their arguments and make a link between the new international law, and actual foreign

---

[80] *FRUS 1929*, III, pp. 6–11; *Documents on British Foreign Policy 1919–1939*, second series, vol. 1, p. 116.
[81] *FRUS, 1929*, I, pp. 371–372.

policy and relations. They had presented various theories and arguments, and in fact a system compatible with their views appeared in the Geneva Protocol. But the Protocol had not gone into effect; instead, the Kellogg–Briand Pact came into force. Because the Pact was not a legally perfect document, international lawyers still had to find a way to control war through the elaboration of the theory embodied in the Pact. On the other hand, precisely because of its general and legally imperfect character, the Pact left room for disagreement.

Observing such disagreement between Hudson and Wright, who shared much of the same ideas, Borchard posed the question "how can it possibly be assumed that in times of crisis all the nations of the world are going to agree on the same interpretation?" He criticized the Pact as being an "ambiguous instrument."[82] Borchard rightly foresaw the probability that the nations of the world would not be able to agree on a single interpretation. But the cause of these different interpretations was not to be found in the text of the Pact itself. The more important issue involved was the extent to which each power appreciated the "spirit" of the Pact and honored that spirit in their interpretations and applications of it.

Japan showed a conspicuous lack of understanding with regard to the idea that war was something to be avoided. While Western scholars of international law were voicing skepticism about the value of teaching the laws of war, Tachi was working on a two-volume interpretation of international law. One volume dealt with the laws of war and the other with the laws of peace.[83] These two volumes, over 1,300 pages in total, were heralded in Japan as the first original and comprehensive Japanese analysis of international law. Although there were some American and European scholars who stressed the importance of the laws of war, they were not as clear-cut in their dualistic approach as Tachi, who had no reservations concerning these laws. Many American scholars shared the view that war should be abolished and agreed with Secretary Kellogg, who stated that "Today probably more than at any time in recorded history, there is a longing for peace."[84] In Japan, however, Sentaro Uyeda, an official in the Foreign Ministry, asserted in a memorandum on the Sino-Soviet conflict over the Chinese Eastern Railway that prolonged conflict would

[82] *Proceedings, ASIL* (1930), 102.
[83] Sakutaro Tachi, *Heiji kokusaiho ron* [International Law of Peace] (Tokyo: Nihon Hyoron sha, 1930); *Senji kokusaiho ron* [International Law of War] (Tokyo: Nihon Hyoron sha, 1931).
[84] Frank B. Kellogg, *The Settlement of International Controversies by Pacific Means: An Address by the Honorable Frank B. Kellogg* (Washington, DC: GPO, 1928), p. 10.

be favorable for Japan, because it would give Japan more opportunity to expand its interests.[85] Peace was accepted as a universal and irresistible value in the United States, but for Japan war was more an opportunity than an evil. This gap in perception was to become apparent in a distinctive way two years later, again in Manchuria.

---

[85] Sentaro Uyeda, "Ro-Shi Fungi ni kansuru Iken" [An Opinion Concerning the Conflict between the Soviet Union and China], July, 27, 1929, To-shi Tetsudo, Teikoku no Taido, JDA.

4

Half-victory

International law and the Manchurian Incident

In the fall of 1929, James Shotwell, Joseph Chamberlain, Quincy Wright and C. Walter Young, all distinguished internationalists or professors of international law from the United States, traveled to Kyoto for a conference of the Institute of Pacific Relations (IPR). The Manchurian problem was one of the most urgent items up for discussion. Arguments similar to Shotwell and Wright's were presented. One argument held that the Manchurian problem was not only important for the three neighboring powers – the Soviet Union, China and Japan – but also for the world as a whole. The "day of local war" had ended, ushering in an era in which "every local conflict now is a potential menace to world peace." In order to face this challenge, the principles embodied in the Kellogg–Briand Pact would have to be constantly borne in mind. However, the proceedings observed that Japan in general tended to rely on the "present *status quo* in regard both to treaty rights and to economic organization." A "typical expression of the Japanese attitude" was seen in their emphasis on geography and proximity. The Japanese stressed that Manchuria was uniquely important to Japan, using such phrases as "a distant and uninterested state" and "the remoter and less deeply concerned nations" to describe the secondary importance of Manchuria to other countries.[1]

The picture presented at this conference would remain unchanged after September 1931, when the Japanese Kwantung Army initiated sweeping military actions in Manchuria. The West and China reminded Japan of her obligations as prescribed in various treaties, but Japan persisted in stressing the economic and strategic importance of Manchuria. Wright had correctly observed that "at Kyoto the feeling was almost unanimous that the unequal treaties were going,"[2] and the Japanese position

---

[1] J. B. Condliffe, ed., *Problems of the Pacific 1929* (University of Chicago Press, 1930), pp. 158, 160, 173, 204.

[2] Quincy Wright, "The Kyoto Conference of the Institute of Pacific Relations," *American Political Science Review* 24 (1930), 454.

was doomed. Three years later, Yosuke Matsuoka, who had presented a paper on Japan's contribution to the development of Manchuria at the Kyoto conference, was to announce Japan's withdrawal from the League of Nations.

Japan's pattern of dissent

In the fall of 1929, at roughly the same time that the IPR was meeting in Kyoto, the League of Nations began discussing the British delegation's proposal to revise its Covenant so that it would accord with the Kellogg–Briand Pact.[3] The Covenant regulated certain types of war, but it did not forbid all types, a position that contradicted the Pact's general renunciation of war. For example, Article 12 of the Covenant stipulated that countries involved in a dispute should "submit the matter either to arbitration or judicial settlement or to inquiry by the Council, and they agree in no case to resort to war until three months after the award." This meant that after three months signatories were legally able to resort to war. Since the Pact prohibited all war, there was a real danger that the two documents would produce conflicting judgments. On September 24, 1929, the General Assembly passed a resolution calling for the problem to be studied. Following the adoption of the resolution, a Committee of Eleven, officially the Committee for the Amendment of the Covenant of the League of Nations in Order to Bring into Harmony with the Pact of Paris, was established. From February to March of 1930, the Committee discussed the issue and then presented its report to the General Assembly. After modification in the Assembly in the fall of 1930, the League sent the proposal to each member country for revision. Each signatory was required to reply by June 1931. The major points in the revision were contained in Article 12 Section 1; Article 13 Section 4; Article 15 Section 6; and Article 16 Section 1.[4]

From the beginning, the Japanese government's attitude toward the revision was not favorable. On September 8, 1929, immediately after the British proposed the revision, the Japanese delegate in Geneva cabled Tokyo the opinion that "if Japan takes independent action and

---

[3] See Kisaburo Yokota, "Senso no zettaiteki kinshi, saikin no Renmei Kiyaku kaisei-an" [The Absolute Abolition of War: A Recent Proposal to Revise the Covenant of the League], *Gaiko Jiho* 632 (1931), 14–31; C. A. Manning, "The Proposed Amendments to the Covenant of the League of Nations," *British Year Book of International Law* 10 (1930), 158–171.

[4] League of Nations, "Amendment of the Covenant of the League of Nations in order to Bring it into Harmony with the Pact of Paris," October 24, 1930, C. 623. M. 245, DLN.

rejects the proposal, the other members will become skeptical of our position."[5] In response, the Foreign Ministry officially proclaimed its general acceptance of the revision, but asked the delegate in Geneva to inform the Ministry as soon as possible whether the revision would "expand and strengthen the Pact."[6] However, in February, 1930, while the Committee of Eleven was meeting, Japan stated its unfavorable opinion more firmly, noting "the Imperial Government expresses its doubts about the revision of the Covenant as a practical matter."[7] The government was afraid that discussion of revision would raise the issue of "war as an instrument of national policy" and that a precise definition of self-defense would be promulgated. The Foreign Ministry, in particular, was worried about the proposal and had consulted with the Ministries of the Navy and Army.[8] Furthermore, Nobumi Ito, a Japanese delegate at Geneva and also a member of the Committee of Eleven, published an article in French to "arouse public opinion" in Japan's favor.[9] Ito's article presented the argument that revision of the Covenant was unnecessary and that maintaining the two separate documents as they were provided a double guarantee.[10]

The official reply to the League in June 1931 appeared simple but was in fact complicated: "The Japanese government is in principle in favor of the draft amendments contained in the report of the First Committee of the Eleventh Assembly, it being understood that these amendments in no way affect the exercise of the right of self-defense."[11] But together with the official reply, the foreign minister, Kijuro Shidehara, also cabled a private communication to Setsuzo Sawada stating that "the Imperial government does not think it necessary to revise the Covenant," but, given the trend in the League and as a sign of her willingness to cooperate, Japan would not insist on her previous position.[12] A careful reading of the reply

---

[5] Delegate to Shidehara, September 8, 1929, Kokusai Renmei Kiyaku Kaisei Mondai Zakken (Documents concerning the revision of Covenant of the League of Nations), JDA.

[6] Shidehara to Delegate, September 11, 1929, *ibid.*

[7] Shidehara to Delegate, February 3, 1930, *ibid.*

[8] For example, see Yoshizawa to Kobayashi, Yoshizawa to Sugiyama, June 30, 1930, *ibid.*

[9] Sato to Shidehara, June 16, 1930, *ibid.*

[10] Nobumi Ito, "Le pacte de Paris et le pacte de la Société des Nations," *Revue Politique et Parlementaire* 37 (1930), 14–36. Ito took the place of Mineichiro Adachi, who could not be present at the meeting, see C. 623. M. 245. 1930. V., 2, DLN.

[11] League of Nations, *Official Journal* (September 1931), 1776; Shidehara to Sawada, May 31, 1931, Kokusai Renmei Kiyaku kaisei, JDA.

[12] Sawada to Shidehara, March 18 1931; Shidehara to Sawada, June 3, 1931, JDA.

reveals the usage of a new term, "exercise," which did not appear in the diplomatic note sent to the United States in May 1928 during the negotiations over the Kellogg–Briand Pact. The phrase "*exercise* of the right of self-defense [italics added]" seemed to connote the direct possibility of concrete action, while "the right of self-defense" could be seen as simply confirming in principle a nation's inherent right.

The Chinese reply, on the other hand, conveyed full support for the revision. Besides endorsing the revision, the Chinese government suggested another proposal, pointing out the danger of military actions that avoided "any legal recognition of war." Such aggression was in opposition to the aims of both the Covenant of the League of Nations and the Pact of Paris. Thus, the Chinese government thought "it would be advisable if some effective measures could also be provided for in the Covenant to prevent this danger."[13] China foresaw the danger that a military action might be launched but not be deemed war. China must have been alarmed by Japan's insistence on the right of self-defense and did not want to be totally unprepared in the event that Japan asserted such a claim.

A legal argument lay behind Japan's attitude toward the revision of the Covenant. Thomas Baty, legal advisor to the Japanese Foreign Ministry, wrote a lengthy and unfavorable memorandum on the revision. He thought the original Covenant, which left room for war, was more desirable and he opposed the revision. He contended that mixing the Covenant and the Pact was like "throwing a spanner into a complicated and delicate machine." For Baty, the spanner was the Pact and the machine was the Covenant. He continued,

> The fact is, the terms of the Kellogg Treaty and of the Covenant do not dove-tail. The Covenant is thinking of all wars, and provides a tentative but obligatory and regular process for dealing with them. The Kellogg Treaty is thinking of some wars and renouncing them in general terms, leaving many loopholes.[14]

Baty stressed that if the Covenant were to prohibit war unconditionally, nations would quite likely resort to war in the name of "self-redress." He thought that it was safer to allow certain types of war and regulate them by specific laws. Otherwise, totally unregulated warfare waged under various names would occur. In May 1930 Baty again wrote a memorandum on the report presented by the Committee of Eleven in which he

---

[13] League of Nations, *Official Journal* (August 1931), 1597.
[14] Thomas Baty, "Kellogg Treaty and League Covenant Proposal to Modify Latter, Further Memorandum," January 10, 1930, Kokusai Renmei Kiyaku kaisei, JDA.

reconfirmed his views. He stressed that "the unqualified renunciation of war will eventuate in the promotion of 'pacific' violence."[15]

Baty's traditionalist argument served Japan's policy, and his position in Western academia as an opponent of the new international law came to be established more firmly and clearly. His support for the old notions of international law dated back to before World War I, and in the mid-1920s Edwin M. Borchard had referred to him to counter the reformers' call for demise of the laws of war, as was discussed in previous chapters. Since the mid 1920s Borchard and Baty had frequently exchanged letters. In one such letter, Borchard straightforwardly expressed his admiration for Baty, writing that "everything you write is valuable and I regard it as a matter of good fortune that we should be the vehicle for the publication of your thoughts to the world."[16] Regarding Baty's article to defend the laws of war, Borchard wrote, "your contribution in the March *Yale Law Journal* has excited much favorable comment among my friends in the Department of State."[17] Baty on his part wrote back a particularly long letter to Borchard. It was dated July 20, 1924, and had been written during Baty's summer retreat in Nikko. In this eight-page letter, Baty not only discussed issues regarding international law, but also touched upon his life in Japan.[18] He acknowledged that Borchard had "so much in harmony with positions I advanced."[19]

Now, with the belief that both of them were in a same camp and opposed to the other, Baty joined the debate between reformers and traditionalists more visibly and assertively, and he did so in the *AJIL*.

The issue concerned neutral rights during war. The debate was set forth by E. G. Trimble of New York University, a student of Borchard's. In the January 1930 issue of the *AJIL*, Trimble had published an article entitled "Violations of Maritime Law by the Allied Powers during the World War." He argued that the Allies, in particular Great Britain, had violated the neutral maritime right guaranteed in international law. Great Britain did not observe the classification of absolute and conditional contraband set forth in the London Declaration of 1904.[20]

[15] Thomas Baty, "Harmonization of the League Covenant with Kellogg Treaty," May 27, 1930, *ibid.*

[16] Borchard to Baty, February 7, 1924, Papers of Edwin M. Borchard (hereafter Borchard Papers), Sterling Library, Yale University, Box 16, Folder 202.

[17] Borchard to Baty, March 31, 1925, Borchard Papers, Box 17, Folder 218.

[18] Baty to Borchard, July 20, 1924, Borchard Papers, Box 16, Folder 207.

[19] Baty to Borchard, February 17, 1925, Borchard Papers, Box 17, Folder 216.

[20] E. G. Trimble, "Violations of Maritime Law by the Allied Powers during the World War," *AJIL* 24 (1930), 79–90.

A year later, James W. Garner responded. Garner argued that the idea of contraband was ridiculous. There was no logical ground for distinguishing between absolute and conditional contraband destined for a neutral port. "The truth is contraband destined to belligerent territory, whatever the character of the port or the public or private status of the consignee, will find its way to the armed forces and be used by them if the government desires."[21]

After reading Garner's article, Borchard wrote to George A. Finch, the managing editor of the *AJIL*, and conveyed his intention to rejoin the debate. He was critical of Garner's argument because it proceeded "on certain fundamental misconceptions of the nature of law." If one regarded international law as "just a matter of convenience, to be set aside when self-interest dictates," it would be "hardly worth devoting much time to its study, and survival would then depend exclusively on force."[22]

The difference between Garner and Borchard's positions appeared more clearly in their respective book reviews of *Maritime Trade in War* by Lord Eustace Percy. The book argued that the existing distinction between absolute and conditional contraband was illogical and arbitrary. Garner gave the book a positive review,[23] but Borchard was critical of it. Borchard asserted that the principle underlying both the distinction between absolute and conditional contraband and the doctrine of continuous voyage was not logic but the need for compromise between two claimants, between belligerents and non-belligerents. Neutral countries were given the right to continue trading with belligerents, and under the doctrine of continuous voyage non-combatants in belligerent countries were similarly entitled to acquire materials necessary for survival. Borchard concluded that this system was based on practical compromise.[24]

However, it was not Borchard but Baty who published an article in response to Garner's approach.[25] Baty argued that among international lawyers some were belligerent-minded and others were peaceful-minded. Garner certainly fell into the category of the belligerent-minded, because

---

[21] James Wilford Garner, "Violations of Maritime Law by the Allied Powers During the World War," *AJIL* 25 (1931), 26–49.

[22] Borchard to Finch, February 2, 1931, ASIL Papers.

[23] James Wilford Garner, review of *Maritime Trade in Law*, by Lord Eustace Percy, *AJIL* 25 (1931), 182–184.

[24] Edwin M. Borchard, review of *Maritime Trade in Law*, by Lord Eustace Percy, *Yale Law Journal* 40 (1931), 492–495.

[25] Baty to Borchard, March 27, 1932, Borchard Papers, Box 1, Folder 14.

his argument would lead to the expansion of belligerents' rights. By abolishing the distinction between belligerents and neutrals, belligerent-minded lawyers did not respect peace in the system of neutrality. Baty recognized the need for legal protection to allow countries to remain neutral in time of war and deplored the deterioration of the system. He stated, "the peaceful neutral has tended less and less to command the respect and admiration of the world." Baty then pointed out that Garner overemphasized the effects of change in international law, which cannot be revised easily to fit new situations.[26]

Baty's conservative view of change was also apparent in his 1930 book *The Canons of International Law*. In its preface, he wrote that his purpose was "to ascertain and to reinforce certain guiding principles, the recognition of which appears to be necessary if the Law of Nations is not to degenerate into a morass of conflicting opinions, or of ukases dictated from Geneva." He viewed innovation in international law as detrimental, because it destroyed law's certainty. Regarding the cries for change since the war, he wrote that "nobody had ever shown what the reasons for change were," and that "investigation would show the old rules were substantially applicable to the circumstances of the present." He reaffirmed his belief that if changes were easily admitted, law would come to reflect the interests of the nation, not of the world.[27]

Even before the Manchurian Incident, a pattern of Japanese dissent had emerged. Japan was not enthusiastic about the efforts to strengthen the framework for prohibiting war and strongly desired to reserve the right of self-defense. Japan found endorsement for its position in the traditional view of international law, in particular as enunciated by Baty. Baty's arguments found supporters, such as Borchard, in the United States.

A treaty-based approach to China

Before introducing the discussions about the Manchurian Incident that took place among international legal theorists, it is important to note that American scholars and diplomats had long been interested in treaty relations in China.

In 1904, William Woodville Rockhill, an American diplomat posted in China, published a book detailing the treaty relationships between

---

[26] Thomas Baty, "Prize Law and Modern Conditions," *AJIL* 26 (1931), 625–641.
[27] Thomas Baty, *The Canons of International Law* (London: John Murray, 1930), pp. vii, 28–29.

China and other powers. It was entitled *Treaties and Conventions with or Concerning China and Korea, 1894–1904: Together with Various State Papers and Documents Affecting Foreign Interests.*[28] At the very outset, Rockhill acknowledged that his book was deeply indebted to a previous work on the subject written by Sir Edward Hertslet in 1896.

In 1921 J. V. A. MacMurray, who had also served as a diplomat in China, issued his own two-volume treatise, which began with the dedication, "To the memory of my former chief, the late William Woodville Rockhill, whose work these volumes are meant to carry on." In the preface of *Treaties and Agreements with and Concerning China, 1894–1919*, MacMurray pointed out that the significance of Rockhill's book lay in its recognition that any study of treaty relationships with China should cover not only formal governmental treaties but also private contractual agreements related to enterprise.[29]

MacMurray also praised Rockhill's objectivity and thoroughness. He stated that the object of his own collection was "to reproduce as fully and as faithfully as possible the available documents embodying that complex of interrelated rights and obligations." As a result of his passion for perfection, MacMurray's two volumes totaled more than 1,700 pages. The work was published under the auspices of the Carnegie Endowment for International Peace, and James Brown Scott, director of the organization's Division of International Law and a former teacher of MacMurray's, wrote in his introduction that it was "a labor of love."[30]

While MacMurray was compiling his monumental work on treaty relations in China, Westel W. Willoughby, a professor of political science at the Johns Hopkins University who had served as a legal advisor to the Chinese government from 1916 to 1917, was also at work on a book about treaty relations in China.[31] Willoughby wrote that he sought to clarify "the rights of the foreigner and the interests of foreign states in China." However, he also wished to elucidate what those foreign rights and interests in turn meant for China, writing, "viewed from the other side, the account will exhibit the limitations under which the Chinese government

---

[28] William Woodville Rockhill, ed., *Treaties and Conventions with or Concerning China and Korea, 1894–1904, Together with Various State Papers and Documents Affecting Foreign Interests* (Washington, DC: GPO, 1904).

[29] John V. A. MacMurray, ed., *Treaties and Agreements with and Concerning China 1894–1919*, vol. 1 (New York: Oxford University Press, 1921), p. xiii.

[30] *Ibid.*, pp. xv, ix.

[31] Westel W. Willoughby, *Foreign Rights and Interests in China* (Baltimore: Johns Hopkins Press, 1920).

is compelled to act."[32] Willoughby's sympathetic attitude toward China was clearly apparent in his treatment of Japanese rights and interests. In a review of the book, William Dennis, who had also been a legal advisor to China, called attention to the author's assertion that he had refrained from inserting his own opinions and had let the documents themselves tell the story. But, Dennis argued that the author had overstepped "the limitations against comment which he placed upon himself" when he dealt with "Japan's 'special interests' in China – The Lansing-Ishii Agreement." Dennis concluded that Willoughby had sought to imply that the United States should not have signed the Agreement.[33]

Willoughby's book was proofread by Paul S. Reinsch, a former American minister to China, and by Stanley K. Hornbeck, then a technical advisor to the State Department.[34] Taking into account the fact that both Rockhill and MacMurray had been China specialists in the State Department, it is understandable that they shared a tendency to look at the situation in China within the framework of the treaty system. This perspective regarded the treaties and agreements as set and thereby fostered a respect for and reliance on formal treaties.

This attitude toward the treaty system can also be seen in Hornbeck's review of Paul Clyde's book *International Rivalries in Manchuria*. In the book's preface, Clyde affirmed that his intention was to look at policies and motives rather than at the treaties themselves, stating "the writer's aim has been to define and interpret national motives."[35] Clyde argued that the American Open Door Policy had been neither fixed nor established as international law until 1922, when the Nine Power Treaty was signed.[36]

Clyde's view challenged the idea that the Open Door was an established international agreement. Several important books on treaty relations, including those by Rockhill and MacMurray, had dealt positively with the Open Door doctrine and the other Powers' replies. As a result, the Open Door came to be regarded as if it had attained the status of a fixed agreement. In focusing on the policies of the United States and other powers, Clyde pointed out the danger that emphasis on treaties alone tended to

---

[32] *Ibid.*, p. iii.
[33] William Cullen Dennis, review of *Foreign Rights and Interests in China*, by Westel W. Willoughby, *AJIL* 5 (1921), 628–630.
[34] Willoughby, *Foreign Rights*, p. v.
[35] Paul Clyde, *International Rivalries in Manchuria, 1689–1922* (Columbus: Ohio State University Press, 1928), p. x.
[36] *Ibid.*, p. 270.

mask the motives behind the policies of each country and to take the legal validity of the doctrine for granted.

Hornbeck defended international law in his critical review of Clyde's book. He had no problems with Clyde's perspective until he came to the section on Manchuria, where Clyde seemed to lose his impartiality and speak "in defense of Japan." Hornbeck argued that all the other powers had agreed to the principle of the Open Door. If readers followed Clyde's interpretation, they would find "confusion between, on the one hand, Hay's doctrine and, on the other, Japan's pledges." Hornbeck ended his review by noting somewhat pointedly that it had "a good bibliography, in which the omission of Moore's Digest of International Law is to be remarked."[37]

Willoughby's book was revised and expanded in 1927. And in 1929, the Carnegie Endowment published *Treaties and Agreements with and Concerning China 1919–1929* as a continuation of MacMurray's book. Other books dealing with treaty relations in Manchuria had also been published during this period. *Manchuria, Treaties and Agreements* was published in 1921, again by the Carnegie Endowment.[38] These books, some of which went into second printings, offered some indication of American interest in treaty relations in China.

The situation in Manchuria was no exception. In 1929, C. Walter Young published a book entitled *International Relations in Manchuria*, which focused on the historical development of treaties and agreements. It was originally prepared for the Kyoto conference of the Institute of Pacific Relations in 1929. It can be argued that Young was at that time the leading specialist on Manchuria in the West. From 1925 to 1927, he conducted extensive research on the politics and economy of Manchuria and wrote prolifically about the situation there.[39] In the author's note, Young stressed that "objectivity was essential," and he warned that as a result of his attempt to maintain objectivity, the reader might encounter repetition and monotony. However, his adherence to objectivity was somewhat obscured by Willoughby's introduction, which argued that Japan had come to exercise political jurisdictional rights beyond the limit inferred from the interpretation of the treaty rights. At the same time, Young

---

[37] Stanley K. Hornbeck, review of *International Rivalries in Manchuria*, by Paul Clyde, *AJIL* 21 (1927), 632–635.

[38] *Manchuria, Treaties and Agreements* (Washington, DC: Carnegie Endowment for International Peace, 1921).

[39] For example, see C. Walter Young, "Sino-Japanese Interests and Issues in Manchuria," *Pacific Affairs* 1(7) (1928), 1–20.

himself offered subjective interpretations on certain matters. He argued that the Washington Conference could not justifiably be labeled the most important event of the decade. For by preserving the agreement of 1915, popularly known as the Twenty-One Demands, it had failed to challenge the Japanese position.[40] Young's view of the Washington Conference was based on a limited perspective that regarded the event only in terms of specific legal relationships that it yielded. He rejected the view that the Washington Conference was important because it purportedly established a multilateral framework that would lead to cooperation in the Far East, an idea that Wright had supported in his 1921 article.

Just as the Japanese army was sweeping into Manchuria, Young was completing a three-volume set entitled *Japan's Special Position in Manchuria; The International Legal Status of the Kwantung Leased Territory*; and *Japanese Jurisdiction in the South Manchuria Railway Areas*. Setting the overall tone for the trilogy, Young argued in the first volume that Manchuria had always been Chinese territory in the legal sense. Even though de facto authority might have been exercised by Chang Tso Lin in the 1920s, *de jure* authority had always been maintained by the central government. With regard to Japan's special position, he wrote, "legally, Japan's position in Manchuria is *quantitatively*, not *qualitatively*, different from that of other foreign states [italics original]." He held that Japan's position in Manchuria could not "be considered under the treaties or international law as an exclusive one." Young referred to the fact that the Japanese government had recently insisted on more "treaty rights," and noted that "certain of these treaty rights are, in themselves, antiquated and out of accord with the spirit of the times."[41]

Wright, a reviewer of the book, found Young's arguments "particularly suggestive."[42] The doctrine that one country could develop into an area belonging to another because it was poor or lacked natural resources was not supported by any principle of international law. And Young held that international law took precedence over the right of any nation to exercise authority over territory.[43] Baty, on the other hand, wrote in a letter to Wright that "Young occurs to me by no means a safe guide," because

[40] C. Walter Young, *The International Relations of Manchuria* (University of Chicago Press, 1929), pp. xi, xiii–xiv, 192.
[41] C. Walter Young, *Japan's Special Position in Manchuria* (Baltimore: Johns Hopkins Press, 1931), pp. 369–371.
[42] Quincy Wright, review of *Japan's Special Position in Manchuria*, by C. Walter Young, *AJIL* 26 (1932), 217–220.
[43] Young, *Japan's Special Position*, p. 323.

"under a cloak of judicial impartiality" he presented the matter "in favor of Chinese assertions." Baty also noted that "W. W. Willoughby's influence may account for this."[44]

Young had dedicated one of the three volumes to Professor Willoughby, but they were far apart during the Manchurian conflict, at the very sites of its development. Willoughby was in Geneva as a technical advisor to the Chinese government at the League of Nations, while Young returned to Manchuria as a technical advisor to the so-called Lytton Commission, which was sent by the League to investigate the cause of the incident.

Theoretical arguments over the Manchurian conflict

On September 19, a day after the Kwantung Army blew up tracks on the South Manchurian Railway and commenced military operations, the Committee of Jurists at the League continued its discussions on the revision of the Covenant. On that very day, the topic of debate was self-defense. Nicolas Politis of Greece, who could be fairly labeled a supporter of the new international law,[45] was of the opinion that any revision of the Covenant aimed at bringing it into accord with the Pact must address both the issue of self-defense and military actions that might evade the definition of war. The discussion did not produce a conclusion about whether the right of self-defense was available through the independent judgment of each country or whether it required an impartial judgment. Nobumi Ito of Japan held that each country was entitled to exercise self-defense freely, but the majority believed that the Covenant did not recognize free exercise. Summing up the discussion, Ito sent a telegram to the Japanese Foreign Ministry: "*The majority of the Committee agreed on the point that both the Pact and the League naturally recognize a right of self-defense, and that current international law does not contain a definitive principle on the right of self-defense* [emphasis original]."[46] For Japan, this cable might have been reassuring, as it reconfirmed the position that ambiguity about the right of self-defense could be beneficial.

Armed with this interpretation, Sakutaro Tachi presented an argument justifying the Japanese invasion. He accepted the position enunciated by his government that Japanese actions in Manchuria had been launched

---

[44] Baty to Wright, April 8, 1932, Wright Papers, Box 19, Folder 15.
[45] See Politis, *The New Aspects of International Law*.
[46] Three delegates to Shidehara, September 21, 1931, Kiyaku kaisei [The Revision of the Covenant], vol. 3, JDA.

in response to an immediate danger precipitated by the Chinese. He also noted that Japan's actions had been based on the right of self-defense, which was to be interpreted broadly enough to include not only the right to defend against immediate dangers from the outside that threatened the survival of the country, but also the right to defend the lives and property of nationals residing in other states. In order to support this expansive interpretation, Tachi cited various academic works that interpreted the notion of self-defense broadly. He also cited as a precedent the US expedition in Mexico from 1915 to 1919, which, he argued, had been conducted in the name of self-defense.[47] He concluded that the Monroe Doctrine and Britain's reservations concerning the right of self-defense in areas of special interest vis-à-vis the Pact could serve as the basis for Japan's claims of self-defense in Manchuria.[48]

Criticism in Japan of that country's actions in Manchuria came from Kisaburo Yokota, a professor of international law at Tokyo Imperial University. Yokota had been a student of Tachi's, but his views on international law differed distinctively from those of his teacher, a difference that can be explained in part by their experiences abroad. Tachi had studied international law and diplomatic history in Germany, France and Great Britain between 1900 and 1904. Yokota was in Europe after World War I, between 1926 and 1928, and from there he went to the United States, where he secured a scholarship from the Carnegie Endowment and studied with Manley O. Hudson at Harvard University. Despite Yokota's short, half-year stay in the United States, he was impressed with Harvard, writing to Hudson that he was very much interested in his case-method in teaching as well as in the codification of international law.[49] Two other professors of international law whom Yokota mentioned in his autobiography, and whom he had visited, were, not coincidentally, Borchard and Wright. Yokota came to share the opinions of the latter.[50] Yokota had hailed the revision of the Covenant as the third major achievement in the

---

[47] Sakutaro Tachi, "Jiei-ken gaisetsu" [An Overview on the Right of Self-defense], *Kokusaiho Gaiko Zasshi* 31 (1932), 317, 329–330.

[48] Sakutaro Tachi, "Saikin Manshu jihen ni kanrenshite Fusen joyaku o yomu" [Reading of the Pact in Connection with the Current Manchurian Incident], *Gaiko Jiho* 649 (1931), 7.

[49] Kisaburo Yokota to Hudson, December 25, 1928, Papers of Manley O. Hudson (hereafter Hudson Papers), Box 83, Folder 6, Harvard Law School Library, Harvard University, Cambridge, Massachusetts.

[50] Kisaburo Yokota, *Watashi no Issho* [My Life] (Tokyo: Tokyo Shinbun Shuppankyoku, 1976), pp. 93–98. Hudson wrote an introductory letter to Wright for Yokota. See Yokota to Hudson, October 20, 1928, Hudson Papers, Box 83, Folder 6.

development of the prohibition of war, following the Covenant and the Pact itself.[51]

Yokota argued that Japan's actions in Manchuria exceeded the justifiable scope of the right of self-defense. Even if the military actions on the night of September 18 had been a response to a Chinese attack on the South Manchurian Railway, the ensuing large-scale military incursions into the city of Kirin and other major cities in Manchuria could not be explained by the right of self-defense.[52] Yokota later wrote, "At that time, I had a strong passion for international law, but the Manchurian Incident ruined international law. So I could not but stand up to defend it."[53] Because of this criticism of Japan's military actions, right-wing patriots and nationalist newspapers launched attacks on Yokota, and he received letters filled with epithets like "betrayer" and "national enemy." Yokota would maintain his position, but doing so was an enormous intellectual and spiritual burden.

It was difficult for Wright to understand why Japanese civilians supported the military actions in Manchuria. A former student of Wright's, Tatsuji Takeuchi, who had received his doctoral degree from the University of Chicago in 1931 and was now back in Japan, wrote to Wright about the nationalistic sentiment in his country. "Both the military and civilian elements are united, apparently, in settling this long-contested question, even if it may bring about very serious international consequences."[54] For Wright this was hard to accept, because he believed that it was normal for people to want peace instead of war. He responded, "I must confess a little surprise at hearing of the unity of the Japanese people upon the methods taken." He then suggested that certain measures needed to be taken against the banditry in Manchuria, observing "it is difficult to reconcile a long occupation of Manchurian territory with the object of promoting Chinese recognition of certain 'fundamental principles,' with the obligations of Japan under the League of Nations Covenant, the Nine Power Treaty, and the Kellogg pact."[55] Wright also expressed skepticism about Japan's assertion of self-defense, writing that although Americans recognized a certain necessity for self-defense in foreign territory, "they find it somewhat difficult to justify such very extensive operations under

---

[51] Yokota, "Senso no zettaiteki kinshi, saikin no Renmei Kiyaku kaisei-an," 14–31.
[52] *Teikoku Daigaku Shinbun*, October 5, 1931.
[53] "Yokota Kisaburo sensei ni kiku" [An Interview with Professor Yokota Kisaburo], *Hogaku Kyoshitsu* 28 (1983), 35.
[54] Tatsuji Takeuchi to Wright, November 20, 1931, Wright Papers, addenda II, Box 25.
[55] Wright to Tatsuji Takeuchi, December 28, 1931, Wright Papers, addenda II, Box 25.

international law and treaties concerning China." Wright came to the conclusion that the American press and public believed that "Japan has violated various treaties to which the United States is a party."[56]

Throughout 1932, Wright and Baty communicated with each other frequently. Baty repeated the claim that Japan's actions were based on the right of self-defense. "If Panama attacked the Canal Zone," certainly the United States would resort to similar actions, Baty wrote.[57] He also pointed out that China did not rule Manchuria, and he criticized Wright for treating the problem "as if the so-called 'Nanking Gov't of Nanking' were the legitimate ruler of all China."[58] Wright responded by saying that "one has to distinguish rather carefully the problem from the standpoint of actual administration and from the standpoint of international relations." He asserted that what was at stake was the principle that "legal title should only change by legal procedure," which was more important than "the applying of a remedy for the disturbed state of Manchuria."[59] In both tone and content, Baty's personal letters to Wright held quite closely to Japan's official position. With regard to Wright's position, Baty wrote, "I should have taken much the same view if I had not been in possession of the full facts, which seem to me, when properly weighted, to point to a different conclusion."[60]

On the other hand, in a letter to Borchard, Baty wrote that the Japanese response to the Stimson Doctrine was written with "no *arrière-pensée*" and "Japan was heartily with America in upholding the treaties and common interests of all the Powers in China." In addition, Baty noted that he had shared Borchard's skepticism toward the League "from the very first." He lamented that "the quasi-diplomats at Geneva are inclined to magnify their office – and really they cannot understand the situation of countries thousands miles away." Baty also pointed out that "the whole root of the present difficulty lies in the want of realism exhibited by the Powers" because they shared the idea that China was united. Thus, the origin and responsibility for the present conflict lay not with Japan, but with China. This was because China had engaged in boycott and violated Japan's interests in the region. Most of Baty's letters in Borchard's archived papers are handwritten, but this one was copied in a typeset format.[61]

---

[56] Wright to Michimasa Soyeshima, March 14, 1932, Wright Papers, Box 6, Folder 4.
[57] Baty to Wright, February 25, 1932, Wright Papers, Box 19, Folder 15.
[58] Baty to Wright, June 2, 1932, Wright Papers, Box 19, Folder 15.
[59] Wright to Baty, June 18, 1932, Wright Papers, Box 19, Folder 15.
[60] Baty to Wright, April 7, 1932, Wright Papers, Box 19, Folder 15.
[61] Baty to Borchard, March 27, 1932, Borchard Papers, Box 1, Folder 14.

It is possible to assume that Borchard, who once remarked that Baty's handwriting was difficult to read, found this letter especially important and had it typed up before sending copies out to his friends in the United States, as he occasionally did with attention-worthy materials.

At the beginning of 1932, the Program Committee of the ASIL was considering what issues to discuss at the Society's next annual meeting in April. Wright thought that the Manchurian problem would "doubtless be a matter of contemporary interest." He suggested that there be three approaches to debate on the issue. There should be a meeting on the Kellogg–Briand Pact and its application with reference to the League of Nations and the Stimson Doctrine, a discussion of the meaning and the instrument of the Nine Power Treaty, and a discussion of the possibility of the United States cooperating with the League.[62]

The annual meeting of the ASIL in 1932 revealed exceptional interest in the situation in Manchuria among American international lawyers. On the night of April 28, 1932, at the opening session of the meeting, introductory remarks were presented by Finch, secretary of the Society. Finch's task was to summarize the important events bearing upon international law in the last year. Most of his talk dealt with the situation in Manchuria, ranging from its history and geopolitical location to the current issues of immigration and Japanese policy.[63]

The next day, both the morning and afternoon sessions were allotted to round-table discussions of the "Treaty Situations in the Far East." A total of nine papers were read, with almost all the specialists on international law in East Asia participating. The meetings were chaired by two of the most authoritative figures on issues involving the Far East, both of whom were closely associated with American policy toward the area. The morning session was led by MacMurray, former American minister to China and editor of the voluminous work on treaties in China mentioned above; the other session was presided over by Hornbeck, chief of the Division of Far Eastern Affairs in the State Department.[64]

The first session was entitled "The Nature and Interpretation of Treaties" and it covered two topics: "Treaties Made under Duress," and "The

---

[62] Wright to Lester H. Woolsey, January 27 1932, Wright Papers, Box 2, Folder 23.
[63] George A. Finch, "Introductory Remarks," *Proceedings, ASIL* (1932), 1–6.
[64] Originally, the ASIL asked Hornbeck to present a paper on the subject "Treaties Made under Duress." Hornbeck declined, however, explaining that his position in the State Department prevented him from doing so. "Conversation, March 25, 1932, Mr. Lester Woolsey, Mr. Hornbeck," Papers of Stanley K. Hornbeck, Hoover Institution, Stanford University, Box 219.

Doctrine of *rebus sic stantibus*." Chairman MacMurray himself provided
the introductory remarks, which revealed his desire to support the existing treaty system and the unequal treaties in China. He proposed that
the system of unequal treaties between the Western powers and China
derived from the necessity of setting up a commercial and trade relationship between the West and China. And he argued that the system "served
its purpose at least tolerably well." According to MacMurray, China was
partly responsible for the current state of affairs, because China had made
very little progress and had ignored or taken lightly the situation created not only by the 1915 treaties but also by those of 1905. He suggested,
moreover, that "the Chinese have been deluded by tolerant sympathy of
the world into attempting the vain and foolish effort to crowd Japan out
of Manchuria by covert and unacknowledged force." MacMurray argued
that if Japan could prove that her military actions were based upon
the right of self-defense, there was room for accepting Japan's claim in
Manchuria in the current conflict. He concluded by reaffirming the "san-
ity" of the treaty system, arguing that "however onerous or distasteful,
so long as they remain in legal effect, states had obligations to adhere to
established treaty obligations."[65]

Following MacMurray, Charles Henry Butler and Edgar Turlington
presented papers on treaties made under coercion. Butler argued that
under the established principles of international law, a nation could
not avoid the obligations of a treaty simply because it had been signed
under duress.[66] Edger Turlington, the third speaker, acknowledged that
the welfare of international society supposed the observance of treaties,
but he believed that some changes should be made. He quoted Dr. Alfred
Verdross of The Hague Academy of International Law, who argued that
a new theory was emerging and that blanket adherence to the validity of
treaties made under duress was being questioned.[67]

Discussion of this issue continued in the following presentation on
the doctrine of *rebus sic stantibus*, which stipulated how treaties could
be revised after claims of changed circumstances. The first speaker was
William C. Dennis, president of Earlham College, former solicitor for the
State Department and former legal advisor to the Chinese government.
He contended that this doctrine was essential but dangerous. No treaty
could remain unchanged forever, but since there was no international

---

[65] J. V. A. MacMurray, "Opening Remarks," *Proceedings, ASIL* (1932), 37–45.
[66] Charles Henry Butler, "Treaties Made under Duress," *Proceedings, ASIL* (1932), 45–48.
[67] Edgar Turlington, "Treaties Made under Duress," *Proceedings, ASIL* (1932), 49–53.

tribunal to judge validity or durability, blanket acceptance of this doctrine could lead to the collapse of the sanctity of treaties.[68] The most progressive interpretation came from the next speaker, Professor Joseph P.
Chamberlain of Columbia University, who was a close associate of James
Shotwell. According to Chamberlain, the doctrine of *rebus sic stantibus*
did not authorize one power to abrogate a treaty unilaterally, but rather
each country was entitled to request from other powers a recognition
of the change in circumstance and to propose that a revision be made.
In the case of multilateral agreements like the Nine Power Treaty, a signatory must persuade all the other signatories, which made the process
more complicated. Chamberlain found a precedent for the application
of this principle in the question of tariff autonomy in China. Signatories
had recognized decisive changes and had worked together for revision of
the treaty. With regard to the Japanese claim of the non-applicability of
the Nine Power Treaty, Chamberlain sided with Dennis, contending that
there had been an increase in trade and investment in China since the
completion of the treaty in 1922.[69]

In the discussion following the four papers, a participant from China
criticized MacMurray's remarks. This participant contended that *rebus sic
stantibus* was essential "to enable modern international law to get abreast
of the times." He also contended that the Treaty of Twenty-One Demands
was not effective, because it was imposed on China in a time of complete
peace, not during war. Wright and Garner, the standard-bearers of the
new international law, also stressed the importance of change. Wright
argued that international law itself was changing, because the Kellogg
Pact legally placed the problem of duress "on an entirely different basis,"
since the Pact clearly stated that war was illegal. Garner contended that the
doctrine of *rebus sic stantibus* would become more important "in this age
of rapidly changing conditions."[70] Contrary to Chairman MacMurray's
opening remark that the system of unequal treaties had some relevance to
the current situation in China, the papers and discussion produced a view
favorable to the revision of treaties, which in turn supported the Chinese
position in the ongoing conflict in Manchuria.

The afternoon session dealt with the topic of "Enforcement of Treaty
Obligations," and included the sub-topics of "Self-help and Self-defense,"

---

[68] William C. Dennis, "The Doctrine of *rebus sic stantibus*," *Proceedings, ASIL* (1932),
53–59.
[69] Joseph Chamberlain, "The Doctrine of *rebus sic stantibus*," *Proceedings, ASIL* (1932),
59–62.
[70] "Discussion," *Proceedings, ASIL* (1932), 63–66.

and "Collective Rights and Duties." As the title of the first sub-topic suggests, these topics were being taken up in response to Japan's claim of the right of self-defense in the war in Manchuria. The first speaker, Harold S. Quigley of the University of Minnesota, argued that self-help was generally allowed in established international law and not treated as unlawful, but that there had been a tendency to limit its legality. He made reference to Charles Cheney Hyde, W. E. Hall and Borchard's skepticism about the legality of the notion. Quigley also noted that the League and the Kellogg Pact had imposed limitations on claims of self-defense. As for the specific Japanese actions in Manchuria, he quoted the remark by Kisaburo Yokota of Tokyo Imperial University that the Japanese had far exceeded the limits of the justifiable exercise of self-defense.[71]

The second speaker, Kenneth W. Colegrove of Northwestern University, contended that international society permitted the means of self-help, but that there had developed a tendency to restrain the unconditional application of the principle. An emerging practice was the submission of disputes to a definite procedure before actions were taken in the name of self-help. Colegrove therefore argued that current international law insisted upon some sort of procedure, which must be followed prior to resorting to self-help or self-defense. In the case of the Sino-Japanese controversy in Manchuria, China had appealed to the League of Nations and followed this procedure at the League without resorting to military action. Japan, however, had rejected these procedures and continued her military actions. Thus, he concluded that "the Nipponese government has fallen short of international standards of correct procedure in resorting to self-help, both in Manchuria and Shanghai."[72]

Wright spoke next on the topic "Collective Rights and Duties for the Enforcement of Treaty Obligations." He argued that before the Great War, the decision about whether an interpretation of a treaty was valid or not had been left to the signatories of the treaty. After the war, collective and multilateral institutions had been established to give direction on the interpretation and enforcement of treaties. He saw the League of Nations Covenant, the PCIJ Protocols, the Washington Treaties and the Kellogg–Briand Pact as all being applicable to the situation in the

---

[71] Harold S. Quigley, "Enforcement of Treaty Obligations: Self-help and Self-defense," *Proceedings, ASIL* (1932), 90–96.

[72] Kenneth W. Colegrove, "Enforcement of Treaty Obligations: Self-help and Self-defense," *Proceedings, ASIL* (1932), 96–101.

Far East. Observing this worldwide trend, the Chinese government had agreed to submit its dispute concerning the validity of the treaty of 1915 to the League, but Japan had insisted on bilateral negotiations. As for the right of self-defense, Wright held that the League was competent to determine whether the facts justified the plea of self-defense.[73]

Finch raised the objection that Wright had merely assumed that a nation was bound to submit to international procedure questions concerning the validity of treaties. But Finch asserted that this was neither "an accepted principle of international law" nor the established practice. Also, if it was argued that a treaty made under duress was not automatically void, then the Japanese insistence on the validity of the treaty of 1915 might be reasonable. Finch remarked that "there is something to be said from the Japanese point of view." Clyde Eagleton, another advocate of collective security, took exception to Finch's position. With regard to the principle of *rebus sic stantibus*, and of self-help and self-defense, he held that if each state were allowed to decide the applicability of these doctrines for itself, "you are not going to get anywhere." He noted, however, "there seems to be general agreement now that there should be a collective judgment substituted for the individual judgment of states, and we are making progress in that direction."[74]

In his concluding remarks for the session, Hornbeck succinctly summarized the points that had been made. He suggested that there should have been more discussion on the question of precedence between bilateral and multilateral treaties and between old and new treaties. The discussions at the ASIL did not produce any definite conclusions in this regard, but the arguments presented by Eagleton and Wright, which favored more recent multilateral treaties over older bilateral ones, had carried the day. The implications for the actual situation in East Asia were that rather than the unequal treaties with China, on which Japan had based its position, the multilateral treaties established since World War I – such as the Covenant, the Nine Power Treaty, and the Pact – would become the legal standard.[75] The discussions at the ASIL were significant in that they favored the new multilateral treaties which were held to present the comprehensive development of a collective framework. The reformers regarded the three multilateral treaties en bloc as a "new treaty system."

---

[73] Quincy Wright, "Collective Rights and Duties," *Proceedings, ASIL* (1932), 101–109.
[74] "Discussion," *Proceedings, ASIL* (1932), 127–128, 131.
[75] *Ibid.*, 134.

The Stimson Doctrine: a great innovation?

Secretary of State Henry L. Stimson, who had tried to invoke the Kellogg–Briand Pact during the Sino-Soviet conflict over the East Chinese Railway in the fall of 1929, initially took a cautious approach to the conflict in Manchuria. But with the Japanese aerial bombing of Chinchow, he began to look for a way to cooperate with the League of Nations. While President Herbert Hoover did not seek active involvement, Stimson succeeded in sending American observers to the League. As a statesman who was sympathetic to Woodrow Wilson's view of international cooperation and who felt that the powers were responsible for maintaining peace in the world, Stimson sought ways to be effective in resolving the matter.[76] In a letter to Elihu Root, Stimson mentioned that he would issue a warning to Japan similar to the one issued in 1915, but he noted "that would be perhaps the minimum which we could do."[77]

Three weeks later, Secretary Stimson sent a diplomatic note both to Japan and China to the effect that the United States would not recognize any situation brought about by means contrary to the treaties.

Wright did not consider the Stimson Doctrine "minimal"; rather he found in it great innovation. He wrote, "No diplomatic note of recent or even more distant years is likely to go down in history as of greater significance in the development of international law than that sent by the United States to China and Japan on January 7, 1932."[78] He had in mind three universal propositions that could lead to radical new developments in international law: "(1) De facto occupation of territory gives no title; (2) Treaties contrary to the rights of third states are void; (3) Treaties in the making of which non-pacific means have been employed are void." Up to that time, international law had given legal recognition to changes effected by the use of force. Wright noted that "recognition has been the magic formula that has converted violation into legality, robbery into title, might into right."[79]

Wright believed that the world had reached a stage of rationality where might should not equal right. He saw the Stimson Doctrine as a progressive step in line with the spirit of the Pact. If Wright's three principles

---

[76] Christopher Thorne, *The Limits of Foreign Policy* (London: Hamish Hamilton, 1972), pp. 152–162, 192–199.

[77] Henry L. Stimson to Elihu Root, December 14, 1931, Papers of Henry L. Stimson, Library of Congress, Washington, DC, Reel 82.

[78] Quincy Wright, "The Stimson Note of January 7, 1932," *AJIL* 26 (1932), 342.

[79] *Ibid.*, 344.

were made effective, then "international law would be revolutionized."[80] It is apparent that Wright did not think that the Stimson Doctrine had already brought about a change in the principles of international law, but he did hold out the hope that in the future it might induce radical change for the positive.

Against this innovative interpretation of the Stimson Doctrine, Sakutaro Tachi replied with an article directly refuting Wright's reasoning. The essence of Tachi's criticism was that Wright's argument had not been accepted as the established principle or understanding of international law. Although Tachi did mention some theoretical works on international law that argued against Wright's position, he mainly favored the use of such stock phrases as "actual international law" and "established international law." For instance, Tachi wrote that "Wright's argument is not compatible with the judicial belief in international law as it has been up to now."[81] Wright's interpretation might have been an effort to develop a new, progressive, and forward-looking principle in international law, but Tachi preferred to stay with the established view.

Kisaburo Yokota fully sided with Wright, stating that the Stimson Doctrine was important "because it would put teeth into the Pact." He focused on the fact that international law was steadily developing around the Stimson Doctrine, and he narrated the course of the Doctrine's development. In January 1932, when the United States government first issued the Doctrine, it had only been the policy of one nation. However, on February 16, it was adopted by twelve signatories at the Council of the League of Nations. On February 24, Stimson reaffirmed the policy. Then, on March 11, 1932, the Assembly of the League of Nations adopted it, thereby making the Doctrine a legal principle. Yokota wrote that the adoption by the Assembly meant that 87 percent of all the countries of the world agreed with the principle. Since the Doctrine gave sanction and assurance to treaties, the observance of treaties would be more secure. Yokota concluded that Wright was quite correct in calling this doctrine a revolution in international law.[82]

---

[80] Ibid., 348. For the Stimson Doctrine, see also Bederman, "Appraising a Century," 33; Zasloff, "Law and the Shaping: The Twenty Years' Crisis," 657–659; Meiertöns, Doctrine of US, pp. 86–95; Grewe, Epochs, pp. 601, 620–624.

[81] Sakutaro Tachi, "Fubar-shugi (ichimei Suchimuson-shugi) no jittai" [Nature of the Hoover Doctrine (in other words) the Stimson Doctrine], Gaiko Jiho 674 (1933), 203.

[82] Kisaburo Yokota, "Manshu jihen to Fubar shugi" [Manchurian Incident and the Hoover Doctrine], Kokusaiho Gaiko Zasshi 32 (1933), 46–86.

Yokota also described the significance of the Stimson Doctrine in the context of the international movement to maintain peace. The Stimson Doctrine adhered to the spirit of the times, a spirit that was at the heart of the Covenant of the League of Nations and the Kellogg–Briand Pact. All these instruments emphasized the pacific settlement of conflicts, the renunciation of war, and collective security. Yokota shared with reformers in the United States the belief that World War I had signaled a turning point in history. The war had taught mankind about the calamity of war and the necessity of a durable world peace, which had become the universal plea of humanity. Since the Stimson Doctrine followed in the wake of these developments, Yokota concluded that it would "take root in the soil of world peace and not vanish like a display of fireworks."[83]

Interest in the Stimson Doctrine among legal specialists was not confined to Japan. British scholars also debated its effects, legal meaning and potential. Arnold D. McNair of Cambridge University argued that the Non-Recognition Doctrine presented the fundamental question that the international community had to answer, which was what the international community was going to do "when faced with the use by one of its members of force, applied or threatened, in order to attain its own ends." McNair held that the Doctrine's significance was that it established the principle for negating the use of force, but he was more cautious in judging its actual effect on aggressors. McNair concluded that the Doctrine should be regarded as "a prelude to concrete action against a wrongdoer."[84]

Another British scholar, Sir John Fischer Williams, viewed the Stimson Doctrine favorably. He had been an ardent advocate of collective security, the League of Nations and the new international law.[85] Similarly to Wright, Williams found in the Doctrine "an important development in international law," since it established the principle that "legality of a title or right acquired by force was not recognized." He compared the new doctrine to "a straw in the wind," and argued that "what is important when straw is blowing is the force and direction of the wind, not the nature of

---

[83] Kisaburo Yokota, "Stimson shugi to sekai no taisei" [The Stimson Doctrine and World Trend], *Chuo Koron* 48 (May 1933), 24–36.

[84] Arnold D. McNair, "The Stimson Doctrine of Non-Recognition: A Note on Its Legal Aspects," *British Year Book of International Law* 14 (1933), 66, 73.

[85] Williams wrote prolifically on topics related to the new international law. See, for example, John Fischer Williams, *Chapters on Current International Law and the League of Nations* (London: Longmans, 1929); "La Convention pour L'assistance Financière aux États Victimes D'Agression," *Recueil des Cours* 34 (1930), 81–174.

the straw." The Doctrine showed that "the world has arrived at the stage of civilization" when mankind would no longer resort to war.[86]

Secretary Stimson himself did not hesitate to view the march toward peace in the context of the Kellogg–Briand Pact. On August 8, 1932, in an address to the Council of Foreign Relations in New York entitled "The Pact of Paris: Three Years of Development," he argued that the Pact "signalize[d] a revolution in human thought ... War between nations was renounced by the signatories of the Kellogg–Briand Treaty. This means that it has become illegal throughout practically the entire world."[87] He noted, moreover, that the Pact had made war the concern of all nations, whereas before it had usually been deemed the concern of only those parties involved in the conflict. This was quite similar to Wright's interpretation of the Pact. Stimson then quoted President Hoover to the effect that the Pact created a "positive obligation to direct national policy in accordance with its pledge."[88] He pointed out that US diplomatic actions during the hostilities between Russia and China in northern Manchuria in 1929 and also during the Manchurian Incident demonstrated US willingness to adhere to the Pact.

Stimson was willing to use the Pact for diplomatic leverage. The Great Depression, Hoover's reserved attitude toward foreign affairs, and American non-participation in the League served as restraints on Stimson's handling of foreign affairs, but the Pact served as an effective tool and he made great use of it whenever possible. It is not certain whether or to what extent he was aware of the implications of his endorsement of the Pact on the development of the new international law, although Stimson himself was a lawyer, but his Non-Recognition Doctrine and favorable attitude toward the Pact, particularly as expressed in his address before the Council of Foreign Relations, had a great impact on theorists. Scholars felt encouraged by his speech and referred to it often. Besides, as time went on, the position set forth in his policies and speech became one of the fundamental principles of the United States. As a result, sixteen years later in February 1948, the speech was quoted during the final summation of the prosecution at the International Military Tribunal in the Far East.[89]

---

[86] John Fischer Williams, "The New Doctrine of 'Recognition'," *Transactions of the Grotius Society* 18 (1932), 110, 127, 129.

[87] Henry L. Stimson, *The Pact of Paris: Three Years of Development* (Washington, DC: GPO, 1932), p. 4.

[88] *Ibid.*, p. 8.

[89] R. John Pritchard and Sonia Magbanua Zaide, eds., *The Tokyo War Crimes Trial* (London: Garland Publishing, 1981), vol. 16, p. 39006.

A new treaty system: work at the League of Nations

The study of international law in China had more in common with the new trends in the United States than with the dominant view in Japan. In the fall of 1931, a meeting of the Institute of Pacific Relations had been scheduled in Shanghai. For this conference, Professor Shu-hsi Hsü of Yenching University in Beijing had prepared a booklet entitled *The Manchurian Dilemma: Force or Pacific Settlement*. In its preface, Shu-hsi noted that the content of the booklet had not been altered despite the Japanese aggression in Manchuria. It started with the sentence "the Briand-Kellogg Multilateral Treaty for the Renunciation of War, signed at Paris on August 27, 1928, by no means confines the renunciation of war to a mere pious wish." The booklet argued that the world had been steadily developing a framework for pacific settlement since the Hague Conference of 1907.[90]

There is an interesting statistic that gives some indication of the difference between Japanese and Chinese attitudes toward the study of international law at around this time. The Carnegie Endowment had sponsored a yearly summer lecture program, The Hague Academy of International Law, at which scholars from many countries taught courses in a variety of subjects related to the field. In the summer of 1929, there were eight Chinese scholars participating in the program, out of a total of 433 – but there were no Japanese participants that year.[91]

After the outbreak of hostilities in Manchuria, the Chinese immediately appealed to the League of Nations.[92] The first meeting of the Assembly was significant in that it indicated the direction discussions would take. The Japanese delegate, Kenkichi Yoshizawa, argued that the Japanese action on the night of September 18 was a defensive measure. The Chinese delegate, Alfred Sze, who himself had a doctoral degree in law and was a close

[90] Shu-hsi Hsü and Robert Moore Duncan, *The Manchurian Dilemma: Force or Pacific Settlement* (n.p., China Council, Institute of Pacific Relations, 1931).
[91] Carnegie Endowment for International Peace, *Yearbook* (1930), 110. The numbers from each country were: Netherlands, 157; Germany, 64; Poland, 41; United States, 26; Italy, 26; France, 19; Great Britain, 14; Egypt, 9; Romania, 9; China, 8; Greece, 8; Hungary, 8; Belgium, 6; Switzerland, 5; Chile, 4; Cuba, 4; Austria, 3; Russia, 3; Danzig, 2; British India, 2; Sweden, 2; Czechoslovakia, 2; Albania, Argentine, Bulgaria, Canada, Colombia, Costa Rica, Denmark, Yugoslavia, Spain, Mexico, and Uruguay, 1 each. Unfortunately, no numbers were given in other volumes.
[92] For the discussions at the League, see Quincy Wright, "The Manchurian Crisis," *American Political Science Review* 26 (1932), 45–76; Welstel W. Willoughby, *The Sino-Japanese Controversy and the League of Nations* (Baltimore: Johns Hopkins Press, 1935); Thorne, *Limits of Foreign Policy*.

friend of Willoughby, countered that at the 36th session of the Council in October 1925 the members had agreed that no nation could of its own accord claim to have taken merely defensive measures.[93]

In response to Sze's remark, the chairman of the session, Viscount Cecil, read the statement by Aristide Briand in October 1925. It noted the danger of resorting to military action in the name of self-defense, because of the possibility that this might lead to war. Instead of pleading defensive measures, members of the League of Nations were required to appeal to the Council. Cecil added that this statement had been approved by Viscount Kikujiro Ishii, the Japanese representative to the League at the time. Cecil continued that the Manchurian Incident was not the "first international dispute of this nature," and he suggested that if Japan had followed the procedures of the League faithfully, she would have appealed to the Council before resorting to military action. Cecil cited the Kellogg–Briand Pact and the Nine Power Treaty as further treaty obligations that Japan and China had to observe, in addition to those contained in the Covenant of the League of Nations.[94]

During subsequent meetings in October, Yoshizawa emphasized that the case of Manchuria was a special one dating back to 1894. He also claimed that there had been certain military actions taken by the Chinese.[95] In contrast, China presented its position in the context of the worldwide movement for peace. Sze proclaimed that "the challenge thrown to us is a challenge also to all nations." He continued:

> The Covenant and the Pact of Paris are our two sheet-anchors, to which we have moored our ship of State and with the help of which we believe we shall ride out this storm. Nevertheless, the Covenant and the Pact of Paris are also the corner-stones of the world wide edifice of peace that has been so laboriously erected in the twelve years since the world war, and if they crumble, the edifice collapses … China has put herself in the hands of the League and abides the issue with confidence in her destiny and in the moral forces of civilization.[96]

The use of phrases that Western liberals found fascinating, such as "edifice of peace" and "civilized countries," must certainly have been applauded by people like Wright.

The impasse at the League led to an investigating commission being sent to Manchuria to examine the origins of the conflict. After several months of investigation in the Far East, the so-called Lytton Report of

---

[93] League of Nations, *Official Journal* (December 1931), 2267–2268.
[94] *Ibid.*, 2269–2270.   [95] *Ibid.*, 2316–2319.   [96] *Ibid.*, 2312.

inquiry was presented to the Council. It focused on the historical causes of the conflict between Japan and China and offered a detailed account of developments in the latter country. In approach, the report was reminiscent of the methodology employed by Young in his book on the Manchurian situation. Concerning the Japanese claim of self-defense, the report clearly stated that the Japanese action on the night of September 18 was not justified. Although the report did not explicitly call for a system of collective security as the condition of settlement, it did mention that a solution should be in conformity with present multilateral treaties.[97]

One of the American advocates for collective security, Arthur Kuhn, wrote a favorable opinion on the Lytton Report. Even though he discussed the content of the report, his positive judgment was mostly directed at its significance as a manifestation of collective procedure. It verified the League's success in achieving a collective method. He wrote, "it is of the greatest interest to international jurists that a procedure has been devised under the auspices of the League" in the event that parties did not agree to submit to arbitration or to judicial settlement.[98]

In Japan, Thomas Baty was very critical of the Lytton Report, because he thought it had not dealt enough with China's repeated violations of the treaties. He even suspected that the first chapters were written by an American, more specifically, by Young.[99] Baty drafted opinions against the report, some of which were adopted in the official Japanese opinion submitted to the League, entitled "Observations of the Japanese Government on the Report of the Commission of Enquiry." Most noteworthy were the sections dealing with the "Special Position of Japan" and the right of self-defense, in which Baty's original was used verbatim. It read,

> The "special position" of Japan in Manchuria, to which so much mystery is attached, is in reality a very simple matter. It is nothing but the aggregate of Japan's exceptional treaty rights in that country, *plus* [emphasis original] the natural consequences which flow from her close neighborhood and geographical situation and from historical associations. Her measures of self-defense must be measured by the extent of their interests.[100]

[97] League of Nations, "Appeal by the Chinese Government, Report of the Commission of Enquiry," October 1, 1932, C. 623. M. 320, p. 72, DLN.

[98] Arthur Kuhn, "The Lytton Report on the Manchurian Crisis," *AJIL* 27 (1933), 100.

[99] Thomas Baty, "Lytton Report Memorandum," in Masakuma Uchiyama, "Manshu Jihen to Thomas Baty hakase" [The Manchurian Incident and Dr. Baty], in *Gendai Gaiko Shiron* (Tokyo: Keio Tushin, 1971), p. 202.

[100] Thomas Baty, "Draft of Observation on the Lytton Report," October 12, 1932, Manshu Jihen zengo shochi kankei, Kokusai Renmei Shina chosain kankei (Documents Concerning the Lytton Commission), JDA.

As a basis for justifying its claim of self-defense, Japan reiterated its previous interpretations of the right of self-defense by quoting both a remark by Secretary Kellogg on the inherent nature of the right of self-defense and the May 19, 1928 British reservation to the Pact regarding areas in that nation's special interest.[101]

The Japanese argument was not completely groundless in terms of legal reasoning, especially for those who held to the traditional approach. Philip Marshall Brown of Princeton University quoted the very section of the Japanese opinion cited above, originally drafted by Baty, and argued that Japan's position was sustainable at least on the point concerning Kellogg's note on reservation of the right of self-defense. Brown argued that Kellogg had stated that the right of self-defense was not hampered in the Pact and that he had "made it possible for Japan to assert that the Pact is inapplicable in these circumstances." Although "the world may not applaud the actions of Japan in Manchuria," the Pact had left room for such a justification.[102]

The Chinese response refuted Japan's position on self-defense. It cited the fact that Kellogg's statement, which Japan had quoted, also included the qualification "If it [the nation invoking the right of self-defense] has a good case, the world will applaud and not condemn its action." Furthermore, it quoted a part of Secretary Stimson's address before the Council on Foreign Relations on August 8, 1932: "A nation which sought to mask imperialistic policy under the guise of the defense of its nationals would soon be unmasked." Thus, a state that invoked the right must demonstrate that it had a bona fide reason to do so. The Chinese response went on to refer to Professor Yokota's argument, in which he had stated that Japan's actions exceeded the limits of justifiable self-defense. The Chinese response concluded by asserting that Japan's opinion was "entirely misleading and cannot be justified in international law or in international practice."[103]

The Committee of Nineteen nominated by the Assembly produced a final report based upon the Lytton Report. It was adopted by the Assembly on February 24, 1933. Its fourth section, entitled "Statement

---

[101] League of Nations, "Appeal by the Chinese Government, Observations of the Japanese Government," November 19, 1932, C. 775. M. 366, pp. 22–25, DLN.

[102] Philip Marshall Brown, "Japanese Interpretation of the Kellogg Pact," *AJIL* 27 (1933), 102.

[103] League of Nations, "Appeal from the Chinese Government, Communication from the Chinese Delegation," December 3 1932, A [Extr.], A. 155, pp. 23–25, DLN.

and Recommendations," clearly proclaimed the principles upon which the settlement of the dispute should stand. "The settlement of the dispute should observe the provisions of the Covenant of the League, the Pact of Paris, and the Nine Power Treaty of Washington." In addition, the same section reiterated the position that members of the League should not recognize any situation, treaty or agreement which might be brought about by means contrary to the Covenant or the Pact of Paris. This was an explicit reference to the Stimson Doctrine. The report concluded that Japan should withdraw her troops from outside the zone of the South Manchurian Railway, because their presence and operation there were "incompatible with the legal principles which should govern the settlement of the dispute." In addition, the recommendation noted that the principles and conditions set down in the Lytton Report should be referred to as guidelines for the settlement of future disputes. The two important guidelines were: "conformity with existing multilateral treaties" and "the establishment of new treaty relations between China and Japan." Taken together, these two guidelines suggested that new Sino-Japanese treaties that conformed with the Covenant, the Pact and the Nine Power Treaty had to be concluded. This, in turn, refuted the Japanese claim, which was based on the old, unequal treaties with China.[104]

The Final Report of February 24 was in significant accord with the arguments set forth by the reformers. Like the opinion that Wright had voiced at the ASIL meeting of April 1932, the League's report treated the three multilateral treaties together and as constituting a collective framework. The report was welcomed by American international lawyers. Hudson's response was nothing short of an unqualified endorsement. He wrote, "It marks a triumph for the collective system of handling international disputes. A new goal has been set in the process of pacific settlement, and a precedent has been established which may serve as a guide for the future."[105] Hudson's enthusiasm for the report did not wane over the next few years, as can be seen in this quote from his 1935 book on the Pact of Paris: "As adopted by the Special Assembly on February 24, 1932, this report is one of the greatest state documents of all time."[106] At the outset of the 1933 meeting of the ASIL, Finch recommended that all the members

---

[104] "League of Nations Assembly Report on the Sino-Japanese Dispute," *AJIL* 27 (1933), Supplement, 147–150.
[105] Manley O. Hudson, "The Report of the Assembly of the League of Nations on the Sino-Japanese Dispute," *AJIL* 27 (1933), 300.
[106] Manley O. Hudson, *By Pacific Means: The Implementation of Article Two of the Pact of Paris* (New Haven: Yale University Press, 1935), pp. 40–41.

read the report. After doing so, they would be convinced that "a full and complete effort has been made by the League of Nations."[107] It is interesting to note that Kuhn, Hudson and Finch, who were not familiar with the details of the Far Eastern situation but were advocates of the collective framework, also praised the Lytton Report and the Final Report without hesitation, though Wright was more reserved in his judgment. He, too, welcomed the report, but at the same time was concerned about the possibility that Japan would withdraw from the League.[108]

Immediately after the Final Report was adopted, the US government issued a statement of support. Most editorials in American newspapers also voiced approval of the report. One contemporary historian, Denna Fleming, conducted a survey of major newspapers in the United States and concluded that favorable opinions were in the majority. Fleming himself contended that "the League saved its soul" with the Assembly's resolution of February 1933, even though the League failed to take decisive steps toward halting aggression in the long term. Because the League was in fact unable to stop military hostilities, one can argue that the League's efforts were limited. But looking at the other side of the coin, what the League achieved in setting up principles and in gaining the endorsement of other countries warrants a more positive evaluation. It was not a perfect victory, because Japan did withdraw from the League and did not abandon its aggression. However, borrowing Fleming's words again, "it [the League] at least refused to vow her."[109] Taking into account what the League accomplished in advancing a collective framework, as well as what remained unachieved, the League's accomplishment might at best be called a half-victory.

The Manchurian Incident occurred just as the old treaty system in China – i.e. the unequal treaties – was being called into question. Multilateral treaties such as the Covenant of the League of Nations, the Kellogg–Briand Pact and the Nine Power Treaty were gaining recognition and emerging as a unified system in the quest for collective security. Japan challenged this "new treaty system" in three ways. First, it adhered to older treaty systems in which its treaty rights were secured rather than recognizing the principles embodied in the Nine Power Treaty, which would have replaced the concept of Japanese special interests in China with territorial integrity or equal opportunity. Second, rather than

[107] *Proceedings, ASIL* (1933), 4.
[108] Quincy Wright, "Some Legal Aspects of the Far Eastern Situation," *AJIL* 27 (1933), 509.
[109] Denna Frank Fleming, *The United States and World Organization 1920–1933* (New York: Columbia University Press, 1938), pp. 454–496.

acknowledging that the Kellogg–Briand Pact and the Covenant were operating together for the general renunciation of war, Japan resorted to overt military actions that could not be justified in any way. And finally, Japan failed to recognize that these three multilateral treaties together constituted a system of international cooperation. One delegate at the Assembly noted that the conflict in Manchuria was a clash between *raison nationale*, which looked at everything in terms of national interests, and *raison internationale*, which was based on a new morale that sought the establishment of a better world.[110] Japan did not want to be a part of this new international framework, as Yosuke Matsuoka made clear in his farewell address to the League. "If China had accepted direct negotiations with Japan, an agreement would have been reached without such difficulties. However, China did not take this method, but appealed to the League of Nations. She intended to hamper Japan with interference from the signatories in the League."[111] The League and the United States had made laborious efforts to elaborate machinery for the maintenance of peace, but the Japanese government disregarded this machinery without the slightest deliberation on the gravity of its actions.

The Japanese were unwilling to accept the new framework, because within it Japan would be unable to hold on to Manchuria. Insofar as Japan's imperialistic ambitions and actions, and the aspirations for peace of most countries of the world were incompatible, conflict was inevitable. Looking at the issue from a broader perspective, one can see that there were different interpretations of and attitudes toward international law underlying the positions of the various parties. These played an important role in establishing an intellectual framework for each position. In Japan scholars who held traditional views, notably Baty and Tachi, were close to the Foreign Ministry, while in the United States advocates of the new international law were engaged in applying the theory of a collective framework to the conflict in Manchuria. At the League, China adroitly presented arguments that were associated with the new international law to support her position.

[110] A remark by Salvador de Madariaga from Spain, December 7, 1932, in Kokusai Renmei rinji sokai kankei ikken, Teikoku daihyo keitai bunsho [Documents Concerning the Special Assembly of the League], JDA.

[111] Gaimusho, ed., *Gaiko nenpyo narabi shuyo monjo* [Major Documents on Japanese Foreign Policy], vol. 2 (Tokyo: Hara shobo, 1965), p. 65.

5

For better or for worse

The debate over neutrality

The debate over neutrality dated back to World War I, when some scholars began to question both the morality of trading arms to belligerents and the feasibility of claiming neutrality. The debate continued after the war and became one of the most heated issues separating the reformers and the traditionalists. The Kellogg–Briand Pact of 1928 was regarded by reformers as providing another reason for revising neutrality, because its multilateral structure required that war become the concern of all signatories. The reformers supported the bill introduced by Senator Arthur Capper in February 1929, which would have given Congress the authority to embargo arm-sales to aggressors, but Congress and the Hoover administration did not show much interest.

After Japan began its military action in Manchuria, the issue of embargoing aggressors was again taken up, this time by Secretary of State Henry L. Stimson. In January 1933 President Hoover sent a message to Congress recommending such a resolution. Senator William Borah introduced an arms-embargo bill, but it was killed by an objection initiated by Senator Hiram Bingham of Connecticut. After Franklin D. Roosevelt took office, an almost identical bill that had originally been suggested by the State Department was introduced in the House of Representatives by Sam D. McReynolds.[1]

By 1933 the government had begun suggesting arms-embargo legislation, and the debate on neutrality, which had been confined primarily to scholars, attracted widespread attention. The scholars, for their part, recognized that their arguments would have more relevance to actual policy than ever. John Bassett Moore, an eminent scholar and a former judge at the PCIJ, and Edwin M. Borchard of Yale Law School played key roles in opposing the bill to impose arms embargoes against aggressors.

---

[1] Divine, *The Illusion of Neutrality*, pp. 32–47.

Stimson and Wright vs. Moore and Borchard

When the embargo bill was introduced in January 1933, Senator Hiram Bingham, who had sought to move for reconsideration, sent the resolution to Borchard for his opinion. Borchard replied that he would support the resolution, provided that the words "country or" were taken out of the phrase "to such country or countries as he [the president] may designate." Their inclusion meant the resolution might be used to embargo only the aggressor. With Borchard's help, Senator Bingham argued that the proposed bill represented a departure from the traditional concept of neutrality. To this Secretary Stimson responded that neutrality was more or less obsolete, and the State Department tried to pressure Senator Bingham to withdraw his opposition. Senator Bingham sought to enlist the support of several scholars at the Yale Law School. One of them was Borchard, who penned a letter to Senator Borah in which he challenged the validity of Stimson's argument. Ultimately Borah's resolution failed to be adopted by the Senate.[2]

When Congressman McReynolds introduced the arms-embargo bill in March 1933, Borchard appeared at a hearing of the Committee of the Foreign Affairs of the House, where he read a letter from Moore that criticized the proposed bill. Moore held that the bill contradicted the traditional notion of neutrality, because "neutrality in the legal sense embraces not only impartiality but also abstention from participation in the conflict." In addition, the bill would enable the President to carry out a war without the requisite declaration.[3]

Borchard then expressed his own opinion. He was critical of Stimson and others in the State Department, complaining that they did not know how to deal with foreign affairs and that they readily became victims of the pacifistic element. In Borchard's view, Stimson was a "good New York lawyer." But since he had only reached the State Department at the age of sixty, he did not have the background of a John Bassett Moore, which was unfortunate. Answering a question on the achievements of the League of Nations, Borchard offered that it did "more harm in the world than [it] will ever do good" because it was not founded on "psychological realities."[4]

[2] Edwin M. Borchard, "Memorandum on the Facts Connected with the 1933 Embargo Resolution," ASIL Papers.
[3] US Congress, House Committee on Foreign Affairs, *Exportations of Arms or Munitions of War, Hearings Before the House Committee on Foreign Affairs*, 72d Cong., 2d sess., 1933, pp. 14, 16.
[4] *Ibid.*, pp. 13, 19, 25.

A month after Borchard's testimony, in April 1933, the ASIL held its annual meeting. The central theme for the meeting was the "sanction of international law," which indicated an interest in the issue of how to *enforce* law. This was a natural consequence of previous developments. In February 1933 the League of Nations had reached a final resolution on the Manchurian Incident, and Japan's actions had been condemned as a violation of existing multilateral treaties. Following this decision, the next step to be considered was enforcement, which led to the issue of sanctions. At the 1933 meeting of the ASIL, a wide range of papers concerning sanctions was read by distinguished specialists, including "The Boycott as a Sanction of International Law" by Charles Cheney Hyde and "Embargo as a Sanction of International Law" by Joseph Chamberlain. In presenting the issue of sanctions, these two papers pointed out that sanctions would entail the possibility of breaching neutrality as it was traditionally defined. Hyde argued that a boycott was "a form of collective intervention," and that it would inevitably abolish the notion of neutrality, according to which non-belligerents were supposed to stay out of conflicts.[5]

In the general discussion, Borchard's disagreement over neutrality with Quincy Wright, James W. Garner and Charles G. Fenwick played out vehemently. The latter group claimed that neutrality had ceased to exist as a viable concept and they condemned Borchard for his indifference toward belligerents. Fenwick stated, "I had thought that the idea of neutrality was pretty well dead, but I see it alive again, starting and disturbing the peace of what we thought was a law-abiding right." Garner argued that international solidarity took precedence over impartiality. Wright even suggested, "Mr. Borchard likes the situation before 1914. He does not want that changed."[6] In response, Borchard laid out the reasons why he had become skeptical of the effort to reform international law. "I got very much discouraged about the World War," he explained, but "the process of romancing in international law, began in 1914, has uninterruptedly continued, and abdication of legal thinking is an incident of it." He also criticized the concept of collective security, arguing that the idea that "when any two peoples lose their head, everybody must go mad, is to me, essential anarchy." He saw collective security as "perpetual war" and "universal fight." Thus, he emphasized the unrealistic and ambitious goals of the new school, adding "you would have to change the whole world as

---

[5] *Proceedings, ASIL* (1933), 71.
[6] *Ibid.*, 55, 95.

it now exists to accomplish the result the 'new school' contemplates with such equanimity if not devotion."[7]

Some scholars, who had been supporting the importance of the traditional approach since the beginning of the 1920s, sided with Borchard. Philip Marshall Brown, protesting the fact that most of the discussion was centered on issues of policy rather than law, cried out, "This is the American Society of International Law!" Dennis P. Myers also noted "a great deal of our discussion has not been in the realm of law, but of policy."[8]

By this time Moore and Borchard had become keenly aware of their role as spokesmen for the traditional school, and they were determined to challenge the reformers. In one of Borchard's submissions to the *Journal*, he repeated his attack on Stimson and the new international law. He wrote that the idealistic and legalistic view of international relations was summarized "in the remarks of an eminent American statesman." Although Borchard did not specify who this statesman was, it was not difficult to surmise given his frequent quotation of Stimson's remarks. Borchard argued that although "his [Stimson's] emotions at least may be respected," his approach to war was dangerous, because "war is a disease to which humanity is likely to be subject so long as the causes of that disease are not checked."[9] His recognition and analysis of the differences between the old and new schools was incisive. Referring to the reformers' views as "the evangelism of new order" and labeling them too ambitious, he criticized the reformers' assumption that "they could, by a stroke of the pen, change human nature or the way of international life." He argued that it was a mistake "to conclude that the system of international relations before 1914 constituted 'international anarchy'." The old order "gave us long periods of tranquility and usually was successful in limiting wars to narrow areas." The traditional methods of conciliation, mediation, arbitration, and of the Hague Conferences had made an important contribution. "They were less ambitious than the 'new' school and, I venture to believe, more practical."[10]

Borchard frequently referred to Stimson as an idealistic statesman. After leaving the office of Secretary of State, Stimson continued to speak for the cause of collective security and emerged as its most eloquent and

---

[7] *Ibid.*, 61, 92, 94. For Borchard and the ASIL around this time, see also Kirgis, *The American Society*, pp. 138–139.
[8] *Proceedings, ASIL* (1933), 100, 173.
[9] Edwin M. Borchard, "The 'Enforcement' of Peace by 'Sanctions'," *AJIL* 27 (1933), 519.
[10] *Ibid.*, 521–523.

distinguished proponent. In the April 1933 issue of *Foreign Affairs*, he reaffirmed his belief that the Kellogg–Briand Pact would serve as the foundation for peace. The Pact established a policy of consultation, as was the case in the 1929 dispute between China and the Soviet Union over the Chinese Eastern Railway. It had also enabled the United States to take cooperative actions with other countries during the period of the Manchurian Incident. For Stimson, the Pact was "a vehicle on the part of the United States for cooperation in the work of world stabilization and peace." Underlying his support for the collective framework was his belief that war had become too dangerous. He argued that modern civilization had become fragile because of the threat of war and that the world had reached the stage when it could abolish war.[11]

In the next issue of *Foreign Affairs*, John Bassett Moore launched an attack on Stimson's viewpoint. The title of his essay, "An Appeal to Reason," reflected his intention to reveal the futility of the other group's position. Stimson had asserted that the Hoover-MacDonald declaration of October 1929, drafted at Rapidan where the two leaders had held preliminary talks about a possible disarmament conference, constituted a "positive obligation to direct national policy." Moore questioned "how a declaration of the parties to a pledge that they mean to keep it can be said to make an epoch." According to Moore, Stimson confused "notions of law and of conduct." While Stimson acknowledged the political effect of the Pact on US policy and regarded it as a rallying point for further action, Moore focused on the narrow and positivistic notion of law, which derived from a literal interpretation of specific treaties.[12]

Moore's pessimism about war was clear. He asserted that "war – its existence is coeval with the history of man" and "to some extent inevitable." Since war could not be abolished, Moore did not question the efficacy of neutrality but instead accepted it as a necessary evil. As proof of the legitimacy of traditional neutrality, Moore cited the international conference held in Washington in 1921–2. The conference dealt with the regulation of radio activities during war, and participating powers attempted to define "the rights and duties of belligerents and of neutrals in time of war." This proved that the world powers had not abandoned the institution of neutrality. Moore was positivistic, writing that not a single member of the League had declared that neutrality was obsolete. Furthermore,

[11] Henry L. Stimson, "Bases of American Foreign Policy during the Past Four Years," *Foreign Affairs* 11 (1933), 384–385, 390–391.
[12] John Bassett Moore, "An Appeal to Reason," *Foreign Affairs* 11 (1933), 550–551.

he opposed economic and military sanctions by the coalition of powers against breakers of the Covenant of the League of Nations or the Kellogg–Briand Pact. Such sanctions, Moore argued, would be military actions "in different name." For Moore, dependence on military force under the name of sanction was a departure from law and would ultimately lead to international anarchy. He also sided with Borchard in noting that it would be difficult to obtain the unanimous consent of the powers for such sanctions, because "we are not all alike."[13]

Borchard occasionally encouraged Moore to publish his views. Moore had once sent a letter to Hamilton Fish III, an isolationist senator. Having had a chance to read a copy of this letter, Borchard recommended that it be expanded and published as an independent article in the *AJIL*. Borchard also asked the managing editor to reprint it "as a separate pamphlet and have it distributed to the members of the Senate and House."[14] Moore wrote that it was his "duty to combat these lawless fallacies."[15] He entitled his article "New Isolation," but this did not refer to his own position. On the contrary, Moore argued that those who held that the international law established before World War I had become obsolete occupied "an isolated position." Scholars like Wright and Fenwick were isolationists because their views were far removed from the mainstream opinion. He claimed that "there is not in the world today a single government that is acting upon such a supposition."[16] For Moore, the standard for judging the mainstream opinion was the official endorsement of government, while for Wright and his group governmental endorsement was not of primary importance, because they themselves endeavored to lead.

. Wright did not remain silent but sent a manuscript to Hamilton Fish Armstrong, editor of *Foreign Affairs*, in which he responded to Moore's criticism. However, Armstrong wrote back that it was not possible to publish the manuscript, because an article by Newton Baker, which was similar to Wright's, had already been accepted and sent to the printer.[17] Instead, Wright published the piece in *World Unity*. He then submitted a detailed critical analysis of Moore's paper to *Foreign Affairs*. First, Wright argued that Moore's criticism of the collective framework was pointless, because the problem with the Kellogg Pact did not lie in its attempt to regulate self-defense but in a lack of support. If there were unanimous

---

[13] *Ibid.*, 558, 560–561, 563.
[14] Borchard to Finch, April 3, 1933, ASIL Papers.
[15] Moore to Finch, April 3, 1933, ASIL Papers.
[16] John Bassett Moore, "The New Isolation," *AJIL* 27 (1933), 607, 622.
[17] Hamilton Fish Armstrong to Wright, August 25, 1933, Wright Papers, Box 8, Folder 11.

support for the Pact, then its effectiveness would be strengthened. Also, the Pact provided an opportunity for each country to seek consultation. With respect to the ideal embodied in the Pact, Wright wrote that "this ideal is alive in our generation and is for the first time incorporated in general international law." Moore had not taken into account the "new will to peace," which was unprecedented in the history of man.[18] As for Moore's reference to the 1921–2 conference on radio activities as an example of the sustainability of neutrality, Wright argued that this conference had been held "long before" the Kellogg Pact was promulgated. Wright regarded the Pact as a turning point in history, and he refuted Moore's assertion that the League of Nations was a war-like instrument. Wright noted that during the Manchurian Incident the members of the Council had never discussed the use of force to impose its will. Rather the significance of the system lay in the fact that its very existence served to prevent war.[19]

Wright noted that Moore's article conveyed an "atmosphere of pessimism," manifest not only in "his deprecatory treatment of all the recent devices" but in "his expression of a basic despair with reference to all possible efforts." In particular, Wright called attention to Moore's statement that war was "coeval," which reflected Moore's resignation over man's inability to change. A belief in the ability to effect change was common to great statesmen like Grotius, Washington, Jefferson and Lincoln, all of whom "devised political changes in conformity with the needs of [their] time."[20]

Wright sent a copy of the article to Stanley K. Hornbeck at the State Department, who wrote back that he had read it with "*very* great interest [emphasis original]." Hornbeck thought that Wright's article raised "a considerable number of points which seem to me very well made."[21] Borchard, meanwhile, had sent a letter to Wright in which he reiterated his opposition to the League. He wrote, "from the very beginning it seemed to me [an] attempt to identify the *status quo*." Wright responded that the League had been used "very effectively by Germany to alter the *status quo*." Nevertheless, Borchard was skeptical of the organization, calling it "a mechanical scheme" that overlooked the nature of human beings, who had "feelings, passions, and interests."[22]

---

[18] Quincy Wright, "The Path to Peace," *World Unity* 13 (1933), 136.
[19] *Ibid*., 122, 144.   [20] *Ibid*., 145, 148.
[21] Stanley K. Hornbeck to Wright, January 10, 1934, Wright Papers, Box 15, Folder 3.
[22] Borchard to Wright, December 13, 1933, December 19, 1933; Wright to Borchard, December 16, 1933, December 21, 1933, Wright Papers, Box 11, Folder 15.

Borchard, who according to Wright, "seem[ed] to consider himself the main defender of Moore's infallibility," could not remain silent in the face of Wright's challenge. He wanted to publish a favorable review of Moore's "Appeal to Reason" in the *AJIL* and sent a manuscript to the editors explaining his motives. He wrote, "As you know the Journal has been pretty well filled for the past fifteen years with what I venture to call international evangelism, partly because there were so few people who were really critical." Borchard insisted that the journal needed to have a balanced and "more legal approach."[23] But the editor, George Grafton Wilson, declined his request because the Society did not have a policy of publishing editorial comments on specific papers.[24] Yet Borchard did not give in. He wrote again, "In my judgment, the merits are all one side and the defects all on the other. One side lives in the world of reality and the other in the world of hallucination."[25] Finally he won out and his comments were published in the journal.

Borchard entitled his essay "Realism v. Evangelism," and this title succinctly conveys his opinion of the two schools. Referring to Wright's paper, Borchard wrote that one of the major differences between Moore and Wright lay in their evaluation of the Covenant and the Kellogg–Briand Pact. While Wright highly regarded both, Moore viewed them as "subversive of law, order, and progress in the world." Another issue that Moore had refuted most vehemently was the new group's call for the demise of neutrality. Borchard wrote, "neutrality, Judge Moore points out, always had the highly moral and expedient object of preventing the spread of war, and of prohibiting acts which contribute to the starting of wars."[26] Borchard concluded that "the world should be grateful for so clear-headed an exponent of reason and practical judgment in dealing with foreign affairs," offering that Moore was "the guide, philosopher, and friend of a confused humanity."[27]

Moore's views were certainly welcomed by some Japanese intellectuals, who accepted his argument as an example that would support the Japanese actions in Manchuria. Dr. Seiji Hishida, Moore's former student, authored a small booklet entitled *Comments on John Bassett Moore's Discussion*. This booklet, published in English, was presumably designed

---

[23] Borchard to George Grafton Wilson, October 23, 1933, ASIL Papers.
[24] Wilson to Finch, October 11, 1933, ASIL Papers.
[25] Borchard to Wilson, December 9, 1933, ASIL Papers.
[26] Edwin M. Borchard, "Realism v. Evangelism," *AJIL* 28 (1934), 110, 111, 113.
[27] *Ibid.*, 117.

to propagate and rationalize Japan's position in West. Japanese Foreign Minister Yosuke Matsuoka and Thomas Baty contributed prefaces to it.[28]

Views on neutrality from abroad

The debate over neutrality among experts in international law was not confined to the United States, but was taken up in Europe as well. Nicolas Politis gave a series of lectures on neutrality at the University of Salamanca, Spain, in November 1933. A book based on the lectures was published under the title *Neutrality and Peace*. Politis took a position against the traditional concept of neutrality, writing that it was "a product of international anarchy" and "a true anachronism" in today's world. He held that the concept was no longer "in harmony with the status of the laws of nations or with the economic necessities and aspirations of the nations." Therefore, neutrality as an institution was "irrevocably doomed" and "destined to disappear."[29]

Politis also argued that the Kellogg–Briand Pact provided a new theoretical ground for rejecting neutrality, because as a result of the Pact war had become illegal for the first time in history. Traditional neutrality had been based on the supposition that war could be waged under extra-legal but not totally illegal conditions. He had no doubt in the significance of the Pact, arguing that "a new era began with the Pact of Paris," and that to regard the Pact as "only ideal" was "profoundly erroneous." It is noteworthy that Politis called attention to American attitudes toward the Pact, mentioning not only Stimson's address before the Council on Foreign Relations in August 1932 but also the diplomatic record from the fall of 1929, when the United States had suggested a multilateral effort to arbitrate the Sino-Soviet dispute over the Chinese Eastern Railway. He claimed that these precedents demonstrated the feasibility of the principles inherent in the Pact. Like Wright, he praised the Stimson Doctrine, writing that "the note of January 7, 1932, marked the beginning of a new era in international relations."[30]

Politis further pointed out signs of movement to strengthen the Pact in the United States. He detailed several bills introduced in Congress that proposed to ban the shipment of arms to aggressors, and he welcomed

---

[28] Seiji Hishida, *Comments on John Bassett Moore's Discussion* (Tokyo: Maruzen, 1933).
[29] Nicolas Politis, *Neutrality and Peace* (Washington, DC: Carnegie Endowment for International Peace, 1935), pp. vii–viii.
[30] *Ibid.*, pp. 8, 58.

them as a positive step to enforce the Pact. He also cited Norman Davis' pledge at the Geneva Disarmament Conference in March 1933. It set out that in the event that an aggressor was determined, "we will refrain from any action tending to defeat such collective effort." Politis even made reference to the 1932 platforms of both the Republican and Democratic parties, both of which had included a reference on consultation based on the Pact. He concluded that "The United States would thus come to reconcile their traditional policy of isolation with their obligation under the Pact of Paris."[31]

On the other hand, Politis also noted that there was strong opposition to the trend for strengthening the Pact. He referred to Moore's article "Appeal to Reason" as representative of views skeptical of the Pact, and he offered that Moore was a traditional isolationist. Despite such opposition, Politis was optimistic about the American attitude, noting that many Americans today admitted that the neutrality was no longer effective. According to Politis, "the logic of events irresistibly drives the United States towards such cooperation."[32]

The issue of neutrality was also debated at the 1932 conference of the International Law Association. Established in 1873, it was the oldest private association for promoting the study of international law. At the 1932 meeting in Oxford, the Committee on Neutrality, which had been working on setting guidelines for interpreting the Pact, proposed that a draft convention be held. The proposed articles of interpretation were largely based on the traditional concept of neutrality: Article 1 proclaimed the impartial treatment of belligerents. However, J. L. Brierly, a professor of international law at All Souls College, Oxford, questioned whether the proposed Article 1 contradicted both Article 11 of the Covenant of the League of Nations and the Pact. He argued that the proposed article was based on "a notion of relations between neutrals and belligerents which was all right in 1899 and 1907, at the Hague Conferences," and "possibly as late as 1913, but which in 1932 belongs to an utterly outlawed order of ideas." After referring to Stimson's speech before the Council on Foreign Relations, which had been made just the day before the meeting, he suggested that the Committee should reconsider the issue of neutrality, be forward looking, and "attempt to lead the nations rather than to look back at the past."[33]

Opinions opposing Professor Brierly's were then heard. Dr. Arthur Wegner from Germany reminded the group that the law of neutrality had

---

[31] *Ibid.*, pp. 68–70.   [32] *Ibid.*, pp. 70–73.
[33] International Association, *Report of the Thirty-Seventh Conference* (1932), pp. 175–177.

a centuries-long history, and he questioned the legal nature of the Pact itself. He acknowledged that the Pact expressed "a great longing of mankind for a new justice for the world," but he argued that it was unrealistic. He suggested that the Brierly's proposal was "too much in favor of the new ideas." It was rather like "going back to the Middle Ages and their discrimination of just wars and unjust wars." Dr. K. Jansma from Holland sided with Wegner. He asserted that "the actual changes that have come about do not justify us in abolishing the law of neutrality altogether." Supporting this view was the fact that the powerful nations of Russia and the United States were still not members of the League of Nations. Dr. Edward Reut-Nicollussi from the University of Innsbruck, Austria, appealed for a cautious approach in labeling war a crime. Some scholars considered war as equivalent to crime, but Reut-Nicollussi held that it was rather a "fact of revolution." Given that there were no definite rules for effecting peaceful change in international relations, war was one means of resisting the status quo.[34]

On the other hand, views favorable to revising neutrality came mostly from the British and Americans. Professor Arnold. D. McNair of Cambridge University asserted that there were two basic factors being challenged in the development of international law at the moment; the whole conception of neutrality and the legal status of war were "in the melting pot." He stated, "I cannot tell you what law of neutrality is today," but whatever it is, it is a "out-worn conception." At the end of the session, it was decided that the draft should be reconsidered and the question of neutrality should be referred back to the appropriate committee.[35]

Two years later, in September 1934, the International Law Association held a meeting in Budapest and devoted one of its sessions to continued debate on interpretations of the Kellogg–Briand Pact. One international lawyer noted in retrospect, "when our Oxford conference took place in 1932, we were fortunate indeed to meet perhaps on the very day when the American Secretary of State, Mr. Stimson, made his famous oration."[36] The Budapest conference proceeded under the chairmanship of Manley O. Hudson. At the beginning of the session on the Pact, Hudson reaffirmed that three legal instruments crafted in the postwar period – the Covenant of the League of Nations, the Statutes of the PCIJ and the Pact of Paris – had great significance for international law. They had brought

[34] Ibid., pp. 181–182, 184.   [35] Ibid., pp. 185, 204–205.
[36] International Law Association, Briand-Kellogg Pact of Paris (August 27, 1928), Articles of Interpretation as Adopted by the Budapest Conference 1934 (London: Sweet & Maxwell, 1934), p. 17.

about "a profound revolution" in international relations and should not be dealt with like ordinary international treaties, because they had a "constitutional aspect" and should thus be regarded as "fundamental laws."[37]

After a general discussion on the draft of the guidelines for interpreting the Pact, the participants debated each article. There was debate on whether it was possible or not to draw inferences concerning sanctions from the Pact. Reut-Nicollussi claimed that while in the text of the Pact, there was no definite statement on sanctions, the proposed articles relating to arms embargoes concerned nothing but sanctions. In the preamble there was a statement that stipulated that violators "should be denied the benefits furnished by the treaty," but this did not specify concrete actions. Reut-Nicollussi argued that the Pact was simply a declaration of policy, not a legal document. He proposed a motion to delete the articles on sanctions from the draft, but this motion was put to a vote and deleted.[38]

Advocates of collective security, on the other hand, sought to make sanctions mandatory. For example, Article 6 of the draft stated that other nations may impose sanctions against a violator. Roger de Level from Belgium proposed to change the word "may" to "shall." Hudson was critical of this motion, complaining that it went "far beyond the text of the Treaty of Paris [the Kellogg–Briand Pact]." The proposal was defeated by a narrow margin. Article 9, which asserted that "the right of self-defense is not affected by the Pact," was deleted as the result of a motion by Hudson. He argued that this issue had already been dealt with in the correspondence relating to the Pact of Paris.[39]

Seven articles of interpretation were adopted at the conference. The most important were Articles 4 (c) and (d) and Article 5. Article 4 stated, in the event of a violation of the Pact, other states may "(c) supply the State attacked with financial or material assistance, including munitions of war," and "(d) assist with armed forces the State attacked." This was a definite departure from the traditional concept of neutrality. Article 5 affirmed the principle expressed in the Stimson Doctrine. It read, "the signatory States are not entitled to recognize as acquired *de jure* any territorial or other advantages acquired *de facto* by means of a violation of the Pact."[40] The conclusions reached by the International Law Association at its conference in Budapest in 1934 signaled the end of the primacy of traditional neutrality.

---

[37] *Ibid.*, pp. 13–15.   [38] *Ibid.*, pp. 48–52.   [39] *Ibid.*, pp. 52–57.   [40] *Ibid.*, pp. 63–64.

Despite their unofficial nature, the Budapest Articles of Interpretation acquired a certain amount of authority and aroused attention in official circles. In Britain, the House of Lords discussed the Articles in February 1935. Lord Askwith opened his remarks by asking whether the British government had paid attention to the Articles. By way of an introduction, he briefly recounted the history of the Pact and its development up to the Budapest conference, including the speech made by Stimson in August 1932. He then posited, "the question is have these gentlemen gone too far?" His answer was "what they decided at Budapest was rather too much." They had gone to extremes, he argued, because the Pact itself did not include concrete sanctions.[41]

The next speaker was Baron Howard of Penrith, who had been the ambassador to Washington at the time the Kellogg Pact was signed. He thought that the Budapest Articles of Interpretation were in the main justified by the correspondence that had passed between the respective governments during the negotiations. For instance, Secretary of State Kellogg had pointed out in his note of June 23, 1928, that any violation of a multilateral anti-war treaty brought about by the aggression of one party would automatically release the other party from its obligations toward the treaty-breaking state. Article 4 of the Interpretation fell within the scope of this note. As for the relevance of traditional neutrality, he cited Stimson's speech and contended that ideas of war and neutrality had been revolutionized since completion of the Pact. As proof that the British government held to this modern conception of "preferential neutrality," which favored one belligerent over another, he cited Anthony Eden's statement of February 4, 1935. Eden had said that the British government informed the League that it was prepared to comply with the recommendation for an embargo on the supply of arms to Bolivia in the Bolivian–Paraguayan dispute. Howard also cited Secretary Hull's statement of February 17, 1935, which reiterated the statement made by Norman Davis in Geneva, as another indication of the trend toward collective action against an aggressor and defying impartiality and toward eliminating indifference to conflicts.[42]

The debate in the House of Lords did not end in complete agreement on neutrality or the Pact. At the end of the session, the Lord Chancellor enunciated the government's position on the Budapest Articles of Interpretation.

---

[41] *Parliamentary Debates, House of Lords*, Fifth Series–Volume XCV (London: His Majesty's Stationery Office, 1935), pp. 1007–1015.
[42] *Ibid.*, pp. 1018–1023.

Although he acknowledged that the work of the International Law Association was well-known and much appreciated by the government, he noted that the Budapest meeting was "a purely private and unofficial conference." The Kellogg–Briand Pact was deliberately drafted in broad terms and its authors wisely declined to be drawn into attempts at precise definitions. He concluded that all the governments would not be ready to accept some of the Articles of Interpretation.[43]

Sakutaro Tachi from Japan also objected to the new interpretations adopted at Budapest. As a basis for his refutation, he referred to the general principles governing how treaties should be interpreted according to international law. Since nothing had been specified about the abolition of the traditional concept of neutrality when the Pact was originally completed, Tachi theorized that the new interpretation was intended to exercise a retroactive power, which the established principles of international law did not allow for. In his arguments, he often used locutions such as, "legal understandings according to established international law do not acknowledge ..."[44]

Tachi wanted to preserve the old notions of international law that were at the heart of his arguments, believing that the already established principles of international law were more important than the progressive aims embodied in the Pact. He saw the new trends as idealistic and based on what he called "the new spirit of the twentieth century in the field of international politics." He suggested that writers in the West confused the idealism of international politics with the realism of international law. He wrote:

> The Budapest Articles of Interpretation of the Pact adopted by the International Association were based on idealism in the study of international politics for the purpose of facilitating cooperation among nations. As a result, these interpretations sought to claim new implications that had not been agreed upon by other signatories at the time of the completion of the Pact. These new interpretations oppose the principles of how to interpret treaties in established international law.[45]

In Europe, and to some extent in Japan, opinions about neutrality were divided. However, it is important to note that those who favored the revision of neutrality and supported the Kellogg–Briand Pact frequently

---

[43] *Ibid.*, pp. 1042–1043.
[44] Sakutaro Tachi, "Fusen joyaku no shin kaishaku o ronnansu" [To Refute the New Interpretations of the Pact], *Gaiko Jiho* 752 (1936), 29.
[45] *Ibid.*, 29.

referred to Stimson's speech of August 1932, to other official American policies, and even to bills in Congress. The US attitude toward the Pact and neutrality was watched carefully by the advocates of the new international law, not only in the United States but also in Europe and Japan.

The American Society of International Law in 1935

Charles Warren, assistant attorney general of the United States from August 1914 to April 1917, had emerged as an authority on neutrality and had brought a new dimension to the debate. He first presented a paper on this subject at the 1933 meeting of the ASIL. In it he argued, from his experience dealing with the American claims against belligerents during World War I, that it was almost impossible to maintain neutral rights regarding trade. Because each belligerent would do whatever it could to secure victory and survival, it was not practical for non-belligerents to expect that such rights would be respected. In the name of "change of conditions and right of retaliation," a new principle that Germany had put forward during the war, the great belligerents had denied the existence of any trade rights claimed by the United States. In the daily conduct of military action, it was not realistic to insist on neutrality rights, particularly in wars fought among great powers. Nor would there be any practicable right of neutrality in future wars. The futility of the notion of neutrality was also indicated by the fact that there existed no mechanism for resolving claims. After the war there had in fact been no effort to settle claims. Warren concluded, "it would be wise not to use the term [neutrality] at all," not only because neutrality was difficult to practice but because the lack of a means of settlement betrayed the emptiness of the concept.[46]

The next year he expanded his thesis and published it in *Foreign Affairs* as an article entitled "Troubles of a Neutral," which gained wide recognition. Before proceeding to the heart of his argument, Warren asserted the validity of his position, writing that this was "not a statement of any theoretical condition; it is the necessary conclusion from what took place in the World War." Bearing in mind the difficulties the United States had experienced, he suggested that if the United States wanted to avoid future involvement in war she should prohibit the sale of arms and ammunition to all belligerents and restrict the travel of American citizens on belligerent ships. He further claimed that the chief source of friction between

---

[46] Charles Warren, "What Are the Rights of Neutrals Now in Practice?" *Proceedings, ASIL* (1933), 130, 132–133.

the United States and belligerents had been "the assertion and attempted enforcement by our Government of alleged rights of trade belonging to our citizens as neutrals." Warren used the locution "alleged rights" because he believed that there were no such rights at all, and because he found the term "right" hopelessly vague and confusing. The frequent usage of this term by President Wilson and the Secretary of State during the last war had led the public to believe in the existence of such rights.[47]

Debate on the issue continued, and by 1935 three positions on the status of neutrality had emerged. First was the position held by the traditionalists, represented by Moore and Borchard, who sought to preserve the old concept of neutrality. The second opinion was that held by the reformers, notably Wright and Fenwick, who advocated the abolition of neutrality in favor of collective security. And last was the new view presented by Warren. The positions of the reformers and of Warren's camp were similar insofar as both rejected traditional neutrality. However, Wright and Fenwick's opposition was based on the belief that the Covenant and the Kellogg–Briand Pact had rendered claims of neutrality meaningless, while Warren focused on the impracticality of neutral rights based on the experience of the last war. The reformers' position was grounded in theoretical arguments, while Warren rejected neutrality in terms of practical difficulty. In addition, the two camps differed in their opinions of what should replace traditional neutrality. Reformers favored sanctions against aggressors, while Warren and his supporters argued for total abstention from war through the curtailment of trade with all belligerents.

Neutrality was the main topic of discussion at the annual meeting of the ASIL in 1935. The timeliness of the issue and the long-standing conflict between the reformers and traditionalists combined to produce the most heated debates yet. The discussions poured light on the chasm separating the two groups. Professor Philip Marshall Brown remarked, "at no meeting have I been so surprised by the statements made by members of this Society." The debate between Borchard and Fenwick raged on. Fenwick, acknowledging that "no member of the society who has attended the meeting in recent years will expect me to come within a mile of agreeing with my brother Borchard," again asserted his belief that international law had changed since 1919 and argued that if the United States maintained the old concept of neutrality it would be a major setback for civilization. In contrast, Borchard cited the importance of limiting the spread of war through neutrality, stating "I think it much safer

---

[47] Charles Warren, "Troubles of a Neutral," *Foreign Affairs* 12 (1934), 372, 382, 386, 389.

for mankind, if these diseases do break out, to confine their ravages as narrowly as possible."[48]

It was Hudson who spoke most eloquently on behalf of the reformers at the meeting. In high spirits at the ASIL meeting, Hudson led the discussion skillfully. He succinctly and precisely summed up the difference between the traditionalists and reformers with regard to the issue of neutrality. According to Hudson, the position set out by the former was "a restatement of the nineteenth century law of neutrality in the light of experience during the World War but with little regard for development." The latter group sought to "escape from nineteenth century conceptions and to construct a new law of both war and neutrality to fit the new conditions of our twentieth century." Hudson agreed with Josef Kunz, the Austrian-American scholar who had presented the argument that the Covenant modified the law of neutrality for members of the League. In particular, Hudson stressed the significance of Article 11, which declared that a war anywhere was the concern of people everywhere. Article 11 was not a "particular treaty law" but set "a new compass."[49]

In addition, Hudson speculated on how the use of force by the community of nations might be perceived. "Force used by a community of States against one State would be looked upon as wholly different from force used by a single State against another to advance its own interests or desires. The latter is war as we have known it, the former might be called something else."[50] Hudson observed, "we are in the midst of a contest between great ideas."

Hudson's remarks precipitated much discussion. William C. Dennis of Earlham College stated that he agreed with the analysis of the struggle between nineteenth- and twentieth-century ideas. However, he called for a more cautious approach and warned that results should not be expected too soon. "I do not believe we can leap from the nineteenth to the twentieth century overnight," he offered. Only step by step could the world make progress. William Hull noted that there seemed to be confusion among the members between law and policy, and objected that members were discussing the issue of neutrality "as if it were a national policy." He suggested that when members discuss the issue of neutrality they should bear in mind that "in this American Society of International Law, we will try to clear up the legal implications and legal possibilities of the doctrine."[51]

[48] *Proceedings, ASIL* (1935), 25–29.
[49] *Ibid.*, 42–43.   [50] *Ibid.*, 44.   [51] *Ibid.*, 51, 150–151.

Hull's comment was to the point, especially as the ASIL had invited Stimson to present a paper. Upon receiving the Society's invitation, Stimson had written to George Finch, "I am not an international lawyer – merely an international politician, and I should wish to approach the subject from the standpoint of future progress rather than existing law."[52] At Stimson's request, Finch forwarded a copy of the 37th Conference of the International Law Association, held at Oxford in 1932. In a letter accompanying the report, Finch referred Stimson to the Association's pamphlet, *The Briand-Kellogg Pact of Paris*, the proceedings of the Budapest Conference of 1934,[53] and called his attention to the connection between the Articles of Interpretation adopted at the Budapest Conference and the neutrality proposals discussed at the Oxford meeting in 1932.[54]

In his address before the ASIL, Stimson noted that war had become more destructive, observing that "the age of steam and electricity has arrived and the world has suddenly become interconnected and interdependent." Given changes in the conduct of war and its increased destructiveness, Stimson asserted that war could not be dealt with by the old methods. Responding to criticism, presumably from Moore and Borchard, that his view was unrealistic, Stimson countered that it was the views of the traditionalists that were in fact unrealistic, because it was very possible that the United States would become involved in future wars. Toward the end of his talk, he referred to the Budapest Articles and reaffirmed their importance as a basis for undertaking collective action and for disregarding traditional neutrality.[55]

Another notable guest speaker at the 1935 meeting was Senator Gerald P. Nye, the leader of the isolationists in the Senate. Nye had been presiding over the Special Senate Committee Investigating the Munitions Industry, which was established to examine the conduct of arms industries during World War I and their relationship to American foreign policy. The Committee had been successful in exposing the fact that companies such as DuPont had reaped tremendous profits by selling arms to belligerents.[56]

The 1935 meeting of the ASIL was indeed a forum for wide-ranging debate on the issue of neutrality, with speakers including a former secretary

---

[52] Stimson to Finch, January 24, 1935, ASIL Papers.
[53] International Law Association, *Briand-Kellogg Pact of Paris*.
[54] Finch to Stimson, March 5, 1935, ASIL Papers.
[55] Henry L. Stimson, "Neutrality and War Prevention," *Proceedings*, ASIL (1935), 123–125, 127.
[56] "Address by Gerald P. Nye," *Proceedings*, ASIL (1935), 172, 177.

of state and the most prominent isolationist in the Senate. The meeting was not exclusively devoted to the exchange of academic opinions.

Stimson sent copies of his address at the ASIL to his colleagues. Nelson Johnson, the American minister to China, wrote back from Peking that he was pleased to find that Stimson "was not pessimistic in regard to collective action for the limitation and prevention of war," although Johnson was "somewhat cynical as regards the will of the nations to limit their activities in the fire of warfare."[57] Herbert Feis of the State Department also responded positively to Stimson's observation that there was a great deal of confusion about the difference between neutrality and impartiality.[58]

At the end of the summer, just when Stimson was receiving these replies, Congress passed the Neutrality Act of 1935, which required the President to impose an arms embargo on all belligerents. At about the same time that the ASIL was holding its annual meeting, Congress and the administration had begun to debate several neutrality bills. On May 7, Senators Nye and Clark had introduced a resolution proposing an embargo of arms on all belligerents. Meanwhile, the State Department had sponsored another bill that gave the president the authority to decide which country or countries should be embargoed. The heated debate in Congress, Nye's Committee expositions, news of Italy's plan to invade Ethiopia and Roosevelt's desire to focus on domestic policy all helped to assure the passage.[59] The Neutrality Act of 1935 was a departure from traditional neutrality insofar as it restricted the right to trade arms to all belligerents. In that embargoes would be imposed on all parties, however, the act adhered to the concept of impartiality. The ideas embodied in the act were Warren's. The positions of both Wright and Borchard had been ignored.

Beyond the Neutrality Act of 1935

Fenwick vigorously attacked the Neutrality Act, arguing that it had nothing to do with the "prevention of war." He claimed, rather, that "it evades that problem altogether" by denying the principle of collective responsibility. In the event that the League imposed sanctions on an aggressor, the act would prohibit US cooperation. The new act was a direct threat to the principle of the Pact. In its impartial treatment of belligerents, the

---

[57] Nelson Johnson to Stimson, August 27, 1935, Stimson Papers, Reel 89.
[58] Herbert Feis to Stimson, August 15, 1935, Stimson Papers, Reel 89.
[59] Divine, *The Illusion of Neutrality*, p. 93.

act refuted the idea that a distinction should be made between a state that resorted to war as "an instrument of national policy" and one that sought "pacific means of settlement."[60]

Immediately after the Neutrality Act was passed, Wright and other advocates of an arms embargo against aggressors began to work for its revision. They joined forces with such internationalists as Clark Eichelberger, director of the League of Nations Association, and James Shotwell of Columbia University. The 1935 Act would expire on February 29, 1936. Opponents wanted to make sure that it was not extended and formed a committee to draft a proposal for revision. The committee was organized under the auspices of the National Peace Conference, a union of twenty-eight peace groups. Eichelberger wrote to Wright, "We have a lot of work to do on neutrality between now and the time Congress meets." Wright suggested that an arms embargo should automatically be imposed on all belligerents until the international community had determined who the aggressor was. After such a determination, the President should impose an arms embargo only on the aggressor.[61]

On October 3, 1935, the committee met in New York City. Among the participants were such distinguished leaders of the peace movement and advocates of collective security as Clark Eichelberger, Frederick J. Libby of the National Council for the Prevention of War, Thomas Lamont, Nicholas Murray Butler, Newton Baker, Senator James Pope, Shotwell and Stimson. Also in attendance were several acclaimed international lawyers: Fenwick, Hudson, Philip Jessup, James Brown Scott and Wright. The committee assigned Wright the task of studying "the obligations of the United States of America under the Pact of Paris."[62]

In the middle of October, Wright finished a memorandum on the relationship between the Neutrality Act and the Pact. He argued that the Pact implied the principle that a party should not take any action "to deteriorate the situation of another party who is the innocent victim of an act in violation of the Pact." He also noted that the Budapest Articles stipulated that a party may furnish financial or material aid to a victim of aggression. With this in mind, Wright suggested that a section be added to the Neutrality Act stating that "the President may revoke such embargo to

---

[60] Charles G. Fenwick, "Neutrality and Responsibility," *AJIL* 29 (1935), 663–665.
[61] Wright to Eichelberger, September 11, 1935; September 16, 1935, Wright Papers, Box 6, Folder 7.
[62] Henry S. Haskell to Stimson, October 4, 1935, Stimson Papers, Reel 89.

any state which had been the victim of aggression in violation of the Pact of Paris."[63]

At the next session of Congress, the central issue was whether and how the restriction of trade in raw materials was to be added to the current neutrality act. The bill sponsored by the administration allowed discretionary authority to the President to decide the items and amounts restricted, while the one presented by Nye provided for the mandatory restriction of all such commodities. The two bills were similar insofar as the restriction of trade was concerned, even though they differed in means of enforcement. But some opposed an extension of the embargo of war materials in any case, including Moore and Borchard.

Borchard again testified when the Senate Foreign Relations Committee held hearings on January 29, 1936. On this day Borchard testified from 10:30 in the morning until 5:05 in the afternoon.[64] He first read a letter from Moore, as he had done at the 1933 hearing before the House. At the beginning of the letter Moore criticized the "Tentative Redraft of the Neutrality Act of August 21, 1935," prepared by the National Peace Conference. He wrote that in spite of it appearing pacific and neutral the Conference's aim was to bring the United States into the League of Nations, because the draft contained the expression "in accordance with its obligations under the Pact of Paris." Comparing the text of the draft with the administration's bill, Moore concluded that they were similar in tone.[65]

Borchard then began to annunciate his own opinions. He argued that the Neutrality Act of 1935 should be kept as it was. He favored the embargo of arms, ammunition and implements of war, but he did not think it wise to enlarge the list to include commodities such as oil and cotton. If the United States were to impose an embargo on the sale of such items as oil to Italy and Ethiopia, it would mean reprisals, retaliation and war. Besides, he was opposed to giving up the right of neutrality, which included the right to trade with belligerents. Responding to the assertion that by continuing to supply oil to Italy the United States was aiding that country in its war in Ethiopia, he suggested that the choice before Americans was "between no embargo helping one rather than the other and an embargo helping one rather than the other." In the first instance, "you cannot be

---

[63] Quincy Wright, "How should the Neutrality Act of August 31, 1935, be Revised?" October 15, 1935, Wright Papers, Box 6, Folder 7.

[64] US Congress, Senate Committee on Foreign Relations, *Neutrality, Hearings before the Committee on Foreign Relations*. 74th Cong., 2d sess., 1935, pp. 171–257.

[65] *Ibid.*, pp. 172–173.

charged with having violated your neutrality," while in the latter case "you are doing something which subjects you to the charge of violating neutrality."

Assistant Secretary of State R. Walton Moore, who attended the hearing, suggested that Borchard and John Bassett Moore may be "in a very small minority when it comes to the opinions entertained by international lawyers." To this, Borchard answered a definitive "no," and asserted vigorously that their position was right.[66]

Regardless of whether or not Borchard and Moore's position was in the minority among scholars of international law, Congress passed the Neutrality Act of 1936, which retained the section on the mandatory embargo of arms and dropped the section on the embargo of war materials, again betraying the hopes of reformers.

Borchard's lengthy testimony had alarmed the State Department, which favored the embargo of commodities indispensable for war. A detailed memorandum analyzing Moore and Borchard's statements was prepared by Charles W. Yost of the Office of Arms and Munitions Control. Joseph G. Green, head of the office, recognized its importance immediately and sent a copy to Secretary of State Cordell Hull, noting that similar arguments might be used again and that Yost's memorandum would "enable the Department to combat those arguments more effectively."[67] After reading the memorandum, Hull asked other concerned officials to read it. Undersecretary of State Sumner Welles, Legal Advisor Green Hackworth, Chief of the Division of Far Eastern Affairs Stanley K. Hornbeck, and others received it.[68]

The memorandum began with an analysis of John Bassett Moore's letter. Yost suggested that the letter was open to criticism because it was lacking in "dispassionate objectivity of tone and content." In particular, Yost refuted Moore's proposition that violations of maritime rules during World War I did not affect the validity of those rules. Yost argued that there was good reason "to believe that they would be violated again in the same way in any future war." Therefore, Moore's insistence that the present rules were sufficient to protect neutral rights in a future war betrayed "the most inexcusable lack of realism." Moore had spent his life compiling and codifying the existing body of international law, and he believed that those rules would protect US rights. Yost offered that Moore's conclusions

---

[66] *Ibid.*, pp. 189, 192–193, 242.
[67] Joseph Green to Cordell Hull, June 22, 1936, 811.04418/177, State Department Decimal Folder, National Archives, Washington, DC.
[68] ETW to Wells, Hackworth, Dunn, Hornbeck, Murray, and Savage, July 6, 1936, *ibid.*

were merely private opinions and of "far less value than his eminent reputation."[69]

Yost asserted that Borchard's statements were simply "an elaboration of the points made by Dr. Moore," and he attacked them for their "static and rigid conception of international law." In Yost's view, Borchard's chief interest was "to uphold the law," but only as it was defined in his works. Yost wrote that Moore and Borchard had "the same predisposition of mind." Both were concerned only with the consequences of the bill for their understanding of international law, while the administration had to consider the issue of neutrality in the broader context of the United States' relationship with the rest of the world. This was why the two scholars were so at odds with the administration.[70]

Despite the unfavorable outcome of the Neutrality Act of 1936 for the reformers, they were not discouraged and continued their discussions. Intensive discussion occurred at the Conference sponsored by the Norman Wait Harris Memorial Foundation and held at the University of Chicago from June 23 to July 2, 1936, under the chairmanship of Wright. Entitled "Neutrality and Collective Security," it consisted of four public lectures and thirteen round-table meetings, and produced a book and a 500-page typescript of proceedings.[71] Four eminent scholars were invited to speak at the public lectures: Sir Alfred Zimmern, a professor of international relations at Oxford University who had served as deputy director of the League of Nations' Institute of Intellectual Co-operation at Paris from 1926 to 1930 and was the author of *The League of Nations and the Rule of Law*;[72] William Edward Dodd, the United States' ambassador to Germany and a professor emeritus of American history at the University of Chicago; Charles Warren; and Edwin Dickinson, a professor of international law at the University of California.

Entitled "The Problem of Collective Security," Zimmern's public lecture was the keynote speech for the Conference. In it, he underlined the importance of the concept of collective security. Zimmern explained the concept with the phrase "the safety of all by all," which meant that "the

---

[69] Charles W. Yost, "Analysis of the Statements on Neutrality Policy by Doctors J. B. Moore and E. M. Borchard before the Senate Foreign Relations Committee," 1, 5, 6,1 0, *ibid.*

[70] *Ibid.*, 10, 13, 22, 25.

[71] Quincy Wright, ed., *Neutrality and Collective Security* (University of Chicago Press, 1936); University of Chicago, Norman Wait Harris Memorial Foundation, "Reports of Round Tables, 1936, Neutrality and Collective Security."

[72] Alfred Zimmern, *The League of Nations and the Rule of Law 1918–1935* (London: Macmillan, 1935).

members of the group had a responsibility to the whole body to aid in the provision of security." He compared the difference between collective security and single state security to the difference between shipboard travel and rail travel. He explained that when one traveled by ship, one was required to obey certain rules and had certain responsibilities, while train passengers did not normally have to worry about the safety of the whole train. The essence of the idea of collective security lay in its emphasis on the whole.[73]

Warren's public lecture presented a concise analysis of the rationale behind the congressional opposition to the neutrality bill sponsored by the administration, which would give the President the authority to decide the items and amounts to be prohibited in an embargo. One opposing argument, presented by Moore and Borchard, sought to preserve traditional neutrality. A second argument was put forward by those who did not want to surrender rights such as "freedom of the seas." A third was that changing the laws of neutrality after the outbreak of hostilities would possibly aid one belligerent at the expense of another. A fourth argument opposed the aggrandizement of presidential discretion. A fifth argument held that by imposing embargoes, the United States would itself become a belligerent. Having summarized these various contentions, Warren concluded that the debate over neutrality was "an example of a confusion of thought and of a singularly incongruous attitude." Finally, he warned that neutrality was not omnipotent, and cautioned:

> If, however, we are resolved to sit on the fence, surrounded by tanks of gasoline, and to watch the match being scratched without taking any part in trying to prevent it, then we ought to make pretty certain beforehand, not only that the house into which we are going to retire is fireproof, but also that the atmosphere will be such that we can comfortably live in the house while the neighborhood is ablaze.[74]

The round-table conferences covered topics ranging from "Factors Tending to Draw Neutrals into War," and "Public Opinion and Neutrality," to "The British Attitude towards Collective Security." More than fifty participants took part in the sessions. Those in attendance included not only Garner, Fenwick and Kenneth W. Colegrove of Northwestern

---

[73] Alfred Zimmern, "The Problem of Collective Security," in *Neutrality and Collective Security*, pp. 4, 6.

[74] Charles Warren, "Congress and Neutrality," in *Neutrality and Collective Security*, pp. 121–138, 153.

University, but also Harold D. Lasswel, a well-known political scientist at the University of Chicago. Most of the international lawyers present were critical of current legislation. In a session on the legal aspects of neutrality, Fenwick pointed out a contradiction in the current legislation, stating that he could not understand "the psychology of the men who think that an embargo on ammunitions will keep you out of war more than an embargo on the key materials." Garner repeated his argument that the practice of neutrality during World War I had been immoral, and asserted that the present legislation "represents a council of cowardice," for which Mussolini was quite likely thankful.[75]

The Neutrality Act was a setback for the reformers because they had been acting on the premise that the Covenant of the League of Nations together with the Kellogg–Briand Pact was to put an end to the old neutrality. Since the end of World War I, the reformers had struggled to contribute to the peace of the world through the elaboration of theories. The emphasis that the reformers placed on multilateral treaties helped to raise the value of the Covenant and the Kellogg–Briand Pact. Their progressive interpretation of the Non-Recognition Doctrine endeavored to make up for the alleged legal weaknesses in the Pact. As a result of the establishment of the Pact and the League's efforts to sustain its principle, the reformers gained confidence that their arguments were compatible with actual policies. The Neutrality Act shattered this illusion. It was a great blow not only to American reformers, but also to some Europeans. The movement to abolish neutrality was also discussed in Europe, and to some extent US policy had encouraged European proponents of the trend. The Kellogg Pact, Stimson's policy and address, and the introduction of embargo bills in Congress were often cited by scholars in Europe as evidence of the vitality of this trend.

The long-standing controversy over neutrality among American scholars did not precipitate or affect the enactment of legislation. The Neutrality Act was closest to the position presented by Warren, a new authority on this issue. The reformers were not solely responsible for their defeat because there were many other factors that led to the act's enactment. On the other hand, Moore and Borchard played a key role in discouraging arms embargoes against aggressors. The debate over neutrality in the mid 1930s caused a new political division. Borchard put a quotation from President Washington's farewell address on the very front page of

---

[75] University of Chicago, "Reports of Round Tables, 1936, Neutrality and Collective Security," pp. 178, 175.

his book on neutrality.[76] It read, "a passionate attachment of one Nation for another produces a variety of evils." Borchard's frequent attendance at congressional hearings cemented his position as an isolationist. On the other hand, Wright and his group now became more closely aligned than ever with the advocates of collective security.

It was also interesting that each side, reformers and traditionalists alike, criticized the other for a lack of realism. Moore and Borchard argued that the reformers' position was far removed from reality and that their views were unrealistic because the reformers seemed to think that they could change the entire world through the power of their theories. After all, not a single government had officially declared an end to traditional neutrality. The reformers had merely been idle dreamers. On the other hand, as Yost at the State Department wrote in his memorandum, and as Stimson once argued, Borchard and Moore's assertion that the powers could have claimed neutrality rights during World War I was "unrealistic." In light of the situation at the time, which side was more realistic? Borchard's reality was past-oriented, while Wright's looked ahead to the future. In the mid 1930s, reality itself was no doubt confusing enough to allow both views. Only historical developments on the world stage could determine which view would ultimately become the real "reality." If the world stayed as it was, Borchard's view would prevail. If humanity entered to a new stage in its history, then Wright would be vindicated.

---

[76] Edwin M. Borchard and William Potter Lage, *Neutrality for the United States* (New Haven: Yale University Press, 1937), p. iii.

6

International law in a lawless world

From the standpoint of reformist scholars of international law who threw their efforts into preventing war, the world situation in the 1930s was not favorable. By the middle of the 1930s, military actions by the powers had become more common. Encouraged by the fact that the League of Nations had failed to take effective steps to halt the Japanese military actions in Manchuria, Italy started a war in Ethiopia in the summer of 1935. In July 1937 Japan and China began an all-out war. Even so, Quincy Wright was determined not to surrender in the face of such lawlessness. In October and November 1936, he gave a series of lectures on the Kellogg–Briand Pact before the Chicago Women's Club, in which he repeatedly emphasized how important it was to uphold the principles of the Pact.[1] His faith in it had not been shaken at all. In May 1938 he wrote to Salmon O. Levinson, "Of all the countries in the world, we are the one that has most interest in restoring law and order."[2] With high spirits and a firm resoluteness, the specialists were going to confront the challenges to their scholarship.

The challenge of military hostilities

In the traditional approach to international law, there was no specific legal term to describe a state that had illegally started hostilities, because war itself was deemed legal. However, when the Pact declared that war as a means of national policy was illegal, and the Covenant of the League of Nations specified the application of sanctions against countries that started wars in violation of the obligations set forth in the Covenant, it became necessary to judge which belligerent had violated the law. This development took a definite form when the League concluded that Japan's

---

[1] Quincy Wright, "The Kellogg Pact and Consultations," "Determination of the Aggressor," Wright Papers, Box 16, Folder 6.
[2] Wright to Salmon O. Levinson, May 28, 1938, Wright Papers, Box 20, Folder 3.

actions in Manchuria had violated both the Covenant and the Pact and when the outbreak of hostilities in Ethiopia brought up the issue of determining which party was the wrongdoer and what sanctions should be imposed.

Wright addressed this problem in terms of the notion of "aggression," arguing that the concept was relatively new to international law. Progress was made concerning actual tests to determine an aggressor during the 1935 Italian action in Ethiopia and the Bolivia–Paraguay dispute. Based on his examination of the practices at the League, Wright defined an aggressor as a state "which employed force against another state, and which refuses to accept an armistice proposed in accordance with a procedure." However, in spite of his academic dedication to clarifying the legal notion of aggression, Wright reluctantly recognized the futility of a legal definition in actual situations, which of itself could not immediately halt ongoing military actions. He wrote that a legal definition was necessary insofar as it would be useful in settling claims in the future and because the accumulation of legal cases by the international court would act "as a deterrent to aggression." But he was frank in admitting that "for the purpose of preventing or stopping hostilities in a given crisis this test of aggression is useless."[3]

The issue of undeclared war also attracted the attention of some scholars. A declaration of war had long been considered a prerequisite for converting actual military activities into a legally recognized state of war. However, since the Pact had declared all war illegal, the use of force without a formal declaration appeared to be an option. In the case of the Italo-Ethiopian War, Wright opined that in the legal sense a state of war existed in spite of the absence of a declaration. The Committee of Six, appointed by the Council of the League to examine this case, reported that the Italian government had resorted to war in violation of Article 12 of the Covenant of the League. Thus, Wright concluded that a declaration was not an indispensable factor in determining the existence of war. It is important to note that Wright argued that "war in the material sense can be converted into war in the legal sense through declaration or recognition of its juristic character by the participants or by other states." In other words, even if the party that initiated military action had not declared war, other parties could jointly determine the existence of a state of war.

---

[3] Quincy Wright, "The Concept of Aggression in International Law," *AJIL* 29 (1935), 395, 388.

If, as the result of an inquiry, nations recognized the existence of a state of war, then the hostilities would acquire the legal status of war.[4]

In July 1937 another war broke out in China. Although vehement and frequent attacks on international law had been heard since the war in Ethiopia, reformers such as Wright, Charles G. Fenwick and James W. Garner did not alter their faith in post-World War I international law. At the 1938 meeting of the ASIL, responding to attacks on international law for its failure to regulate military action, Garner quoted Sir Frederick Pollock, a well-known scholar of jurisprudence, that law did not cease to exist merely because it had been violated. Garner then remarked that the issue at stake was pessimism, which of itself would discourage the whole system of international law. He did not believe that it was "necessary for this Society at this time to answer the attacks against international law that have been made from the beginning by a few cynics and skeptics." Reformers did not agree that the League was a failure; nor had they given up the idea of international organization. Arthur Kuhn argued that "however immature the efforts to organize the League" might have been, the League must go on. It was necessary to "learn by our failures to proceed in a way that is more likely to succeed." Fenwick clearly stated his motivation for supporting the League, arguing that "the system was not wrong because it went too far, but because it did not go far enough." He ascribed the cause of its failure to members' hesitation "to suppress violence by collective action."[5]

At the same time, Fenwick did not abandon his long-standing faith in collective values as a basis for a durable international order.

> The principle of law which must remain dominant is the principle that the collective judgment of the community of nations must replace the right of each State to be the judge in its own case and the collective power of the community be substituted for the old right of the individual State to take the law into its own hands.[6]

Never once did Fenwick abandon either his belief in the significance of collectivity or his opposition to the old notion of individuality.

But where could effective measures for enforcing principles be found? The concepts of "recognition" and "denunciation of treaty violations" were based on the premise that the established

---

[4] Quincy Wright, "The Test of Aggression in the Italo-Ethiopian War," *AJIL* 30 (1936), 47, 51–52.

[5] *Proceedings, ASIL* (1938), 33, 39–40.

[6] Charles G. Fenwick, "The 'Failure' of the League of Nations," *AJIL* 30 (1936), 506.

system was appropriate and workable. Garner argued that using "the term 'recognition' or 'non-recognition' to describe the attitude adopted by other governments" had become "almost as well-established in recent years" as a principle of international law. According to Garner, refusing to recognize the fruits of aggression had become tantamount to a legal obligation for each state, because "a number of multipartite treaties or pacts have been widely entered into by states," and those treaties were believed to create "an obligation for the parties not to recognize territorial acquisitions." As proof to support this position, he cited the Budapest Articles of Interpretation, the Stimson Doctrine, and the fact that most states had not recognized Manchukuo. Responding to criticism that the policy of non-recognition had been unable to prevent an aggressor from launching a war, Garner nevertheless defended the policy, because "its moral value, if employed by the whole body of States, is not to be ignored."[7]

Wright also endorsed the policy of non-recognition, but he went further than Garner and argued for a new concept of "denunciation." Referring to the statement issued by Secretary of State Cordell Hull on October 6, 1937, that "the action of Japan in China is contrary to the provisions of the Nine Power Treaty and to those of the Kellogg–Briand Pact," Wright raised the question of the appropriateness and expediency of issuing a formal criticism. As to whether a state had the duty to formally protest violation, Wright held that while "states were free to remain silent and to withhold protests," "certain treaties impose a duty to denounce certain types of illegal behavior by other states." The Kellogg–Briand Pact fell into this category, because it "solemnly declares in the name of their respective peoples that they condemn recourse to war for the solution of international controversies." Wright focused on the phrase "in the name of their respective peoples," and argued that since the declaration was of a formal and public nature, the protest against a violator must likewise be formal and public. Secondly, he raised the question of whether a state was free to remain silent if a formal protest would damage its relationship with the alleged law breaker. He wrote that one of the important sanctions of international law was "public opinion." Thus, by issuing denunciations states should show "their interest in general respect for that law and for treaties to which they are parties," because the endorsement of law was more important than the deterioration of relationships.[8]

[7] James Wilford Garner, "Non-Recognition of Illegal Territorial Annexations and Claims to Sovereignty," *AJIL* 30 (1936), 679–681, 684, 686.
[8] Quincy Wright, "The Denunciation of Treaty Violators," *AJIL* 32 (1938), 527, 531–532.

Wright did not argue for denunciation of every breach of international law, but clearly specified when denunciation was necessary. He wrote that states should refrain from comment unless the violation involved a breach of a general treaty embodying "a fundamental principle of the community of nations." In other words, the violation would have to be of a law or treaty that had an impact on the order and security of the whole community. More specifically, the League Covenant, the Pact, and other such agreements whose breach was "the business of every state" fell into this category. Wright even suggested that breaches of fundamental treaties might be characterized as "crimes against the community of nations."[9]

With the prospects of war and calls for appeasement becoming urgent, Wright advocated for the US role of upholding international law. He wrote to Sumner Welles that the issue at stake was not national interest, but international order. Wright asserted that it was desirable that "governments, even though their own or their citizens' material interests are not directly involved, should voice vigorous protests against violations of fundamental principles of international law, of general treaties, and of humanity wherever they occur."[10] Wright also exchanged letters with Thomas W. Lamont, writing in a similarly passionate tone that the issue was not whether Americans had any call to save Ethiopia from conquest. Rather, what was involved was "whether Americans had an interest in preserving respect for treaties to which they are party, and for general international law." Wright closed his letter to Lamont with the admonition "if the whole structure of law and treaties crumbles, we will live in a jungle." He strongly criticized the policy of isolation, writing that "the United States will eventually have to make up its mind whether or not it is a member of the family of nations." Wright defined US interests not in terms of tangible material interests but as the "real interest we have in the maintenance of treaties, international law, and international cooperation."[11]

The legal situation in the Far East

In the course of the general debate on the relevance of international law, the Far Eastern situation drew the attention of some specialists. In April 1934 Eiji Amau, the official spokesman of the Japanese Foreign Ministry, made a statement that Japan's special position in China gave

---

[9] *Ibid.*, 533–534.
[10] Wright to Sumner Welles, June 6, 1938, Wright Papers, Addenda I, Box 27.
[11] Wright to Thomas W. Lamont, February 25, 1938, Wright Papers, Box 16, Folder 15.

it dominance, and hence Japan would object to further undertakings by other powers that might undermine its position. Charles Cheney Hyde of Columbia University analyzed Japan's legal position on the relationship between the statement and the previous treaty obligations. With regard to Japan's claim for a Monroe Doctrine in Asia, Hyde wrote that in theory such a claim was not totally baseless because the power that Japan sought to wield over Asian nations had been exercised by the United States over Latin American nations. However, he emphasized the significance of the Nine Power Treaty, by which the powers had acknowledged China's independence and agreed to a policy of non-interference. The Treaty had become the standard of conduct for contracting nations, and "excuses for interference were to be tested by that instrument rather than by customary international law." In Hyde's view, Amau's statement was in "contrast to the terms and theory of the Nine-Power Treaty." But Hyde was realistic enough to acknowledge the difficulty of enforcing the Treaty, because it was possible that "as a matter of diplomacy" some contracting parties might not regard Japan's actions as detrimental for fear that it would harm their relationship with Japan.[12]

Before Amau issued his statement, Sakutaro Tachi had published an article entitled "Manchuria and Panama," in which he elaborated the argument that Manchuria was to Japan what Latin America was to the United States.[13] Wright had also compared American and Japanese foreign policies. He agreed that the American policy toward Latin American countries had once had "resemblance to the Japanese policy vis-á-vis Manchuria." But this was no longer true, because the current Roosevelt administration's Good Neighbor Policy had abandoned the imperialistic designs. Furthermore, Wright noted that there were certain differences between Japan now and the United States in the past; that the world had been less integrated economically and politically than it was now; and that the United States had been under no treaty obligations to refrain from aggression.[14]

Between 1934 and 1935, Tachi developed a theory on the Open Door principle. He argued that the original principle, set forth by John Hay in 1899, had been applied only to the sphere of interests held by the

---

[12] Charles Cheney Hyde, "Legal Aspects of the Japanese Pronouncement in Relation to China," *AJIL* 28 (1934), 431, 438, 441.

[13] Sakutaro Tachi, "Manshu to Panama" [Manchuria and Panama], *Gaiko Jiho* 698 (1934), 1–14.

[14] Quincy Wright, "Analogies between Japanese and American Foreign Policies," Wright Papers, Box 10, Folder 11.

powers, but not to China. However, the principle was transformed at the Washington Conference, expanding its scope to cover all of China. By pointing out the difference between the Open Door principle as it existed in between 1899 and in 1922, Tachi attempted to set forth the contention that the old principle remained valid. If the old principle was valid, Japan's claim was secure.[15] Tachi seemed to be confident that his theory would be accepted by foreign scholars. In February 1934, at a sending-off party before his trip to Europe, where he would attend a meeting of the International Academy, Tachi announced his desire to publish his work abroad.[16]

Tachi sent his article on the Open Door principle to the *AJIL* for publication and Wright, who was then serving on the editorial committee, reviewed it. Wright occluded that Tachi's article was "exceedingly disappointing" and judged that it was not fit for publication. Wright argued that the Hay note of 1899 and Tachi's broad interpretation of it could not be applied "retroactively in any sense." In Tachi's writing, Wright found only a politically motivated desire to defend Japan's action. It was "clear that Japan is anxious to do away with the Open Door legally in the Far East, having already abolished it in a considerable measure practically, but I hardly think that we should honor their arguments by publication."[17]

Wright also judged harshly an article submitted to the ASIL for publication by Mr. Ninomiya, another international lawyer from Japan. According to Wright, the argument set forth in "The Kellogg–Briand Pact Re-examined" could best be characterized as "special pleading" to justify Japan's position. Wright suggested that "Japan, having violated the Kellogg Pact in the general opinion of the world, appears now to be trying to persuade the world that the Pact never meant much of anything anyway."[18] Wright reviewed two other Japanese articles for the journal, again recommending that they not be published. He dismissed one for simply "threshing over old straw" and "below our standard from every point." Admitting it was unfortunate that Japanese views had not been presented in the journal, he expressed his desire that the Japanese scholars argue "not merely from a purely theoretical point of view, but from the

---

[15] Sakutaro Tachi, "Monko kaiho–shugi o ronzu" [To Discuss the Monroe Doctrine], *Gaiko Jiho* 724 (1935), 7, 8, 11.

[16] See *Gaiko Jiho* 702 (March 1934), 218. Several high-ranking officers form the Japanese Army attended this party for Tachi. This seems to indicate that Tachi had a close relationship with the Army.

[17] Wright to Finch, October 9, 1935, Wright Papers, Box 2, Folder 23.

[18] Wright to Finch, April 18, 1935, Wright Papers, Box 2, Folder 23.

practice of state [*sic*] interpreting the Pact."[19] For people like Tachi, who had cherished the traditional positivistic approach, the words in a treaty were the primary object of research. At the same time, only a theoretical interpretation of the treaty could allow for Japan's conduct.

When Japan started another war with China in July, 1937, Fenwick did not hesitate to express his overwhelming faith in international law. He labeled the Japanese attack an outright breach of international law, writing that "the conduct of Japan constitutes an international crime of the first magnitude and a challenge to international law and order." According to him, while in old diplomacy "you must not speak unless you were prepared to back up your words with armed force," in the new diplomacy there were two new forces: "the moral force of condemnation of wrong by the public opinion of other states" and the "economic force of the refusal of individual citizens of other states to hold commercial inter-course with a state that breaks the law." With regard to the latter force, official condemnation of the violator would become important insofar as it served to arouse public opinion.[20]

Tachi countered that Fenwick's argument was "totally groundless," and insisted that Japan had not violated the Nine Power Treaty, because the term "independence" in Article 1 could be interpreted in two ways. In a broad sense it meant the lack of restraints on freedom of action for a country, while in a narrow sense it meant the political independence of China. Following the latter interpretation, Tachi argued, if a country conquered China or subordinated it completely, this would constitute a breach of political independence. But under the current situation, Japan was simply waging a war of self-defense in China, which did not result in a breach of China's independence. Furthermore, Tachi refuted the opinion that the Nine Power Treaty was a law-making treaty, which had a normative value for contracting members, because the treaty merely set guidelines for pol-icy and not rules of international law.[21]

Elihu Root had once presented an opinion similar to Tachi's that the treaties signed at the Washington Conference signified policies but not law. From the traditionalist perspective, the post-World War I treaties were not regarded as "law" because law should be confined to concrete agreements between nations concerning specific rights and obligations in

---

[19] Wright to Finch, November 9, 1935; Wright to Finch, January 24, 1936; Wright to Finch, April 18, 1935, Wright Papers, Box 2, Folder 23.

[20] Charles G. Fenwick, "The Nine Power Treaty and the Present Crisis in China," *AJIL* 31 (1937), 671, 674.

[21] Sakutaro Tachi, "Kyukoku joyaku" [Nine Power Treaty], *Gaiko Jiho* 794 (1938), 1–27.

treaties. Garner responded vehemently to the narrow interpretation of the Hay Note that Tachi presented in his article. Garner wrote, "I am worrying less over the interpretation of the Nine-Power Treaty than I am over what seems to me to be this virtual repudiation by the present Japanese government." He continued, "Whatever may be our views regarding the meaning of the open door in that treaty, there can be no doubt that Japan pledged herself to observe the open door and to respect the sovereignty, independence, and territorial integrity of China."[22] Tachi's position, which reflected Japan's official stance, tended to refute the value of postwar treaties. In 1938 Tachi published a book on international law and the Sino-Japanese War, in which he wrote that "since the Kellogg Pact reserved broad rights of self-defense, it was meaningless from the beginning."[23]

In 1939 Wright compiled a book for the Institute of Pacific Relations that presented an overall analysis of the legal situation in the Far East. Although he provided a detailed description of the content of each treaty and the status of Far Eastern territories, his main purpose was to establish that there had been a gap between the *de jure* and de facto situations in the region. The ability to draw a concise, sensible picture from the detailed description of the legal machinery was a hallmark of Wright's work. In the simplified picture he provided in this book, the problems in the Far East were treated as being indicative of the discrepancy between law and facts. This discrepancy made the situation chaotic, and stability could be achieved only when "the existing *de jure* situation has been restored in fact," or when "a new situation has been developed by legal procedures from that *de jure* situation." It should be noted that Wright did not acknowledge the possibility that the de facto situation could change the *de jure* one. He also pointed out the contrast between how the Stimson Doctrine had been applied in Europe and Asia. Although the Doctrine had been "generally observed in connection with the Far East," it had not been applied in the case of Germany's annexation of Austria and Italy's annexation of Ethiopia.[24]

An expanded version of Wright's book was published in 1941. It featured essays on Non-Recognition by Hersch Lauterpacht of Cambridge University and by Edwin M. Borchard and a new conclusion by Wright. Lauterpacht went a little beyond Wright in suggesting that the Non-

---

[22] Garner to Tachi, January 22, 1938, Garner Papers.
[23] Sakutaro Tachi, *Shina jihen kokusaiho-ron* [International Law and the Sino-Japanese War] (Tokyo: Shoka-do, 1938), p. 10.
[24] Quincy Wright, *The Existing Legal Situation as it Relates to the Conflict in the Far East* (New York: Institute of Pacific Relations, 1939), pp. 7, 6, 3–4.

Recognition Doctrine was essential to maintaining the validity of international law. The Doctrine was important, because it entailed "a vindication of the legal character of international law as against the 'law-creating effect of facts'." If Non-Recognition was abandoned, legal principles would be subordinated to facts. A "weighty factor in the maintenance of authority of international law" was at stake. Lauterpacht pointed out that the Non-Recognition Doctrine had developed from a policy into a legal obligation during the discussion of Japan's invasion of Manchuria at the League. With the resolution of the Council of the League on February 16, 1932, and that of the Assembly on March 11, 1932, the policy of Non-Recognition was transformed into an obligation.[25]

Borchard agreed with Lauterpact that the League's resolution of February 16, 1932, marked "the apotheosis of strength for the Doctrine of Non-Recognition." But he cautioned that Manchukuo and Italy's absorption of Ethiopia had continued to "exist as political facts and to be dealt as such in practice," while the world gave "lip service to the theory of their non-existence" by upholding the Non-Recognition Doctrine. He noted that insistence on the Doctrine would itself lead to a dangerous and unstable situation: "The old view that the law follows the facts, however unpleasant, had a certain stabilizing function, which the theory of refusing *de jure* recognition to facts which some nations regard as 'illegal' does not have, whereas its destructive potentialities are all too apparent."[26]

Wright responded with a concise summary of the two interpretations of the Doctrine; "the Non-Recognition Doctrine, which favors modifying facts to accord with law" and "the *de facto* doctrine which favors modifying law after military or political action has succeeded in creating a new situation in violation of legal rights." He endorsed the former and reiterated his criticism of Borchard for his "profound pessimism with respect to the capacity of man to improve the world by law."[27]

It should be noted that the debate over the Non-Recognition Doctrine among the three specialists did not address particular legal issues directly

---

[25] Quincy Wright, ed., *Legal Problems in the Far Eastern Conflict* (New York: Institute of Pacific Relations, 1941), pp. 137, 147. For Lauterpacht, see Koskenniemi, *Gentle Civilizer*, pp. 353–412; Renee Jeffery, "Hersch Lauterpacht, the Realist Challenge and the 'Grotian Tradition' in 20th Century International Relations," *EJIL* 12 (2006), 223–250; Anthony Carty, "Hersch Lauterpacht: A Powerful Eastern European Figure," *Baltic Yearbook of International Law* 7 (2007), 1–28.

[26] Wright, *Legal Problems in the Far Eastern*, pp. 172–173, 175.

[27] *Ibid.*, pp. 115, 120.

concerning the Far East. What was important to these scholars was, for instance, not the interpretation of the Nine Power Treaty but the relationship between law and facts. The Far Eastern situation served as a case, a clear and symbolic case that addressed the fundamental issues in international law.

In the 1930s, the reformers attempted to catch up with as yet unfolding events by elaborating legal notions within the framework of the new international law. They created and advocated legal concepts such as aggression, Non-Recognition, denunciation, and peaceful change. However, their discussions revealed the practical limitations of legal notions in preventing war and solving actual problems. Even in 1941, when relations with Japan were deteriorating, they continued to engage in a philosophical debate, as the discussions on Non-Recognition held at the Institute of Pacific Relations showed. Were their discussions totally meaningless and futile? To answer this question, we must examine the implications of the study of international law on American foreign policy.

Cordell Hull and the study of international law

Cordell Hull, Secretary of State in a critical period in American foreign policy before and during World War II, wrote in his memoirs that while managing American foreign relations in the late 1930s "we sought again and again to revitalize international law."[28] Thus, it is necessary to examine Hull's understanding of international law and his relationship with the scholars. In the collection of Hull's papers, there was an unpublished manuscript written by Wright entitled "The Far East and the World Peace Machinery." Attached to it is a note that reads "Return to Hull," dated July 14, 1934. The existence of this manuscript among Hull's papers provides some indication of Hull's interest in the field and suggests that he himself was more or less committed to the study of international law.[29]

On July 16, 1937, a week after the outbreak of war between Japan and China, Hull proclaimed general guidelines for American foreign policy. At the outset, he stressed that any "tensions and strains" in international relations would be of "inevitable concern to the whole world," and he asserted that "there can be no serious hostilities anywhere in the world

---

[28] Cordell Hull, *The Memoirs of Cordell Hull*, vol. 1 (London: Hodder & Stoughton, 1948), p. 537.
[29] Quincy Wright, "The Far East and the World Peace Machinery," Papers of Cordell Hull (hereafter Hull Papers), Library of Congress, Washington, DC, microfilm edition, Reel 11.

which will not one way or another affect interests or rights or obligations of this country." Hull noted that the United States had "deep concern" for the situation in the Far East. He emphasized that solutions to international problems should be reached "by orderly process carried out in a spirit of mutual helpfulness and accommodation" and that "international agreements" and "established obligations" should be faithfully observed. "We stand for revitalizing and strengthening of international law," he posited. In addition, Hull stressed the importance of economic stability for world peace, such issues as "economic security," "lowering the tariffs in international trade" and "equal commercial opportunity."[30]

Former Secretary of State Henry L. Stimson praised the speech. "I think it is an admirable statement of principles of our nation towards its neighbors, and that, put forward at this time, it may serve as a powerful moral appeal in a world where many people and some governments think that those principles are obsolete and may be safely disregarded." Stimson regarded the Japanese attack on China as a fundamental assault on the established international order, cautioning that "Japan's present attempt on China cannot be taken as less serious or fundamental than the attacks of the Mongol invaders upon the civilization of Europe fifteen centuries ago."[31] Both Hull and Stimson recognized that the Japanese action represented a fundamental challenge to the principles of international order. Both also had faith in moral values and believed that the making of moralistic statements could bring about concrete and positive results. This was clearly shown in the fact that Hull sought to make public the replies from various governments to his July 16 statement.

When Hull sent copies of the statement to other governments, he specifically instructed his representatives abroad to obtain each country's reply for publication.[32] He explained his aim, "My plan has been to get the maximum beneficial effect by assembling replies from all governments and publishing them en bloc."[33] Hull was so determined to publish the replies that he set a deadline of August 4 for their return. He asserted that his message was not intended to apply to any particular situation, but that if he received positive replies from all over the world, this would indicate that other governments accepted "as the norm for international relations" the principles he had set forth. Therefore, "the cumulative effect

[30] *FRUS*, 1937, I, pp. 699–670.
[31] Stimson to Hull, August 30, 1937, Hull Papers, Reel 15.
[32] Hull, *Memoirs*, vol. 1, pp. 535–537; *FRUS*, 1937, I, pp. 697–802.
[33] *FRUS*, 1937, I, p. 711.

upon publication would be enormous and would do much to strengthen international law and international morals."[34]

Hull's high regard for legalism might be attributed in part to his personal relationship with Salmon O. Levinson, who started the movement for the outlawry of war in 1920 and who is considered one of the original advocates of the Kellogg–Briand Pact. After Hull assumed the office of Secretary of State, the two communicated with each other on the issue of international relations quite frequently. Levinson shared his views with Hull and there is some indication that Hull appreciated them.[35] Beginning in the mid 1930s, Levinson and Wright also began to correspond frequently, particularly concerning Hull's policy and their strategy to support him.

For instance, between the fall of 1934 and the spring of 1935 Levinson repeatedly proposed that a conference of all the powers be held in Washington. Levinson's views were largely shaped by moralistic concerns. In March 1938 he wrote to Hull that the world was "at the moral cross roads" and warned that "If America does not stand firm for international decency, moral conduct and the legal sanctity of treaties freely entered into, the peoples of the world will give up hope and the night of anarchy will have encompassed civilization."[36] Expressing his gratitude for Levinson's advice, Hull wrote back, "I am circulating your views and suggestions among suitable officials and others here ... I want you to know how much I appreciate your fine spirit of cooperation."[37]

On March 17, 1938, Hull gave an address on foreign policy. This was his first formal pronouncement after Germany's annexation of Austria. The address was broadcast not only in the United States, but in Canada, Great Britain, and other European countries by short-wave radio. The address was based on Hull's statement of July 1937 and reaffirmed the importance of upholding principles. Though the United States did not have an intention of policing the world, its policy would be "one of firmness in support of right principles and justice in international relations but not a policy of positive action." He reiterated the importance of order based on law. "Only by making our reasonable contribution to the firm establishment

[34] *Ibid.*, p. 748.
[35] For the relationship between Levinson and Hull, see the Papers of Salmon O. Levinson (hereafter Levinson Papers), Regenstein Library, University of Chicago, Box 23, Folder 16 and 17, and Box 24, Folder, 1 and 2.
[36] Levinson to Hull, March 13, 1938, Levinson Papers, Box 24, Folder 2.
[37] Hull to Levinson, March 28, 1938, Levinson Papers, see also Levinson to Hull, April 12, 1938, April 22, 1938, Wright Papers, Box 20, Folder 3.

of a world order based on law can we keep our problem of security in true perspective." The next day, the address appeared in the *New York Times*. Directly beneath it was the headline, "Approves Hull's Speech, but London Paper Says Europe Must Act, Not Talk Ideas."[38]

While some were skeptical of Hull's policy, Levinson and Wright were satisfied and they supported his views. Two days before the address, Levinson had asked Wright to "write Mr. Hull upholding his Non-Recognition Doctrine."[39] In a letter to Hull after the speech, Wright proclaimed that it had "established a standard which is bound to be of great value in the long run." Wright referred to the Non-Recognition Doctrine and argued that he did not regard it as an obstacle to change, but as "an assertion that change shall become legal only when validated by proper legal process." If the United States opposed the use of force, it logically followed that the United States would deny the fruits of use of force. He concluded by asserting that the United States should play a positive role in restoring "the morale of the law-abiding states."[40]

In June 1938 Hull delivered a speech entitled "The Spirit of International Law" before the American Bar Association. He asserted again and again how important the revitalization of international law was for a stable international order, stating that "international law, both in its development and in its potentialities for the future, is today a factor of crucial importance in the relations among nations." The speech also conveyed Hull's endorsement of the Kellogg–Briand Pact, which he saw as "a milestone in the process of transmitting this idea into political reality." Hull stressed that the world was a community and that each state had a responsibility in it, using phrases like "responsibilities of organized society" and "responsibilities as a member of the family of civilized nations." Despite the fact that international law had been violated so frequently and easily, he argued for a long-term view of history and observed that "progress has always been slow and its road has always been strewn with difficulties, interruptions, set-backs, temporary disappointments." Because the world was facing just such setbacks now, it was all the more important to faithfully promote the principles of law. "At this crucial juncture of history," he asserted, the United States should contribute to preserving and advancing "the principles of international law and of the orderly and

---

[38] *New York Times*, March 18, 1938.
[39] Levinson to Wright, March 15, 1938, Wright Papers, Box 20, Folder 3.
[40] Wright to Hull, March 19, 1938, Wright Papers, Box 20, Folder 2.

cooperative process of international relations."[41] Hull's distinct commitment to international law was no doubt encouraging for scholars, while for Hull himself his public commitment to it necessarily colored the direction and tone of his policies.

In the meantime, at the ASIL James Brown Scott was suffering from ill health, requiring a new president to be chosen. Scott had been president since 1930 and he suggested that Stimson be his successor.[42] Scott wrote to Stimson, requesting that "you follow in the footsteps of your distinguished predecessors in the Department of State." The previous presidents had been Elihu Root and Charles Evans Hughes, while Scott's presidency was supposed to have been only of a temporary nature until such time as the Society could find "the appropriate successor to the two Secretaries of State."[43] Stimson declined the position, however, because he had already accepted the presidency of the American Bar Association, which would last until May 1939.[44]

Hull was re-elected vice-president of the ASIL in 1938 and he accepted this result with pleasure. It seems that Hull had cultivated a good relationship with the ASIL and its members, and he used the Society's mailing list to distribute copies of his June 3, 1938 address, "The Spirit of International Law."[45] His esteem for the ASIL was more than merely token, as shown by his somewhat lengthy letter declining the invitation to the 1939 meeting. Correspondence of this sort was more than just a formality for a man of such high office.[46] For Scott and others who wished to have a prominent figure for president, the idea of getting Hull could not have been far from their minds.

However, some members voiced strong opposition to having another Secretary of State for president. Philip Jessup noted that the ASIL had had only three presidents, Root, Hughes and Scott, and he suggested that "we need a president of that type in order to interest the public in our activities." Some older members as well as many of the younger ones thought that their society should "follow the practice of the other scientific societies like those of the historians, political scientists, and economists, who

[41] Cordell Hull, "The Spirit of International Law," Papers of Stanley K. Hornbeck, Hoover Institution, Stanford University, Box 209.
[42] Finch to Philip C. Jessup, April 19, 1938, ASIL Papers. See also Kirgis, *The American Society*, pp. 157–159.
[43] Scott to Stimson, April 22, 1938, ASIL Papers.
[44] Stimson to Scott, April 26, 1938, ASIL Papers.
[45] Hull to Finch, May 27, 1938, Hull to Finch, July 5, 1938, ASIL Papers.
[46] Hull to Scott, April 1, 1939, ASIL Papers.

elect annually a new president selected in general because of his current contributions to the science."[47] In spite of such views, however, Hull was elected president at the executive meeting of 1939. In his letter of acceptance, Hull expressed the hope that "we, in working together, may find it possible to do something of a constructive character in the field of international law, the principles of which are being sorely tried in these troublous times of international relations."[48] Hull's leadership gave great encouragement and enormous prestige to the ASIL at a pressing moment in world affairs.

It is interesting to note that Fenwick played an important role in getting Hull elected president, all the more so because the former had been opposed to having Hughes as president twenty years earlier. In 1921 Fenwick had claimed that Hughes had not contributed enough to the study of international law, but now he rejected a proposal that scholars serve as president on a rotating basis.[49] His change of heart may be attributed to the realization that by having the Secretary of State in charge there was a greater likelihood that the scholars' views might be translated into actual policy. Fenwick visited Hull at the end of April 1939 as a representative of the American Union for Concerted Peace. At that time, Congress was debating the revision of neutrality legislation, and Fenwick suggested that a new section be added to a proposed amendment to the neutrality act. He proposed a resolution stating that the United States should not furnish munitions of war to a state that was at war in violation of a treaty to which the United States was a party. Fenwick observed that the proposal was in accord with Hull's position, asserting that "it is the principle which you have yourself enunciated so often – the principle of the integrity of treaty obligations and the vital interest of the United States in the maintenance of international law and order."[50]

At the annual meeting of the ASIL in April 1940, Hull gave the presidential address, which was broadcast on NBC radio. After mentioning that Elihu Root and Chief Justice Charles Evans Hughes had previously served as presidents of the Society, the NBC announcer introduced Hull. The new president started his address by stating that those who were interested in this field were "profoundly conscious of the fact that today the subject of international law has an extraordinary significance ... Never

---

[47] Jessup to Wright, April 10, 1939, Wright Papers, Box 2, Folder 23.
[48] Hull to Scott, May 5, 1939, ASIL Papers.
[49] Finch to Fenwick, May 3, 1939, ASIL Papers.
[50] Fenwick to Hull, May 3, 1939, Hull Papers, Reel 17.

before has it been so fraught with import for the future of mankind." Hull proceeded to outline the development of international law, describing it as a gradual movement toward the regulation of the use of force. Currently, international anarchy was threatening to destroy a civilization founded on law and order. International lawyers had a special obligation to "persistently search for ways and means of strengthening the study of international law and of making more effective the translation of principles into firmly established international practice."[51] This address was delivered six months after the outbreak of war in Europe. Hull, Secretary of State and president of the ASIL, took the opportunity to affirm his faith in international law.

International law during the war in Europe

The European war, which began with Germany's invasion of Poland in September 1939, did not shock most of the American international lawyers as much as the outbreak of World War I had. This was partly because the coming of war had been anticipated. Nor was the faith of the lawyers in the principles of international law shaken as it had been in the last war, so that they were less pessimistic. Most of the reformers were overwhelmingly determined to uphold international law. No major change can be found in the writings or discussions of the scholars immediately before and after the outbreak of the European war.

In his analysis of the causes of the war, Fenwick frankly admitted that international law had "failed in its primary task" of preventing war. He did not find any fault in the principles themselves, but argued that the weakness of the present system lay in other factors. Vital issues such as economic and social justice had not been addressed or included in the legal framework. Moreover, the concept of collective security set forward in the Covenant of the League of Nations had not been upheld when tested by the Japanese invasion of China. In particular, Fenwick regretted the lack of responsibility on the part of the powers in maintaining collective security, which he described as "the complete abandonment of the conception of community responsibility for acts of aggression." What was at stake was not just the rescue of China, Abyssinia or Czechoslovakia, but "the larger principle of whether the old right of self-help was to be allowed to reassert itself." He argued that "the United States has a vital national interest in the maintenance of international law and order" and claimed

---

[51] *Proceedings, ASIL* (1940), 12–16.

that the United States might have prevented the present catastrophe if it had acted differently.[52]

Wright likewise attributed the failure of international law to the incompleteness of the system, not to the principles behind it. He wrote that the idea of collective security had never really been tried; the refusal of the United States to enter the postwar system had meant that "one third of the total industrial and raw materials production of the world had refused to go into that system."[53] Eagleton also felt that "the fault does not lie in the law – it lies with the nations which have refused to put behind it any better sanctions." More specifically, it was the United States' fault, because by rejecting the idea of collective security, the Americans had set "an example of sovereign independence and irresponsibility which other nations have not been slow to follow and to expand." The present catastrophe could have been avoided "if the American people had been willing to build and uphold the law of nations."[54]

Not all international lawyers shared Wright and Fenwick's views. Philip Marshall Brown sided with Wright and Fenwick insofar as he reaffirmed that it was the role of international lawyers to defend international law, and that the doctrine and principles of international law did not cease to exist merely because Russia, Germany and Japan had violated them.[55] However, he was critical of the post-World War I development of international law. Above all, he did not endorse the reformers' central premise that "international law is the prevalent conviction of the community." Brown proceeded to remark, "I feel that many of us have been seriously thrown off our balance since the World War," and he argued for caution with regard to the reformers' too ambitious aspirations. Another member stated, "I have often felt in our discussions here in the Society in recent years a desire to construct an entirely new order."[56] Jessup similarly criticized the reformers' grandiose ambitions, stating that "those who were so sure that the Covenant of the League of Nations and the Pact had ushered in a new era and who therefore scorned much of the law built up painfully through the centuries must bear a share of responsibility for the feeling of hopelessness which is today so prevalent." He argued, moreover, that most international activities, such as the regulation of radio, were

---

[52] Charles G. Fenwick, "International Law and Lawless Nations," *AJIL* 33 (1939), 743–746.
[53] *Proceedings, ASIL* (1940), 44.
[54] Clyde Eagleton, "The Needs of International Law," *AJIL* 34 (1940), 701–702.
[55] Philip Marshall Brown, "Changing Concepts of International Law," *AJIL* 34 (1940), 504–505.
[56] *Proceedings, ASIL* (1940), 153–155.

still governed by international law. It was agreements of this kind, not the ambitious Covenant or the Pact, which formed the basis of international law and would remain unaffected by the course of the war.[57]

The gulf separating the reformers and the traditionalists was as pronounced as ever at the 1940 meeting of the ASIL. Wright did not abandon his faith in the importance of having an international legal order of a mandatory nature, arguing that "if international law flows only from the consent of the states ... then a state can renounce its consent at any time, which means there is no international law." In order to establish legally binding principles, he emphasized the importance of the Non-Recognition Doctrine, which, he said, should be regarded as deriving from the fundamental principle that "violence, in itself, cannot destroy existing rights." To this Borchard responded vehemently, charging that the Non-Recognition Doctrine ought to be called "the doctrine of making faces." It created "bad blood" among nations and was "the perfectionists' approach." Borchard believed it was "an instrument of that moralistic world which was supposedly built up after 1919, a world of mechanical devices." He called the reformers a "theological school" and argued that the doctrine was "theoretically beautiful" but had no basis in the realm of physical fact or law.[58]

The outbreak of war in Europe immediately raised the issue of neutrality again, but the actual war between the Allies and Germany did not change the scholars' positions, and the division over the issue remained. While Brown wrote that the basic principle of impartiality embodied in neutrality should not be given up, Fenwick noted that "the existing neutrality legislation favors those who had themselves been guilty of violation of the most sacred of all laws."[59] As the revision of the neutrality act came to attract public attention in the fall of 1939, the debate among international lawyers moved into the pages of the *New York Times*. Hyde and Jessup submitted letters to the paper opposing the revision of the neutrality act. Their contention was that if the embargo of arms were relaxed, it would effectively aid Britain and France. For them the essence of neutrality lay in its strict impartiality, and they argued that the modification of law after the outbreak of hostilities would violate international law. They also suggested that supporters of the revision ask themselves whether they

---

[57] Philip C. Jessup, "In Support of International Law," *AJIL* 34 (1940), 505–508.
[58] *Proceedings, ASIL* (1940), 155, 89, 96, 97.
[59] Philip Marshall Brown, "Neutrality," *AJIL* 33 (1939), 727; Charles G. Fenwick, "The Revision of Neutrality Legislation in Time of Foreign War," *AJIL* 33 (1939), 728.

would still favor it if the situation were reversed, and the revision would aid Germany. Opponents of the revision also posited that the real issue was one of policy and not of international law. Clyde Eagleton responded by asserting that the most vital issue was that of peace. He wrote that "the principle of common action against the lawbreaker" was the issue at stake: "How else have human beings ever had peace than through upholding law?"[60]

The *New York Herald Tribune* also took up the issue and asked international lawyers, "Would a repeal of the arms embargo at the present time constitute, under existing international law, a violation of the neutral obligations of the United States?" Borchard, Hyde and Jessup answered in the affirmative, while Eagleton, Fenwick, Kuhn and Wright answered in the negative.[61]

Wright asserted that neutrality was "far from discouraging war" and that "neutrality has tended to encourage aggression of the strong against the weak." He argued that the system on which neutrality was based was established during the *Pax Britannica*, when imperialism and war were not banned as improper and when the immoral actions of states were not questioned. In essence neutrality signified international anarchy. He asserted, however, that it was all the more important at this critical moment that international law must recognize that "the whole is greater than the parts." A world community intent on preserving the peace of the whole community would have "little use for the concept of neutrality."[62] When President Roosevelt announced the transfer of old destroyers to Great Britain on September 3, 1940, Wright presented the argument that the United States was not a neutral in relation to the European hostilities. Referring to the terminology of the Harvard Draft on Rights and Duties of States in Case of Aggression, Wright defined the United States as a "supporting state." The Harvard Draft convention was a product of the Harvard Research in International Law, which had started in 1930 with the collaboration of the ASIL and had been working on drafting codes in various fields of international law. In the Harvard Draft on neutrality, a supporting state was defined "as one which assists a defending state without armed force." According to Wright, this concept was also adopted in the Budapest Articles of Interpretation. The President and Secretary of

---

[60] *New York Times*, September 21; September 28; October 5; October 15, 1939.
[61] Clyde Eagleton, "The Duty of Impartiality on the Part of a Neutral," *AJIL* 34 (1940), 98, footnote 1.
[62] Quincy Wright, "The Present Status of Neutrality," *AJIL* 34 (1940), 409, 411, 415.

State had publicly declared that Germany and Italy were violating international law, and as a result the United States had acquired the status of a supporting state. In addition, Wright noted that about thirty-five nations had recognized that Germany had started the hostilities in violation of its obligations under the Pact. Given the official US declaration and the positions of other governments toward Germany, Wright concluded that the United States was, with respect to international law, no longer neutral.[63]

Borchard argued that Wright's idea would lead to "perpetual war and a counsel of anarchy," because it would be practically impossible for nations to reach a unanimous agreement as to which state was the aggressor. Even though Borchard was also a member of the Harvard Research in International Law, he wrote that "the 'draft convention' on 'aggression' is an evangelical expression of moral convictions." He stressed that if the United States persisted in its aid of Great Britain, this would run counter to the concepts of neutrality in international law.[64]

When the Lend-Lease Bill was passed in March 1941, Wright praised it as an abandonment of impartiality and a movement "toward responsibility for world order." Impartiality, which could be labeled as synonymous with indifference and isolation, meant the denial of community. He justified his position by referring to the Pact and the Budapest Articles of Interpretation. In addition, Wright found in Hull and Stimson's public statements a clear endorsement of the principles contained in the Pact and the Budapest Articles. He regarded the bill as historically significant: "The Lend-Lease Act constitutes the first legislative endorsement since the Napoleonic period of measures other than war openly against some belligerents and in favor of others."[65]

Wright's position received semi-official endorsement, as seen in the fact that Robert Jackson, the attorney general, followed the reformers' views in his endorsement of the Lend-Lease Bill. Jackson used the term "new international order" and quoted Elihu Root's statement that a breach of peace is a matter of concern to every member of the community of nations. Jackson noted the gradual development of international law over the past twenty years and pointed to the law's vitality.[66]

---

[63] Quincy Wright, "The Transfer of Destroyers to Great Britain," *AJIL* 34 (1940), 685, 688–689.

[64] Edwin M. Borchard, "The Attorney General's Opinion on the Exchange of Destroyers for Naval Bases," *AJIL* 34 (1940), 696–697.

[65] Quincy Wright, "The Lend Lease Bill and International Law," *AJIL* 35 (1941), 308, 311, 313.

[66] "Address of Robert H. Jackson, Attorney General of the United States, before Inter-American Bar Association, Havana, Cuba, March 27, 1941," *AJIL* 35 (1941), 353–359.

Wright commended this remark, writing to Jackson, "It is a pleasure to those of us who have been expounding these principles for years in journals of international law to find them so ably set forth by one in your position of authority."[67] On the other hand, in his comments on the attorney general's statement, Borchard wrote, "the 'new international law' is thus found in the vague and illusory monuments to the myth called 'collective security'." He was doubtful of the legal effect of the Budapest Articles of Interpretation, and regarded them as nothing more than a private statement drafted by a group of scholars. He argued that "international law is not made in that way," noting that not a single nation had adopted these private resolutions. Borchard proceeded to argue that the Roosevelt administration's decision to aid the allies was agreeable, but that it should not have been made in the name of law. "These are political acts which an independent and sovereign country is to take." He asserted that this policy should have been presented "more forthrightly by not invoking the jargon of collective security."[68]

The war in Europe intensified, but in general the attitude among international lawyers was not pessimistic. Jessup wrote, "We are all accustomed to the popular scoffing at international law. We were accustomed to it during the last World War."[69] Experts in international law were united in their faith in scholarship, although they held different positions on specific issues.

This faith was seen in the planning for the ASIL's 1941 meeting. Brown confided in a letter to Wright, "We must have the courage to reaffirm these principles in defiance of a general cynicism and defeatism, much as Grotius boldly spoke up in a time of black despair for Europe."[70] Wright replied that he "entirely agreed," and he proposed that the 1941 meeting deal not only with technical problems but with "fundamental issues from the point of view both of enduring principles and of the readjustment of the interpretation of these principles in our present world of interdependent states if international law is to require the role." He suggested that the meeting be "oriented very definitely toward the future," and proposed in particular topics such as: "the protection of the civil liberties of the individual under international law," "the protection of national and cultural autonomy by international law," "the protection of backward races and of

---

[67] Wright to Robert H. Jackson, April 3, 1941, Wright Papers, Box 6, Folder 10.
[68] Edwin M. Borchard, "War, Neutrality, and Non-Belligerency," *AJIL* 35 (1941), 618, 623, 625.
[69] *Proceedings, Seventh Teachers* (1941), 6.
[70] Brown to Wright, December 11, 1940, Wright Papers, Box 2, Folder 23.

the Open Door in backward areas by international law," "the protection of the state against aggression by international law" and "the problem of international legislation."[71]

At the 1941 meeting, Wright presented a paper entitled "International Law and Commercial Relations." He argued that economic problems were one of the causes of war, and that the economic sovereignty of states must be limited by rules of positive law. Growing interdependence would necessitate the establishment of general principles of economic relations and hence of international economic organization.[72]

A fresh round of criticism

Although ardent reformers like Wright and Fenwick did not abandon their faith in scholarship, it is true that the outbreak of hostilities in the 1930s led to criticism of the study of international law. Thomas Baty, who had doubted whether a new international law had in fact emerged during the previous twenty years, resumed his long-standing attack on the reformers. This time, he was particularly critical of their presentation and manipulation of the legal notions of "recognition" and "war." Baty pointed out the futility of playing with the legal notion of recognition when a state of war actually existed. If a country like Manchukuo existed in terms of its actual function and relationship with other countries, then, Baty asked, what was the meaning of legal recognition? Similarly, he argued that if a country attacked another country's territory with an armed force, war existed, and the intention to wage war on the part of the attacking country should not matter. He deplored the fact that the legal situations had become chaotic as a result of the notion of illegal war constructed by the legalists. Baty particularly blamed the Pact, because it "abolished the name of war and thereby denaturalized the whole theory of international conflict."[73]

Baty proceeded to argue that the debate over defining terms such as "recognition" and "war" pointed to the more fundamental problem of determining who was entitled to change legal concepts. According to Baty, the body of accepted law, in other words the positive treaties and agreements among nations, should be the only source of authority in the

---

[71] Wright to Brown, December 16, 1940, Wright Papers, Box 2, Folder 23.
[72] Quincy Wright, "International Law and Commercial Relations," *Proceedings, ASIL* (1941), 37–39.
[73] Thomas Baty, "The Trend of International Law," *AJIL* 33 (1939), 658, 663.

application of international law. However, if one accepted the reformers' argument that the notion of war had changed, then this might imply that scholars could change legal concepts and principles simply by pushing forward and elaborating their arguments. Why and when had the legal concepts of war and recognition changed, and who was entitled to effect such change? Baty proclaimed that the arbitrary creation of legal concepts involved great danger, and wrote, "I am only the innocent child pointing out that the Emperor has no clothes on."[74]

A much more comprehensive critique of international law came from Hans Morgenthau, who after the war would become the founder of the so-called realist school of international relations. In one of his early writings on neutrality, published in February 1939, he sought to analyze the relationship between the status of international law and the international political situation. At a time when most scholars were focusing on the legal aspects of neutrality and its implications for American policy, Morgenthau took a long-term historical view of neutrality and its relationship to the international system. He divided the history of international law into three periods. The first period began with the collapse of the Holy Alliance and ended with the close of World War I. Morgenthau termed the second period the era of "post-war international law, the 'new' international law of Geneva." The third period started with the collapse of the system of collective security as shown in the demise of the League. During the first period, the legal order was based on the balance of power and neutrality, when the interest of states relied upon temporary modus vivendi of antagonistic political interests. The legal order of collective security, on the other hand, was based upon "the assumption that there exists in international field a permanent harmony of interests." Morgenthau pointed out that the second period had not achieved a complete conversion to collective interest and that former elements of the balance of power and neutrality remained. He cited as an example the powers' unwillingness to impose economic sanctions as well as the several treaties of mutual assistance that coexisted with the League of Nations. He concluded that "a formal and legalistic science of international law" had too long neglected the relationship between the rules of international law and the underlying political and military conditions.[75]

[74] Ibid., 663–664.
[75] Hans J. Morgenthau, 'The Problem of Neutrality,' University of Kansas City Law Review 7 (1939), 109, 117, 122–123, 128. For Morgenthau and international law, see Koskenniemi, Gentle Civilizer, pp. 436–493.

Morgenthau criticized the new, postwar international law for its formalistic nature. He suggested that its devices and schemes would not pass the test of history and charged that the internationalists took "the appropriateness of the devices for granted and [tended] to blame the facts for the failure." In particular, one of the failures of the science of international law was that it had not developed a criterion for distinguishing between "seemingly and actually valid rules of international law." Some of the rules, which the new international law claimed to be legal, were merely "alleged legal rules" or "speculations." He even questioned whether the Covenant of the League of Nations was "valid international law" and argued that the Pact and some new conceptions such as the concepts of aggression and Non-Recognition were based on speculation. In many respects, Morgenthau's views were in agreement with Baty's. In fact, Morgenthau wrote that "[an] excellent contribution to the understanding of this problem is to be found in Baty."[76]

Criticism of the new international law also surfaced at the meetings at the ASIL and the Conference of the Teachers of International Law. Opponents pointed to a lack of reality in the study of international law, and some went so far as to characterize the current scholarship as being nothing more than "wishful thinking." According to these opponents, international law had been destroyed as a science by people who "indulge in wishful thinking" and "teach international law as they wish it to be and not as it is."[77] They admonished such "wishful" scholars to acknowledge the fact that their theories set out "what they wish international law to be in the future." In this critical atmosphere, Wright was also attacked because, according to his critics, he was "expecting too much from international law in the way of improving and strengthening the conditions of international law." These critics argued that establishing concrete organizations to regulate economic activities, such as a world bank, was much more important than coming to agreement on principles.[78] Wright responded that the establishment of a world bank and other such institutions was indeed important, but noted that agreement on general principles would make it easier to negotiate treaties to establish such institutions.[79] Some reformers argued that international lawyers should talk about fundamentals or "general principles" for the very reason that

---

[76] Hans J. Morgenthau, "Positivism, Functionalism and International Law," *AJIL* 34 (1940), 266, footnote 22.
[77] *Proceedings, Seventh Teachers* (1941), 70.
[78] *Proceedings, ASIL* (1941), 48.
[79] *Ibid.*, 50.

it was such a chaotic period for the world. Bessie C. Randolf posited that "the teaching of international law and related subjects is a matter of morals, a matter of conviction, and a matter of determined judgment of what we ought to do."[80]

At the 1941 Conference of the Teachers of International Law, the general direction of the teaching of international law was questioned, and it was suggested that too much emphasis had been placed on international law and not enough on international relations. One participant claimed that by teaching only international law to students, "we are giving them a warped picture of the world. We are giving them a picture of a legal world, when we are living in a political world." He suggested "taking the body of international law and injecting into its blood stream suitable transfusions of the red blood corpuscles of economics, politics, sociology and geography." Most critics suggested paying more attention to other factors in international relations, particularly to the role of power. Edward Mead Earle of Princeton University argued that "during the last twenty years, we must admit that we have underemphasized the role which military force may play in international relations." In addition, he suggested that clear definitions of such terms as "security" and "strategy" were necessary.[81]

Some of the criticisms of the new international law that had been voiced at the meetings were similar to those raised by Baty and Borchard. Baty had decried the lack of positivism in the new international law that had emerged since World War I. Given that the new criticism coincided with the old, it might be prudent to ask whether the new international law had gone too far. It is worth noting, however, that some of the criticisms of the new international law raised by the new generation of international lawyers had in fact been voiced even before World War I. Calls for a more functional approach and for a reevaluation of relationship between law and politics fall into this category. Paul S. Reinsch had discussed the need for a functional approach even before World War I. Fenwick, on the other hand, had claimed that by enlarging the scope of law, it would become possible to include and regulate political activities, which hitherto had been excluded from the subject of legal restraint. For reformers, the fact that international law had begun to deal with issues of war and the use of force was evidence that law was entering into the political field, because issues of war had until then been the exclusive domain of politics. During the previous twenty years, international law had succeeded in enlarging

---

[80] *Proceedings, Seventh Teachers* (1941), 59–60, 73.
[81] *Ibid.*, 69, 70, 41, 58, 61.

the scope of subjects falling under its jurisdiction, but other factors that could not be dealt with in a legal framework had become apparent to a younger generation. The new factors were power, security and military force. This new generation of scholars, notably Morgenthau, argued that law was not omnipotent, but that it had limits, beyond which power and security mattered more.

James Wilford Garner died on December 9, 1938, and Salmon O. Levinson on February 2, 1941. Both had dedicated most of their lives to the effort to regulate war through international law, and both must have died in despair because their efforts had not prevented war from recurring. After Levinson died, Wright continued to correspond with Hull, commenting on and supporting the secretary of state's policies. In a letter dated November 27, 1941, he wrote that he was happy and relieved to discover in a statement Hull had made to the press concerning the ongoing negotiations with Japan that "the fundamental principles of international policy sent to all the governments in July 1937 still represented the position of this government."[82] Wright also noted that under both the Pact and the Nine Power Treaty, Japan had a definite obligation to end its hostilities in China. When violations of these agreements had ceased, the United States would begin negotiations with Japan for a new commercial treaty. Wright appreciated the coherency and continuity of Hull's policies and was convinced that the policy of the United States was legally justifiable.

Two weeks before he wrote this letter to Hull, Wright was composing the foreword to *A Study of War*. The two-volume work, more than 1,500 pages, was hailed as a monumental analysis of war from every possible perspective. It appeared to break new ground in Wright's scholarship because it applied a multidisciplinary approach to legal concerns. Wright was frank in admitting the failure of international law, but he repeated his previous argument that this failure could not be attributed to the law itself, but to the lack of political, sociological and psychological foundations to support it.[83] The book's final chapter, entitled "Toward a Warless World," consisted of three sections: policy of each government, institutional framework, and functional approach such as education and world welfare. In the second section on institutional framework in which Wright put forward his views most strongly, his long-standing hopes for international organization were clearly expressed. He discussed the

---

[82] Wright to Hull, November 27, 1941, Wright Papers, Box 20, Folder 2.
[83] Quincy Wright, *A Study of War* (University of Chicago Press, 1942), vol. 2, p. 938.

reorganization and remolding of the League that he believed would serve as the foundation for the future.[84]

It is true that the new international law had failed in its primary task of preventing war. However, according to the legal reasoning enunciated by reformers like Wright, Germany, Italy and Japan were clearly violators of international law, and therefore steps against them were justified. From the perspectives of the reformers, US assistance to the Allies even before Japan attacked Pearl Harbor constituted a form of collective sanction against law breakers. According to the logic of the reformers, the war launched by the Axis powers and the war waged by the Allies were of a totally different nature. In addition, the Roosevelt administration had made use of the reformers' position when the Lend-Lease Bill was passed, and to that extent their position had received semi-official endorsement.

Nor did the reformers perceive any major faults in their scholarship. It is remarkable that the outbreak of the war in Europe did not shock them as greatly as had the outbreak of World War I, when most of them had felt that the study of international law faced a serious challenge. This time, the reformers concluded that the system itself was appropriate but incomplete. Moreover, Japan and Germany had been denounced for violating the Covenant and the Pact by the League and other countries, and it was easy to identify which countries had challenged the postwar international order and were responsible for the present catastrophe.

Still, just as Wright's generation had challenged the traditional approach to international law – represented by Root and Scott – the next generation had begun to criticize the scholarship of the new international law. The criticism voiced by this new generation bore resemblance to the objections raised by the traditionalists, as can be seen in Morgenthau's commendation of Baty's work. If the new and the old criticism identified the same weaknesses in the new international law, did this mean that the traditional international law was more appropriate? Had the reformers, Wright, Garner, Fenwick and others, who strove to achieve a peaceful international order accomplished nothing durable and tangible? Should their efforts be regarded as little more than an aberration of the interwar period? To answer these questions, we must further explore and examine the outcome of World War II – post-World War II international order, and lawyers' role in its formation.

---

[84] *Ibid.*, pp. 1326–1352.

7

Reconstructing the world order once again

On Sunday, December 7, 1941 Quincy Wright, Clyde Eagleton, Charles G. Fenwick and Clark Eichelberger were in New York City. They were working together on the drafting committee of the Commission to Study the Organization of Peace (hereafter CSOP). At around noon, Margaret Olson, secretary for the meeting, went to her apartment for her lunch break. It was there that she heard radio news of a Japanese attack on Pearl Harbor. Olson immediately phoned the office to inform her colleagues. In shock and dismay, Wright, Eagleton and Eichelberger hurried to the latter's apartment – only a few blocks away – to confirm the news. Fenwick, having returned the day before from a meeting with Secretary of State Cordell Hull in Washington, did not believe the news and decided to continue his work in the office. After the others telephoned Fenwick to corroborate the news, he finally joined them.[1] Following the shock of the Pearl Harbor attack, they would redouble their efforts to reconstruct world order throughout the war years.

Debates over the postwar international organization

The CSOP, a group that aimed to examine and spread public awareness about the problems of postwar international organization, was established in November 1939, shortly after the outbreak of war in Europe. It was one of the most active groups involved in such studies.[2]

Wright and Eagleton in particular were original founding members of the CSOP, and they frequently exchanged opinions regarding

---

[1] Clark M. Eichelberger, *Organizing for Peace: A Personal History of the Founding of the United Nations* (New York: Harper & Row, 1977), p. 186.

[2] Other active groups were: the Council of Foreign Relations, the American Association for the United Nations, the Federal Council of Churches of Christ in America, Americans United for World Organization, and the Foreign Policy Association. See Ruth B. Russell, *A History of the United Nations Charter: The Role of the United States, 1940–1945* (Washington, DC: The Brookings Institute, 1958), p. 215, footnote 9.

various matters on the Commission. During its formative stage, Wright suggested who should be recruited and invited to join. His recommendations included figures such as John F. Dulles and Allen Dulles, Manley O. Hudson, Sarah Wambaugh, Arnold Wolfers, Phillip Jessup and Thomas Lamont.[3] Eagleton, on his part, suggested to Wright that the aims of the CSOP should include a greater focus on the United States' general responsibility in world affairs. He wrote to Wright that he did not want to be "too precise in stating the details of organization" because the primary importance was to win over the American people to acceptance of responsibility.[4]

In December 1939, Wright received an assignment from the CSOP to study political international organization. At the start of his research, Wright sent out preliminary questionnaires to his colleagues and asked for their critical opinions. For instance, he asked, "Is a general political international organization desirable and if so should it be a stronger or a weaker organization than the existing League of Nations?" To this, Hudson replied, "Certainly such an organization is desirable, and it should be stronger than the League of Nations." Another question was whether international organization should be universal, regional or "confined to democratic states." Hudson's reply stated that there was a need for a "universal organization," but noted that "some regional organization is not inconsistent with universal organization." Including only democratic states was "a red herring," Hudson answered, because such states would be difficult to define. With regard to the need for sanction, Hudson wrote, "I don't lay very much stress on sanction." Other issues Wright inquired about in this letter were a design for the organization's structure, whether the organization should guarantee individual rights, and so on.[5]

Based on the replies from Hudson and other members, Wright prepared a memorandum on international political organization for the CSOP. After a discussion held on March 17 in New York and further exchanges opinions over the issue, Wright presented a revised version.[6] James Shotwell commended Wright's revised draft, writing in April 1940

[3] Wright to Eagleton, December 8, 1939, Wright Papers, Box 5, Folder 11. For the CSOP, see also Glenn Tastuya Mitoma, "Civil Society and International Human Rights: The Commission to Study the Organization of Peace and the Origins of the UN Human Rights," *Human Rights Quarterly* 30 (2008), 607–630; Hillmann, "Quincy Wright and the Commission," 485–499; Bucklin, "Quincy Wright's Blueprint," 227–240.
[4] Eagleton to Wright, December 19, 1939, Wright Papers, Box 5, Folder 11.
[5] Hudson to Wright, December 18, 1939, Hudson Papers, Box 100, Folder 9.
[6] Wright to Eagleton, March 25, 1940, Wright Papers, Box 5, Folder 12.

that "we are all indebted deeply to you for the labor and thought you have put into it."[7]

Five days after Pearl Harbor, Eagleton sent the members of the CSOP a memorandum recommending that it further step up to work on plans for postwar international organization. Given the experience of failing to join the League, the CSOP above all realized the need to educate the American public and set up local chapters for that purpose. Wright was chairman of the Chicago chapter, where he organized a series of public lectures.[8]

Eagleton did not miss the opportunity to address the aim of the CSOP to the readers of the *AJIL*. In a regular article – "Organization of the Community of States" – he stressed the role of international lawyers under the changing conditions of the world. A scholar of international law must use his expert knowledge to explain to the people and persuade statesmen that "the choice before them now is a world organized by force by some strong man or group, and a world organized by agreement of the community of nations to bring war under force." He then detailed the Preliminary Report of the CSOP.[9]

Wright, who had had strong faith in postwar international organization and US participation in it, devoted his efforts to enlightening the public. In the journal *Free World*, he argued that the balance of power system would simply not work according to his observations of contemporary developments. To catch up with new trends and make postwar peace durable, he proposed four points on a prospective organization. Firstly, he maintained that "the world organization must rest on a world public opinion, and not merely upon the contracts of government," a view that reflected his strong belief that institutions without public support would neither be effective nor durable. Secondly, the world organization needed to be universal. Thirdly, the world organization must have a central agency controlling the military force of national governments and possess its own international military force. Finally, postwar world order should include several institutions that would be operated through a functional approach, by which he meant that different international bodies would respectively deal with economic problems, political problems and human rights issues.[10]

---

[7] Shotwell to Wright, April 1, 1940, Wright Papers, Box 5, Folder 12.
[8] Robert A. Divine, *Second Chance: The Triumph of Internationalism in America during World War II* (New York: Atheneum, 1967), pp. 53–55.
[9] Clyde Eagleton, "Organization of the Community of Nations," *AJIL* 36 (1942), 230–241.
[10] Quincy Wright, "Responsibilities of the United States in the Post-War World," *Free World* 5 (1943), 35–48.

Wright argued that it is important for the general public to develop a sense of world citizenship. Significantly, this proposition was connected with his other important argument – that human rights should be guaranteed by international society and individuals' responsibility for committing serious crimes against humanity should be tried by international society. Wright had already proposed at one meeting of the CSOP in 1940 that postwar international relations should deal with the protection of human rights. In 1943 the CSOP published a pamphlet entitled *Human Rights and the World Order* authored by Wright.[11]

It is significant to note that Wright's pamphlet was mentioned and discussed in a 1943 State Department document on human rights, explicitly stating that "extended treatment of the subject is to be found in a paper, entitled 'Human Rights and the World Order' presented to the Commission [CSOP] by Quincy Wright." The governmental document summarized Wright's concrete proposal to enhance human rights, and quoted his conclusion to a considerable length.[12]

Another interesting aspect of Wright's views concerning an international organization was that it should be equipped with more forcible measures – namely an "international police force." In his November 13, 1943 memorandum, he pointed out the possible conditions, difficulties and effects of such a force. Since international policing should be imposed upon the aggressor, Wright argued, such a mechanism implied the existing rules of international law clearly stated that aggression by any government would be illegal. Then, such force should consist of "the most mobile type or armament," namely an air force. If the force composed of volunteers from many nations was located on islands of strategic importance under the jurisdiction of the international authority, it would serve as "a powerful deterrent" against a would-be aggressor, he concluded.[13]

In another memorandum, "The International Organization of Security and Welfare" dated January 27, 1944, Wright argued that an international organization should perform security as well as welfare functions. He wrote that while security organization must be universal, coercive,

---

[11] Mitoma, "Civil Society," 614–615.
[12] "Permanent International Organization, Functions, Powers, Machinery, and Procedure, Promotion of Observance of Basic Human Rights," July 23, 1943, Papers of Leo Pasvolsky (hereafter Pasvolsky Papers), Library of Congress, Washington, DC, Box 4, Folder 8.
[13] Wright, "International Police Force," November 13, 1943, unpublished memorandum, Wright Papers, Addenda I, Box 54, Folder 8.

centralized and negative at this stage, welfare organization must be limited, voluntary, decentralized and positive.[14]

In the meantime, Eagleton, Eichelberger and Wright – active members of the CSOP from the outset – all came to assume wartime positions at the State Department. Eichelberger became a consultant from August 6, 1942. Eagleton, too, assumed the position of consultant from October 12, 1943, then became regular officer from December 16, 1943. And finally, Wright also served as consultant during August 1944.[15] According to one official record, Eagleton and Wright "participated in a single meeting or series of meetings on problems in their field" in 1944.[16] Eagleton – a "shy and retiring" man – "moved out of his libraries to promote his beliefs" and eventually became assistant secretary at the Dumbarton Oaks Conference and an official delegate to the San Francisco Conference.[17] At the Dumbarton Oaks Conference he regularly attended the meetings for American delegates, and thereafter he was engaged in "off the record discussion" on the official proposal with various interested groups elsewhere in the United States.[18] Eagleton had taught classes on the subject of international organization since he first proposed it at the Second Conference of Teachers of International Law and Related Subjects in 1925.[19] His wartime position was the natural culmination of his lifelong faith in and commitment to international organization.

The same could be said for Wright, whose influence and imprint on policy was considerable. Wright's former students were an acknowledged presence in wartime Washington. They formed "the Q club in Washington – the Q standing for his first name," one of his students later recalled.[20] Wright, on his part, spent the summer of 1944 in Washington as consultant to the State Department.

After returning to Chicago, Wright maintained a correspondence with Leo Pasvolsky, a special aide at the Department who was in charge of the

---

[14] Wright, "The International Organization of Security and Welfare," January 27, 1944, unpublished memorandum, Wright Papers, Addenda I, Box 54, Folder 8.

[15] Department of State, *Postwar Foreign Policy Preparation, 1939–1945* (Washington, DC: GPO, 1949), Appendix 22, "The Research Staff (February 3, 1941-January 14, 1944)," pp. 518, 523; Appendix 32, "The Research Staff, (January 15 1944-April 24, 1945)," p. 568.

[16] *Ibid.*, p. 249.

[17] Richard N. Swift, "Clyde Eagleton," in Warren F. Kuehl, ed., *Biographical Dictionary of Internationalists* (Westport: Greenwood Press, 1983), p. 231.

[18] Division of Public Liaison, "Policy Interpretation and Group Relations," November 1944, Box 4, Folder 19, Papers of Green H. Hackworth (hereafter Hackworth Papers), Library of Congress, Washington, DC.

[19] Clyde Eagleton, *International Government* (New York: Royal Press, 1948), p. v.

[20] *New York Times*, October 18, 1972.

planning of postwar international organization.[21] In one letter, Wright noted that Pasvolsky "hoped I might maintain a similar relationship with the Department of State."[22] In November 1944, Wright wrote to Pasvolsky, expressing his thoughts on the Dumbarton Oaks Proposals. "In general, I think the Proposals," he wrote, "are excellent and a real advance on the League of Nations, especially in emphasizing the corporate character of the Organization and its capacity to act effectively in the maintenance of international peace and security." However, Wright expressed certain reservations on the dominance of great powers, stating that it seemed "smaller states are likely to insist upon such clarification in order to assure themselves that they would not be the victims of arbitrary action by the great powers."[23]

Furthermore, in a detailed eight-page memorandum on the Dumbarton Oaks Proposals, Wright laid out important points with his usual insights and analysis. He suggested that membership should not be confined to "peace loving" states. Instead, enemy states might be denied the "privileges" of the organization until they have established governments generally recognized as peace-loving. He also thought it was undesirable to have special agreements, "whereby one state agreed to make available contingents for the defense of another if attacked, but not in all cases of aggression."[24]

Wright's correspondence with Pasvolsky continued into the winter of 1945. Of particular significance is one letter containing Wright's analysis of a memorandum on "Military Advice for the Security Council."[25] In it he argued it was not feasible or realistic to expect the Military Staff Committee – "composed of the Chiefs of Staff of the permanent members" – to work out military policy for the international organization. The experience of the League of Nations clearly showed the difficulty of attaining cooperation from national militaries, which put primary emphasis on their own national policy, not worldwide considerations. Hence, it was "utopian" to suppose that wartime cooperation would be continued by the militaries of member states permanently on the Security Council after the

[21] For Pasvolsky, see Stephen C. Schlesinger, *Act of Creation: The Founding of the United Nations* (Boulder: Westview Press, 2003), pp. 33–51.

[22] Wright to Pasvolsky, September 14, 1944, Wright Papers, Box 13, Folder 19.

[23] Wright to Leo Pasvolsky, November 9, 1944, Wright Papers, Addenda I, Box 54, Folder 2.

[24] Quincy Wright, "The Dambarton Oaks Proposals," undated memoranda, Wright Papers, Addenda I, Box 53, Folder 2.

[25] Wright to Pasvolsky, February 23, 1945, Wright Papers, Addenda I, Box 54, Folder 11.

war, for the Allies during the war can "forget their rivalry and exchange plans and information to defeat the common enemy," but this could not be expected in peacetime.[26] Instead, he suggested the establishment of a military policy committee distinct from the Military Staff Committee. In the end his suggestion was not to be adopted by policy makers, and the UN Charter followed the original idea of Military Staff Committee. Yet, as later history unfolded, Articles 45, 46 and 47 of the UN Charter were doomed to fail.

Meanwhile, Fenwick was involved with the activities of the Inter-American Juridical Committee, established by the Third Meeting of Foreign Ministers at Rio de Janeiro in January 1942. He conveyed the Committee's critical opinion of the Dumbarton Oaks Proposals to high officials in Washington. Officials took Fenwick's viewpoints seriously because they feared that he had unofficial but important channels with Latin American countries concerning the future international organization. His criticism was mainly based on the points that the proposal did not support the principle of equality of states, that it included no Latin American representation at the Security Council, and that it did not pay due respect to the Inter-American system.[27] State Department officials instructed Pasvolsky and Green Hackworth, legal advisor of the State Department, to pay attention to Fenwick's opinion and drafted a memorandum in preparation for a possible talk with him.[28]

During the same period, Hudson's leadership in organizing and presenting American and Canadian views on the future course of international order was clearly manifested and also drew official interest.[29] As early as 1942, a number of Americans and Canadians began to consider the possibility of presenting "a community of views with reference to the steps which might be taken at the end of the war to increase the usefulness of international law." Starting at a meeting in Washington on April 24, 1942, these scholars held more than twenty meetings in Washington,

---

[26] Quincy Wright, "Military Advice for the Security Council," February 7, 1945, Wright Papers, Addenda I, Box 54, Folder 11.

[27] Charles G. Fenwick, "Reactions of Certain of the American Republics to the Dumbarton Oaks Proposal," January 17, 1945, Pasvolsky Papers, Box 2, Folder 9.

[28] "Dr. Fenwick and the Inter-American Juridical Committee," January 2, 1945; John C. Dreier to Hackworth, January 2, 1945; Hackworth to Dreier, January 2, 1945, Hackworth Papers, Box 6, Folder 1. See also Dreier to Pasvolsky, January 19, 1945, Pasvolsky Papers, Box 2, Folder 9.

[29] For instance, Hudson's name was underlined by a red pencil in an official memorandum when the International Law of Future was mentioned. See "Permanent International Organization," July 24, 1943, p. 38, Pasvolsky Papers, Box 4 Folder 7.

DC, New York, Boston, Chicago, Philadelphia, Montreal, Ottawa, Los Angeles, San Francisco and Denver. At those meetings, first, second and third drafts were respectively circulated, discussed and revised. Finally, on January 1, 1944, "The International Law of the Future," was proposed. Participants included not only scholars of international law, but also professors of political science, judges and government officials. All the reformers participated in it, while traditionalists such as Edwin M. Borchard and John Bassett Moore were absent. Other notable names among its participants were Robert H. Jackson (Justice of the United States Supreme Court) and John Foster Dulles (Member of *Sullivan & Cromwell*).[30]

The text of their proposal was published in the *AJIL*, the *American Bar Association Journal,* the *Canadian Bar Review* and *International Conciliation*. French, Spanish and Portuguese translations were also published.

Hudson, the leader of the project, not only contributed an article about the project to the *AJIL*, but also delivered a speech on it at the annual meeting of the ASIL in April 1944.[31] Hudson maintained in his article that "the central conception is that of a Community of States, for which effective organization is required. International Law is the law of this Community of States."[32] Specifically, the statement proposed the establishment of a "General Assembly," "a smaller body of [the] Executive Council" and the General Secretariat, in addition to the continuation of the PCIJ, and the International Labor Organization. Thus, the design generally followed the example of the League of Nations. Furthermore, he proposed to have more enforceable measures to "proscribe the use of force" since "it must be realized that a mere pronouncement is not enough."[33] Hudson concluded that "the statement merits careful consideration by those who will be the architects of the 'general international organization' fostered by the Moscow Declaration of October 30, 1943."[34]

This group extended its activity, and after a further series of fifteen conferences over a period of several months issued a document entitled "Design for a Charter of the General International Organization"

---

[30] "The International Law of the Future," *Supplement, AJIL* 38 (1944), 41–135.
[31] Manley O. Hudson, "The International Law of the Future," *Proceedings, ASIL* (1944), 9–19; Hudson, "The International Law of the Future," *AJIL* 38 (1944), 278–281.
[32] Hudson, "The International Law of the Future," *AJIL*, 278–281.
[33] "The International Law of the Future," 108.
[34] Hudson, "The International Law of the Future," *AJIL*, 278–281.

on August 1, 1944. Again, Hudson took the initiative, and Wright, Eichelberger, Shotwell and Jessup – international lawyers who were active supporters of the League – participated in this project as well.[35] Its basic structure included an Assembly, Council and a permanent Security Committee of the Council.

These two initiatives by Hudson were highly regarded among policy makers.[36] Around the time Hudson's second initiative was being published, an official document, "United States Tentative Proposals for a General International Organization, July 18, 1944" [Tentative Proposal] was under final review. In mid-July, before Hudson's Design was officially published, the State Department compared its official "Tentative Proposals" with the League Covenant as well as other "significant" unofficial proposals, which examined only three plans – "The International Law of the Future," "Draft Pact for the Future International Authority" by Lord Cecil and "A Design for a Charter of the General International Organization." Two of the three unofficial proposals were produced under Hudson's leadership. This official memorandum, in fact, referred to the "The International Law of the Future" as "Hudson's Draft." The memorandum – in total fifty pages long – compared the official Tentative Proposal with the League Covenant and the three private plans, commenting on them in detail.[37]

While both the CSOP and Hudson's initiative were projects that the main figures of this book actively participated in, it is impossible to determine the definite author for various concepts that were adopted in the final form of the UN Charter, as plans had to go through complex processes of negotiation and revision. However, suffice to say that during the planning stages, their views and presence were not completely unrecognizable, as indicated by frequent references to and attention given to them by State Department officials.[38]

---

[35] Manley O. Hudson, "A Design for a Charter of the General International Organization," *AJIL* 38 (1944), 711–714. "Design for a Charter of the General International Organization (GIO)," *AJIL, Supplement* 38 (1944), 216–223.

[36] "The International Law of Future" was covered with more length than other plans presented by the CSOP, Friends Conference on Peace and Reconstruction, and the World Federation. See "Permanent International Organization, Functions, Powers, Machinery, Procedure, I Political Settlement of International Disputes," n.d., Pasvolsky Papers, Box 4, Folder 7.

[37] "Comparison of the Tentative Proposal for a General International Organization with the League of Nations and Significant Unofficial Proposals," July 15, 1944, Pasvolsky Papers, Box 4, Folder 8.

[38] See "Permanent International Organization, Functions, Powers, Machinery and Procedure," July 27, 1943, Pasvolsky Papers, Box 4, Folder 8; "International Organization:

On the other side of the Atlantic, American jurists' work, to a degree, inspired their counterparts in Britain. As Hersch Lauterpacht wrote to his son, "last year the American international lawyers appointed an enormous Committee (including your friend Judge Hudson) to draft projects of post-war international organization. They held various meetings in distant parts of the USA and eventually produced an elaborate report which they sent here to the British international lawyers."[39] However, as he wrote later, the British meeting was "annoying" because scholars were "very realistic" and only produced proposals that the government would accept.[40] In the end, British lawyers did not reach any agreement on a future international organization that was as concrete as Hudson's plans.

In the meantime, some academic gatherings resumed in the UK. The conference of the Grotius Society was held on April 29–30, 1944, at Burlington House in London under the presidency of Sir Cecil Hurst, with 134 jurists in attendance. Arnold McNair discussed "the method whereby international law is made to prevail in municipal courts." V. R. Idelson and Latuterpacht held a discussion on "The Law of Nations and the Individual," which maintained that while only the state was the subject of international law twenty-five years ago, documents such as the Atlantic Charter opened the way to address this issue. In addition, "The Organization and Functions of the Future of International Authority" was presented by C. J. Colombos, Honorary Secretary of the Society. It was recorded that Professor Goodhart of Oxford University pointed out the importance of "a just peace, the general strengthening international bonds and the enforcement of peace by the peace loving Powers." However, some expressed concerns about the great powers' dominance in a future international organization while another noted that "the judicature be elevated to its proper place. 'Put the judge first; a policeman has only to support the judge.'"[41]

Thus, legal scholars – whether they were members of the ASIL or those who gathered at the meetings in London – were mostly supportive of

Comments and Developments, December 6–8, 1944," Hackworth Papers, Box 4, Folder 14; "Dumbarton Oaks Proposals: Current Developments and Comments," December 11, 1944, Hackworth Papers, Box 4, Folder 14.

[39] HL to EL, November 23, 1943, Elihu Lauterpacht, *The Life of Hersch Lauterpacht* (Cambridge University Press, 2010), pp. 238–239.

[40] HL to EL, April 6, 1944, Lauterpacht, *The Life of Hersch Lauterpacht*, p. 246.

[41] Roman K. Kuratowski, "International Law Conference of the Grotius Society," *AJIL* 38 (1944), 474–475.

general direction in establishing a postwar international organization. Hudson noted that:

> the only alternative to Dumbarton Oaks would seem to be nothing in the way of general international organization, and that alternative is as *impossible for those interested in international law* as it is for all who would seek to do everything that can be done in our time which may help to prevent another world war [italics added].[42]

Contrary to Hudson's statement about the impossibility of opposition, Borchard took a public stand as a scholar of international law that disagreed with the trend. He argued that it was erroneous to assume that international law could be advanced by strengthening enforcement like municipal law, because its units – sovereign nations – were totally and fundamentally different from individuals. He then questioned the intellectual fallacy of international community, which in fact was the embodiment of great power control. In addition, Borchard warned others to "stop chasing the presently unachievable rainbow of collective security."[43]

Borchard's critical attitude remained and even grew stronger after the Dumbarton Oaks Proposals were officially promulgated. Particularly, he paid attention to the dominance of the great powers. The Big Five "can never be declared an aggressor" in the Proposal, which would prove to be "a stultifying reservation," because it would place them "above law and subject." Furthermore, China and France could not send their troops abroad, and Russia and Britain usually would not act outside of their sphere of influence, thus, "the brunt of burden will fall on the United States." Worse still, he observed that "the United Nations are very loosely united, a coalition for war purposes only."[44]

The fact that the ASIL allowed Borchard to publicize his critical view indicated that the Society and its journal provided a precious space for the exchange of diverse views, yet his stand appeared to be an isolated one. This time, no support came from John Basett Moore. Despite Borchard's harsh comments, steady progress was made towards the establishment of the UN, overcoming difficulties among the powers. A conference was convened in San Francisco in April 1945 to finalize and agree on the Charter of the United Nations. Forty-three members of the CSOP

---

[42] Manley O. Hudson, "An Approach to the Dumbarton Oaks Proposals," *AJIL* 39 (1945), 95–97.
[43] Edwin M. Borchard, "Flaws in Post-War Peace Plans," *AJIL* 38 (1944), 284–289.
[44] Edwin M. Borchard, "The Dumbarton Oaks Conference," *AJIL* 39 (1945), 97–101.

including Eichelberger, and Eagleton – now a member of the official US delegation – travelled to the city.[45]

War of aggression as crime

Wright's interest in trying state leaders for responsibility in initiating war dated back to even the immediate post-World War I period. In the February 1919 issue of the *American Political Science Review* he contributed an article on the subject. It presented a three-tiered legal system that should be respectively applied to define war crimes: municipal law, law of war, and international law. Typically, Wright not only mentioned law of war but also international law as an applicable body of law, implying that there existed a type of legal liability different from the violation of law of war. However, he specified neither the definition of international law, nor any particular treaty or conventions. Referring to Grotius' thought that a king who undertook a war "cannot be accused with any injury done to his enemies," he argued that the view was still accepted, "however incompatible with the solidarity hoped for in a league of nations." As a concrete example of a breach of faith by a state that was recognized as an offense against international law, he suggested the case of Napoleon's imprisonment at St. Helena. However, he frankly admitted that for Napoleon's case "consideration of legal responsibility cannot be separated from those of political consequences."[46]

Among regular contributors to the *AJIL*, managing editor George Finch touched off on the issue of war crimes, contributing an editorial comment on "Retribution for War Crimes" in January 1943. Finch also indicated the case of Napoleon as a precedent of trying state leaders.[47]

The 1943 annual meeting of the ASIL devoted one whole session to the topic of war criminals. Charles Cheney Hyde of Columbia University detailed the practical difficulties associated with actual procedures at military tribunals. Specifically, he pointed out difficulties in obtaining evidence, calling witnesses, determining who should serve as a judge – the Allied persons or neutrals, and the location of the tribunals – in Allied countries, enemy countries or neutral countries. He suggested that the President call a conference to examine these problems.[48]

---

[45] Mitoma, "Civil Society," 625.
[46] Quincy Wright, "The Legal Liability of the Kaiser," *American Political Science Review* 13 (1919), 120–128.
[47] George A. Finch, "Retribution for War Crimes," *AJIL* 37 (1943), 81–88.
[48] Charles Cheney Hyde, "Punishment of War Criminals," *Proceedings, ASIL* (1943), 39–46.

The following speaker, Edwin D. Dickinson of the US Department of Justice, also mentioned the issue of what bodies or courts should try war criminals. More fundamental, however, was the question of which law should be applied. To this he proposed that "we shall be a little conservative," by which he meant that trials should limit war crimes only to cases when violation of the law of war was clear and the evidence supporting its violation was sufficient. His presentation touched upon the problem of "retroactivity," warning that "we shall be accused of imposing *ex post facto* penalties." In general, he based most of his argument on the laws of war, and was cautious of putting Axis individuals on trial.[49]

Yet, in following discussions Charles Warren remarked, "I must regret that I must differ from almost everything that has been said by the two preceding speakers." He presented his view that the Allies should go beyond ordinary and customary procedures because Axis officials not only violated "the Hague Convention but the laws of humanity." Also, "the right to punish is not a right conferred upon victorious belligerents by international law, but it flows from the fact of victory." As the basis for his argument, Warren referred to James W. Garner's 1925 work, *Recent Developments in International Law*, which argued that it was a matter of policy and expediency to try state leaders who initiated war. Warren, too, mentioned the precedent of Napoleon, when England, Austria, Prussia and Russia agreed to try him as their common prisoner.[50]

Finch also supported Warren's position, saying that "the punishment of Hitler, Mussolini, Tojo" should be "purely a political matter." Wright agreed with Warren on the point that the trial could not escape from its political nature, but he was a little more cautious. Specifically, Wright proposed three conditions: firstly, a trial should be based on the principles of civilized justice; secondly, it should prevent the arousal of a sense of reprisal from the enemy nations; and finally it should separate the masses of the enemy population from their leaders. In addition, he argued that if the Allied forces had violated the laws of war, which he hoped was not the case, the trial should apply to all the armies. Typically and symbolically Wright referred to the Pact of Paris, arguing that since the Axis had violated it and other treaties, "the offense should be described as one against the community of nations as a whole."[51]

Wright's interest in war crime was rekindled, and he wrote in May 1943 that Warren's plan "that the treatment accorded Napoleon be followed

[49] Edwin D. Dickinson, "Discussion," *Proceedings, ASIL* (1943), 46–50.
[50] *Ibid.*, 51–53.   [51] *Ibid.*, 55–57.

as a precedent in treating war criminals" seemed to have "much merit as a means of dealing with five or six of the Nazi and Fascist leaders."[52] In September, he wrote to Raymond L. Buell that war crimes trials "could make an important contribution to the establishment of individual responsibility for compliance under international law." Wright believed that such trials could have a positive effect on the future development of international law. Another concern for Wright was the possibility that the Allies might be tried. He pointed out the difficulty of solely relying on the laws of war. If the laws of war were to be applied to both sides of belligerents, the Allies would not be exempted from charges. However, if the war was regarded as "a criminal revolt against the community of nations, in violation of treaties, including Pact of Paris" this problem could be evaded.[53] Thus, at this point in 1943 Wright was proposing the possibility of deducing legal foundation from the Pact for treating aggressive war as a crime.

Meanwhile, war crime was emerging as a topic of interest among scholars in Europe, where a few unofficial bodies began to discuss the issue. Members of the Faculty of Law of Cambridge University, and scholars and officials from occupied countries of Europe – Belgium, Czechoslovakia, France, Greece, Luxembourg, the Netherlands, Norway, Poland and Yugoslavia – called a conference in November 1941. This conference set up a committee to discuss the rules and procedure over "Crimes against International Public Order." In May and June 1942 this committee submitted its opinion on the definition of war crimes, focusing mainly on offenses against the laws of war. Its interim conclusion was that the jurisdiction of war crimes committed against the laws of war mainly falls to municipal courts, although the possibility of setting up an international court was not totally rejected. The overall contribution of this body was "the creation in official and semi-official circles of an atmosphere favorable to the conception of punishment of war criminals."[54]

Lauterpacht, who was the member of the Cambridge Commission, contributed an article to the 1944 *British Year Book of International Law*. The article was based on a memorandum submitted in July 1942 to the Commission on Crimes against International Public Order

---

[52] Wright to Oscar Cox, May 18, 1943, Wright Papers, Addenda I, Box 58, Folder 2.
[53] Wright to Raymond L. Buell, September 8, 1943, Wright Papers, Addenda I, Box 58, Folder 2.
[54] The United Nations War Crimes Commission, *History of the United Nations War Crimes Commission and the Development of the Laws of War* (London: His Majesty's Stationery Office, 1948), pp. 94–99.

chaired by Arnold D. McNair.[55] In this article, Lauterpacht argued that the punishment of war crimes was "a problem of politics rather than of law." However, he argued that scholars of international law should bear in mind that "war crimes are crimes against international law." He then pointed out difficulties, stating that it was "legally inadmissible to punish the state, the corporate entity of the State," and that "punishment upon individuals" was questionable. Furthermore, he stressed that the judicial process should be "fair and impartial." Overall, his argument was mostly limited to the law of war, and did not pay special attention to the new concept of crime derived from the Kellogg Pact.[56]

Another notable unofficial activity was carried out by the London International Assembly, which had been established under the auspices of the League of Nations Union and was headed by Viscount Cecil. Although it was not an official organ, its members were sent by the exiled Allied governments in London, thus facilitating discussions between scholars and officials. Its original purpose was to make recommendations to the Allied governments on various maters, but as the time went on the question of war crime emerged as its major concern. Under the London International Assembly, the Commission on War Crime was set up in March 1942, eventually holding a total of about thirty meetings and producing a report. Delegates to this Commission engaged in active discussion on whether aggressive war could be claimed as international crime. The most notable presentation was that of Bohuslav Ečer, a representative from Czechoslovakia who supported the notion of crime of aggressive war after examining the Pact and the unratified Geneva Protocol.[57]

With groundwork laid by the above-mentioned unofficial activities, the Allied nations finally agreed upon setting up an official body to discuss the issue of war crime, and the United Nations War Crime Commission (UNWCC) was established on October 20, 1943. Starting its official activities on January 11, 1944, Australia, Belgium, Canada, China, Czechoslovakia, France, Greece, India, Luxemburg, the Netherlands, New Zealand, Norway, Poland, South Africa, the UK, the United States and Yugoslavia participated in the Commission. Certain members who had participated in unofficial discussions held at the Cambridge Commission as well as the London International Assembly became official delegates

---

[55] Hersch Lauterpacht, "The Law of Nations and the Punishment of War Crimes," *British Year Book of International Law* 21 (1944), 58, footnote 1.

[56] *Ibid.*, 58–96.

[57] *History of the United Nations War Crimes Commission*, pp. 99–101.

to the UNWCC, namely M. de Baer (Belgium), B. Ečer (Czechoslovakia) and M. Colban (Norway).

The UNWCC assigned its legal committee to work on the notion of aggressive war as international crime. The resulting majority report was prepared and submitted by McNair, who was a technical expert. The Report observed that "acts committed by individuals merely for the purpose of preparing for and launching aggressive war, are *lege lata,* not 'war crimes.'" At the same time, it also pointed out that aggressive war should one day be declared a criminal act, even though it was not yet a firmly established notion in positive international law. In contrast, the minority report submitted by the Czech delegate, Ečer, reaffirmed the point he delivered at the London International Assembly and stressed the viewpoint that the Geneva Protocol and the Kellogg Pact made it possible to define aggressive war as an international crime. In the subsequent meetings in October 1944, both reports were considered. The minority report was supported by the delegates of Australia, China, New Zealand, Poland and Yugoslavia, while the delegates of France, Greece and the United States supported the majority report.[58]

Significantly, one of the supporters of the minority report was Lord Wright, the Australian representative and future chairman of the UNWCC. He favored the Czech view, but the fundamental reasoning for his position lay in the argument that international law, much like common law, was progressive. The comparison between international law and common law was another important argument in formulating the notion of aggressive war as a crime.[59]

In Washington, US officials were closely following the UNWCC's discussions in London and began to reconsider their views on the criminality of aggressive war.[60] Due to the political weakness of the State Department, the initiative on this matter fell into the hands of the War Department, headed by Henry L. Stimson.[61] In the beginning Stimson was rather skeptical of aggressive war as a crime against peace, largely because he thought it would go beyond international thought of the day. However, Stimson eventually emerged as one of its advocates, and his support would later determine the fate of the notion.

[58] *Ibid.,* pp. 180–183; Onuma, *Senso Sekinin-ron,* p. 218.
[59] *History of the United Nations War Crimes Commission,* p. 183.
[60] Bradley F. Smith, *The Road to Nuremberg* (New York: Basic Books, 1981), p. 91.
[61] Harvey Strum, "Henry Stimson and the Nuremberg War Crimes Trial," *Mid-America* 65 (1983), 3–13.

In late November 1944, William Chanler, deputy director of the Civil Affairs Branch in the War Department and a close friend of Stimson's, submitted a memorandum entitled "Can Hitler and the Nazi Leadership be Punished for their Acts of Lawless Aggression, thus Implementing the Kellogg Pact and Outlawing War of Aggression?" He proposed that the Pact of 1928 be used to establish the legal foundations for the claim of aggressive war as a crime.[62]

However, in the War Department Chanler's position did not immediately prevail because it was regarded as a radical change in legal thinking.[63] The debate continued within the Department over whether aggressive war could be claimed as a crime in international law, mainly on the basis of the Pact. On December 18, Alwyn Vernon Freeman, a legal aide in the Department, presented a memorandum that rejected the idea. Freeman's memorandum noted that "volumes have been written about the meaning of two articles and the preambles [of the Pact]." Freeman cited Wright's and Hans Wehberg's treatises in his footnotes as representative scholars who weighed progressive interpretation on the Pact, while he mentioned the name of Borchard, as a representative of the skeptical view. After examining both arguments, he concluded that violations of the Pact did not mean that aggressive war was made a crime, and that "it is the only conclusion compatible with existing principles of positive international law." Thus, he concluded that "the position taken by the majority of the sub-committee appointed by the United Nations War Crimes Commission is believed to be legally correct."[64] From this memorandum, we can observe how scholars' opinions and views from preceding years were a significant influence on wartime policy making. When officials in Washington were discussing war crimes, they inevitably turned to such scholarly studies.

These counterarguments did not discourage Chanler, who continued to write further memoranda to his superiors. Here, too, he recognized the fact that although legal scholars such as Wright and Eagleton supported the Budapest Articles of Interpretations resolved at the International Law Association in 1934, other scholars such as Jessup, Borchard and Hyde held the opposite position. As the historian Bradley F. Smith claimed, by referring to reform-minded scholars as the basis for his viewpoint, Chanler

---

[62] Bradley F. Smith, *The American Road to Nuremberg: The Documentary Record, 1944–1945* (Stanford University Press, 1982), pp. 68–74; Onuma, *Senso Sekinin-ron*, pp. 251–276.

[63] Smith, *Road to Nuremberg*, pp. 99–100.

[64] Smith, *Documentary Record*, pp. 81–82.

naturally came to support the cause of legal innovation that progressive scholars had been advocating for the preceding two decades.[65] Those in the War Department who sought to draw legal implications for aggressive war as a crime from the Pact inevitably recognized scholarly debates on the Pact during the interwar period, and came to endorse the reformers' view.

Chanler eventually prevailed and won Stimson's endorsement of the charge of aggressive war as a crime. His commitment and support was critical in formulating the concept of crimes against peace as an official notion to be tried by the Allies. It is true that the notion of war as a crime did not originate from Stimson, but as this book has argued, Stimson played a key role in advancing progressive interpretation of the Pact by delivering speeches in support of it following his Non-Recognition Doctrine.[66] For him, it was neither a deviation nor a change from his original position.

Wright's works were often referred to by officials in Washington when they needed an authoritative legal source on progressive interpretations of the Pact, but he was not directly involved in the governmental process of formulating the notion of aggressive war as a crime. Instead, Wright promoted his views through journal articles. In an April 1945 *AJIL* article, he presented his position on which law can and should be applied to trials. To the three bodies of law that he discussed in 1919 – municipal law, law of war and international law – he added "universal law." It was a new category that included the Pact. Wright argued that the Axis powers, as parties to the Kellogg–Briand Pact, were under an obligation not to resort to armed force, and the violation of this obligation has been determined by general recognition of the members of the community of nations. However, at the same time, he wrote that "prosecutions under universal law would have the disadvantage from the juridical point of view of resting upon a controversial legal foundation." Trials of this kind "would look towards the future rather than to the immediate past, but it is believed that sufficient legal materials exist to nullify the suggestion that they would rest upon *ex post facto* law."[67]

When the San Francisco Conference on the International Organization was convened in April 1945, the US government submitted a memorandum on war trials to the British, Soviet and French foreign ministers. At

---

[65] Smith, *Road to Nuremberg*, p. 106.
[66] *Ibid.*, p. 106.
[67] Quincy Wright, "War Criminals," *AJIL* 39 (1945), 257–285.

the Conference, the four powers held only informal discussions, and more substantial discussion was to be conducted at the London Conference in June 1945.

At this juncture, it was significant that in May 1945, President Truman nominated former Attorney General Robert H. Jackson as US Representative in charge of the matters on war crimes. As was noted in Chapter 6, Jackson had already endorsed the progressive view on international law when he delivered a speech in Havana in support of the Lend-Lease Bill in 1941. Jackson read a paper on war crimes at the annual meeting of the ASIL in April 1945, arguing that if the Allies were to try war criminals the process had to be a legal and not political one.[68] Before he was officially nominated, Jackson had conveyed to Samuel Rosenman, assistant to the President, that his official view had been fully addressed in the speech delivered at the ASIL. Jackson recorded in his diary, "I wanted both him and President Truman to be fully informed about the speech in case it should be used publicity-wise to my disadvantage and that any appointment of me should be made only after full knowledge of it."[69] Stimson on his part naturally supported Jackson's nomination. Recalling a telephone conversation with Stimson, Jackson wrote Stimson thought his speech "completely expressed the viewpoint that he had been fighting for and he wanted to be of personal help and wanted his whole Department to be of help at any point in the proceedings."[70]

Prior to the London Conference, Jackson prepared a report to the president in early June. In the section of the report concerning the US legal position, he stressed state conduct in formulating legal principles, writing that "innovation and revisions in International Law are brought about by the action of governments designed to meet a change in circumstances … Hence I am not disturbed by the lack of precedent for the inquiry we propose to conduct." Jackson then traced the gradual development of the principle of "unjustifiable war," citing the Kellogg–Briand Pact, Stimson's speech, the Geneva Protocol of 1924, and other efforts during the interwar period. Above all, the Pact was important because the United States "relied upon the Briand-Kellogg Pact and made it the cornerstone of our polity." Furthermore, he recognized that US policy would have a positive effect on future developments because "any legal position asserted on behalf of the

---

[68] Robert H. Jackson, "Address," *Proceedings, ASIL* (1945), 10–19.
[69] Robert H. Jackson, "Diary," April 27, 1945, Papers of Robert Jackson (hereafter Jackson Papers), Library of Congress, Washington, DC, Box 95, Folder 4.
[70] Robert H. Jackson, "Diary," May 1, 1945, Jackson Papers, Box 95, Folder 4.

United States will have considerable significance in the future evolution of International Law."[71] This report especially pleased Stimson, who sent Jackson his "hearty approval and congratulations." Stimson went on to declare that he was "particularly gratified to see the battle for which we fought in 1932 in a fair way to be won. 'Truly the world do move!' "[72] From such statements, it is clear that Stimson found Jackson's position compatible with the principle of the Non-Recognition Doctrine he had issued in January 1932 following the Manchurian Incident. Jackson's report was later published in Europe as well as in the United States, and was widely accepted as a semi-official statement of the position of the United States.

A final round of diplomatic negotiations among the four powers was held at the London Conference from June 26 to August 8, 1945. The resulting Charter of the International Military Tribunal was signed on the final day of the Conference. Article 6 (a) of the Charter defined "Crimes against Peace" as the "planning, preparation, initiation or waging of a war of aggression," thereby constructing the notion of aggressive war as crime.

After the London Conference, Jackson admitted in a letter to Stimson that the process had been a difficult one. Success was not a certainty, and Jackson was concerned that he might need to "confess a failure to get acceptance for the principles of outlawing aggressive war."[73] Later, in early September Stimson and Jackson finally had an opportunity to meet in person. Jackson wrote, "As I left the President's office, Secretary Stimson was coming in and I had a chat with him about his letter to me and he said he had received a gratifying answer."[74] On the same day, Jackson also had a brief meeting with Quincy Wright, in which they discussed the trial of the Japanese.[75]

However, Wright was not sent to Tokyo. Instead, he was nominated as a technical advisor to the US delegation for the International Military Tribunal in Nuremberg. In his correspondences, one can observe the importance of the scholarly activities of the ASIL. In early December 1945 he wrote to Finch from Nuremberg, asking for necessary reference materials shipped by air mail, including several volumes of the *AJIL*

[71] "Report to the President by Mr. Justice Jackson, June 6, 1945," in *Report of Robert H. Jackson, United States Representative to the International Conference on Military Trials* (Washington, DC: GPO, 1949), pp. 52–53. See also Robert Jackson, "Nürnberg in Retrospect," *Canadian Bar Review* 27 (1949), 761–781.

[72] Stimson to Jackson, June 25, 1945, Jackson Papers, Box 110, Folder 3. See also Strum, "Henry Stimson," 8.

[73] Jackson to Stimson, August 21, 1945, Jackson Papers, Box 110, Folder 3.

[74] Robert H. Jackson, "Diary," September 5, 1945, Jackson Papers, Box 95, Folder 5.

[75] *Ibid.*

Supplement. Wright thought the shipment would be "a considerable load," but was sure that it would help "enlighten the work of this Tribunal." He had discovered that there were "few materials" on international law available in Nuremberg, and clearly thought that a shipment of such scholarly works would provide important assistance.[76]

After coming back from Nuremberg, Wright kept in touch with Francis Biddle, the primary American judge at the Tribunal, with whom he exchanged views regarding the development of the Tribunal as well as the reception of the Tribunal by the American public. In one letter, Wright noted that public opinion over the Tribunal was "a good deal divided ... In Chicago the *Tribune* has one editorial a week attacking them vigorously." Thus, Wright worked to increase public support for the trials, reporting that he gave talks to local people and his colleagues at the university who were in general friendly to the trial, but businessmen and lawyers in downtown were less supportive.[77]

Judge John J. Parker also wrote to Wright from Nuremberg, "We have missed you a lot over here and I wish that we had you with us so that I could talk with you about some troublesome questions of international law."[78] Around this time, Wright also corresponded with Lord Wright, head of the UNWCC. In one letter, he requested copies of Lord Wright's works, which were considered important reference material for the American judges of the Tribunal.[79] Lord Wright replied with information on where copies could be found, noting that one was in print on the *Law Quarterly Review,* and the other was being sent to the birthday volume in honor of Roscoe Pound.[80] Such letters clearly indicate Quincy Wright's close relationship with high officials involved in war trials, which in turn might have enhanced his commitment to the effort.

Wright's 1947 article – "The Law of the Nuremberg Trial" – candidly acknowledged that the trial had both champions and critics. For those who supported it, the trial established important precedents on the definition of aggressive war as a crime and the criminal liability of individuals. Wright's tone in this article was again forward looking, stating that "these principles, if established, will add important sanctions to the numerous international agreements, including the Kellogg–Briand Pact and the

---

[76] Wright to Finch, December 6, 1945, Wright Papers, Addenda I, Box 57, Folder 3.
[77] Wright to Francis Biddle, January 17, 1946, Wright Papers, Addenda I, Box 57, Folder 3.
[78] John Parker to Wright, May 7, 1946, Wright Papers, Addenda I, Box 57, Folder 3.
[79] Wright to Lord Wright, January 18, 1946, April 4, 1946, Wright Papers, Addenda I, Box 57, Folder 3.
[80] Lord Wright to Wright, February 20, 1946, Wright Papers, Addenda I, Box 57, Folder 3.

Charter of the United Nations, outlawing war as an instrument of national policy." Interestingly, he argued that critics of the Tribunal "appear to dislike the trend of international law recognized in the [UN] Charter." The trend, in his observation, made "inroads upon national sovereignty" and change in "the foundation of the international community from a balance of power among sovereign states to a universal federation." Regarding the *ex post facto* issue, he wrote that the Tribunal took pains to show that "the rules of international law which they applied were not *ex post facto*." Supporting the Tribunal's position, he cited Lord Wright's argument that "international law is progressive," much like common law.[81]

In the process to construct and define the concept of aggressive war as crime, reform-oriented American scholars were not directly involved in the policy making process, whereas in Britain, even though not to a very significant degree, some scholars participated in the discussions held at informal activities as well as at the UNWCC. Before the London Conference met and the Nuremberg Charter officially promulgated, most scholarly argument had pointed out that the trial would involve both legal and political aspects, and that defining the notion of aggressive war as a crime based upon the Pact could face legal opposition. Lauterpacht, McNair and Wright, who had been supporters of the Non-Recognition Doctrine, all realized that there could be opposition, but they believed that acceptance of the notion was nonetheless right and desirable for future. After all, on this issue the line between *lex lata* and *lex ferenda* was not an absolute one for them. They were determined to step beyond the line, and decided to become social reformers in international relations, even with the possible charge of going too far.

Officials in Washington and London who were perhaps more politically motivated to establish the notion of war as an international crime found it valuable and expedient to coat their claims with legal reasoning from the reformers' arguments. Thus, Lord Wright, when he discussed the development of differential treatment of belligerents in international law during interwar years in his introduction of the official history volume on the UNWCC, referred to the names of Hersch Lauterpacht and Quincy Wright as "some of the greatest writers on international law of the time."[82]

---

[81] Quincy Wright, "The Law of the Nuremberg Trial," *AJIL* 41 (1947), 42, 47, 59.
[82] *History of the United Nations War Crimes Commission*, p. 16.

Changing orientation in the discipline:
from international law to international relations

The Conference of the Teachers of International Law and Related Subjects, which had guided the teaching of international law throughout the previous three decades, held its first postwar meeting in April 1946.

Wright, serving as director for this Eighth Conference, delivered the keynote speech, entitled "The Teaching of International Law in the Postwar Period." The address stressed the expansion of the discipline through integration with other related fields. Calling attention to the meeting on "Teaching and Research in International Relations" held in February 1946 under the auspices of the New York Council on Foreign Relations, he remarked, "I note that our own program at the present meeting is concerned as much with international politics, the United Nations, and the atom bomb as with international law." He then explained that the change was not caused by "a decline of interest in international law but an increase in interest in other aspects of international relations." Wright also made a noteworthy confession about his past optimism, saying that "the problem of establishing a law-governed world is perhaps less simple than we thought a generation ago."[83]

Although Wright in principle admitted that a broader subject – International Relations – should be taught, he cautioned that it would be "dangerous to allow international law to step out of the curriculum altogether." In particular, he recommended that fundamental and basic elements of international law should be taught because too much emphasis on "technical and professional studies" may result in "professional distortion."[84]

Wright then proceeded to address the ties between international law and other aspects of international relations. "International law examines the entire field of international relations from the universal point of view," whereas "other aspects of international relations tend to proceed from particular and practical points of view," he argued. If teachers put too much emphasis on the practical side of the subject, the values would be forgotten. On the other hand, too much attention to ideals would overlook the actual conditions of the world. Therefore, it was necessary for scholars to approach international relations "with due consideration to both the general and particular, to both the desired and observed." It

[83] *Proceedings, Eighth Teachers* (1946), 23–24.
[84] *Ibid.*, 24–25.

could not and should not be discussed in isolation from other fields, such as international politics, geography and diplomatic history.[85]

Topics of recent interest that were dealt with at the Conference included "The Impact of Scientific Discovery and Technological Change on International Relations" and "The United Nations Assembly Meetings in London." The Conference also included one session that indicated a new orientation for the discipline: "The Teaching of International Relations in the Postwar World." In this noteworthy session, invited speakers stressed the need to broaden the field from one mainly composed of international law and diplomatic history to one more encompassing international relations. More specifically, one speaker, Harold M. Vinacke, a professor of political science at the University of Cincinnati, maintained the importance of studying the notion of "power," arguing that "we brushed power politics aside on the assumption that international relations were conducted on a higher level than power relationships of the state against state."[86] A similar opinion was expressed by Charles E. Martin of the University of Washington in the discussion that followed. Martin argued that the content of the conference revealed that teachers and students of international relations would face the problem of dualism between "the area of institution of peace which are related to the adjustment of disputes" and "the area of power politics and war." It was a mistake for teachers in the interwar period to "glibly" write off the institution of war and studies on the influence of power politics.[87]

The discussion also featured another interesting indication for the future course of the fields of international studies. Frank M. Russell of the University of California pointed out the important issue of "underdevelopment." Russell did not think that the study of international law and international relations would be enough to understand the life of "backward" peoples. Anthropology, economics, political geography and social psychology would be more important. "In the next twenty five years we are going to make efforts to solve the issue of 'backward nations' that had been under control or tutelage," he maintained.[88]

In all, the trend and direction of the papers and discussions at this conference signaled the significance of expanding the field to a more inclusive one, with particular emphasis on the study of "power" and "power politics." Two years after this 1946 meeting, Hans Morgenthau published the widely acclaimed and widely read *Politics among Nations*, a book that argued for the importance of power in the study of international

---

[85] *Ibid.*, 26.   [86] *Ibid.*, 53.   [87] *Ibid.*, 66.   [88] *Ibid.*, 71.

relations. It is important to note that some scholars had already shared and expressed such a view at this conference.

In a similar vein, when an independent session on the teaching of international law was held at the ASIL's 1947 annual meeting, the changing focus of the discipline was unmistakably clear. Three papers were read in this session: "The Teaching of International Law in Law Schools," "The Teaching of International Law in Undergraduate and Graduate Courses in Political Science" and "The Teaching of International Law in Adult Education of the General Public." This categorization of dividing the field into three groups already showed the contemporary scholars' realization that the teaching of international law should be differentiated depending upon the audience. Wright – though he was not a speaker at the meeting – unsurprisingly put emphasis on the third category. Times had changed, and teaching to the general public had greater importance because governments now sought to obtain greater public endorsement for policy. With his usual resolve, Wright argued that "we must realize that international law depends, more than any other types of law upon world public opinion, not only on public opinion of this country but in other countries." However, a contending opinion was also expressed. One participant maintained that scholars and professionals should abstain from "propaganda" work, and should only focus on scientific and scholarly tasks.[89]

Most notably and significantly, a rising star for postwar American scholarship in the field of international law made an impressive debut at this annual meeting. Myres S. McDougal, who introduced himself as "a newcomer to this organization," confessed that he was "just a little shocked and disappointed by what I heard last evening and so far this morning." His targets of attack were, in his words, the "canonized doctrines of international law." For instance, *pacta sunt servanda* was "just to ignore the kind of world in which we live and what we are trying to do. That fact is that agreements must change as values and conditions change." In addition, he pointed out that these doctrines were used by "people at certain foci of power to get certain consequences." He was also critical of the Harvard Research Draft Conventions, saying that devoting time to "merely duplicating the Harvard Research" would be a wasted effort. In addition, he perceptively observed that "the world has become more and more bipolar in appearance."[90]

[89] *Proceedings, ASIL* (1947), 95, 174, 177.
[90] *Ibid.*, 47–50. See also Kirgis, *The American Society*, p. 212.

McDougal's remark inspired participants to a considerable degree, with one labeling him as "our devil's advocate of the day." Philip Marshall Brown was among those who took note of McDougal, saying, "I have been tremendously impressed with some of the things that have been said … especially by Mr. McDougal." Brown believed there were two different concepts of international law, the Western concept and the Communist concept. If the Soviet idea prevailed in a large part of Europe and Latin America, Brown thought that scholars "must seriously revise our whole basic concept. To that extent I am heartily in sympathy with the challenge that Mr. McDougal has thrown out."[91]

Another participant and former student of Wright, Charles Prince, notably criticized his mentor and sided with McDougal. Prince stated that "regretfully there has crept into our thinking among our teachers, including my own teacher, Professor Quincy Wright, some misconception as to what the Soviet attitude toward international law really is." Responding to those critical statements, Wright himself stated that McDougal "interpreted law as simply the implementation of somebody's values." However, since the world was filled with heterogeneity of opinion rather than homogeneity, "there are very few values which command the allegiance of all the members of the community of nations" and developing universal values was very slow, Wright argued. That was the very reason why codification was necessary and useful.[92]

At this annual meeting, international lawyers were also perceptive enough to recognize the emergence of the Cold War. As mentioned above, some scholars called attention to the conditions, policy and jurisprudence in the Soviet Union. Within the context of developing political conditions, great power and US attitudes toward international law became a matter of concern. Eagleton lamented that "the practice of the members of the United Nations, it seems to me, has shown very little respect for the law." He went on to state that the United States was "disregarding the United Nations with respect to Greece and Turkey."[93] As Eagleton correctly observed, the US government issued the Truman Doctrine in March of that year, gradually formulating the policy of containment to the Soviet Union.

In March 1943, Borchard wrote to Wright regarding their ideological differences, stating that "sometimes I wish I could see the world through

---

[91] *Proceedings, ASIL* (1947), 55, 51–52.
[92] *Ibid.*, 54–55.
[93] *Ibid.*, 53.

your rose colored spectacles, even though I knew I should get a rude awakening."[94] Did this debate between "rose colored spectacles" and "a rude awakening" result in a clear-cut victory for one side over the other?

Borchard had to admit the victory of new international law, but he would not accept the arguments of its supporters. This was clear in his short 1946 account entitled "The Effect of War on Law" in which he wrote that "the most serious inroad upon international law has been the purported abolition of neutrality, which has been underway since the organization of the ill-fated League of Nations in 1919." Borchard saw the establishment of the United Nations as an invitation for "universal intervention as the road to peace." On this point he was more pessimistic and critical, arguing that "the United Nations should not have been assigned the inappropriate task of preserving the peace, especially by force." Moreover, the Big Three were "not united and cannot be." Borchard believed that smaller states would become "appendages or satellites" of larger neighboring states.[95] In sum, he acknowledged the fact that new international law had become more firmly established and institutionalized, but never changed his perspective that it would further endanger rather than contribute to the peace of the world.

The triumph of new international law can be attributed in part to the fact that some major progressive legal scholars were mobilized into the government, either as consultants or regular staff, thereby utilizing their professional knowledge to influence the course of policy whenever they could. Wright's legal expertise was frequently sought by government officials. This is evident in an April 1945 letter to Wright from George H. Blakeslee of the State Department's Office of Far Eastern Affairs, and a former professor of history and international relations at Clark University: "We are having frequent perplexing problems in international law, and need your assistance ... I know that [Joseph] Ballantine, [Eugene] Dooman and other are very anxious to have you here."[96]

However, it was not only the scholars' objective and professional knowledge of international law that helped to shape the course of postwar international law and organization. More importantly, the reformers had shared a common faith in international law and a commitment and will to use it for the betterment of the postwar world. Hudson, writing in 1942 to thank Borchard for sending him a note on E. H. Carr's *The Twenty*

---

[94] Borchard to Wright, March 19, 1943, Wright Papers, Box 19, Folder 6.
[95] Edwin M. Borchard, "The Effect of War on Law," *AJIL* 40 (1946), 620–621.
[96] George H. Blakeslee to Wright, April 20, 1945, Wright Papers, Box 13, Folder 19.

Years' Crisis,[97] stated that "on the whole he [Carr] seems to me to give too little weight to the factor of 'will'." Hudson compared the situation to "the man climbing a mountain."[98] For reform-minded international lawyers, international order was a mountain that had to be conquered. With "will" they resolutely believed that they could overcome it.

Lauterpacht was not favorably depicted in Carr's work.[99] However, as Hudson correctly observed, Lauterpacht was someone who believed that an international lawyer was a social engineer endowed with the power and capability to make international law more effective and workable. Lauterpacht himself wrote, when he was considering a plan for postwar international organization:

> Some of my colleagues are what they believe to be very realistic. This means that in making proposals they do not wish to consider what is sound and rational, but what the Governments are likely to accept. What they forgot is that what Governments will think will to some extent be influenced by what we think is the right course.[100]

Wright, Fenwick, Eagleton, Hudson and Lauterpacht all shared the belief that lawyers can and should go a step further and that their academic efforts could lead and reorient the course that policy makers would pursue.

---

[97] E. H. Carr, *The Twenty Years' Crisis, 1919–1939* (London: Macmillan and Company, 1939).

[98] Hudson to Borchard, January 20, 1942, Hudson Papers, Box 97, Folder 9.

[99] See Carr, *The Twenty Years' Crisis*, pp. 259–260.

[100] HL to EL, April 6, 1944, Elihu Lauterpacht, *The Life of Hersch Lauterpacht*, p. 246.

Conclusion

Thomas Baty wrote in his last book, *International Law in Twilight*, published in 1954, "It is useless to urge that the Law of Nations has been changed, suddenly and precipitately, and that the treaties must carry consequences which their framers never intended. Who clothed Lord Wright and Professor Q. Wright with authority to alter the international law?" Changes in international law, he continued, "cannot be effected by the opportunist declaration of a coterie of professors and journalists, however eminent they may be."[1] Baty died at the age of eighty-five just before the book was published. He had remained in Japan during World War II, and after the war the British government deprived him of protection as a British subject on account of his collaboration with the Japanese government. To the very end of his life, Baty did not alter his beliefs.

As for his philosophical opponents, Lord Wright, chairman of the UNWCC, contended in his famous article of January 1946 that "International law is progressive." Quincy Wright, an advocate of the new international law, as has been discussed in this study, served as a technical advisor for the Nuremberg War Tribunal.[2]

The issue of whether international law had changed was raised during the Tokyo War Tribunal. The prosecution presented its summation on February 11, 1948. In it, Comyns Carr, one of the prosecutors, endorsed changing international law. He asserted, "international law, like common law, is not a static, but a continually growing body of legal concepts."[3] One defendant, however, Kenzo Takayanagi, pointed out that the view of international law presented by the prosecution had not been universally acknowledged and was in fact held only by the so-called revisionist

---

[1] Thomas Baty, *International Law in Twilight* (Tokyo: Maruzen, 1954), pp. 185–186.
[2] Lord Wright, "War Crimes under International Law," *Law Quarterly Review* 62 (1946), 40–52; Wright, "The Law of the Nuremberg Trial," 38–72.
[3] R. John Pritchard and Sonia Magbanua Zaide, eds., *The Tokyo War Crimes Trial: International Military Tribunal for the Far East, Proceedings, Exhibits, and Judgment* (London: Garland Publishing, 1981), vol. 16, pp. 39006–39014.

school. Takayanagi took the position that Japan had followed the orthodox interpretation of international law. He explained Japan's position in the following words: "If international law had rapidly and bewilderingly transformed itself during the war, of which we were unaware, it is palpably *ex post facto* action."[4] The contest that emerged during the early years of this century between the traditional and the new school of international law was carried into the military tribunals held after World War II.

The difference between the two schools was brought into sharp focus by Wright's proclamation, "international law must recognize that the whole is greater than the parts."[5] The reformers, represented by Wright, Charles G. Fenwick and Manley O. Hudson, attached great importance to "the whole." They believed in the existence of an international society, in which war was to be abolished and a peaceful and equitable international order would prevail. The concept of law in this school of thought was general enough to function as equivalent to a constitution in domestic society. In particular, the reformers regarded multilateral treaties such as the Covenant of the League of Nations, the Nine Power Treaty and the Kellogg–Briand Pact as comprising the fundamental legal code of international society. On the other hand, the traditionalists – Baty, John Bassett Moore and Edwin M. Borchard – held that "the parts," that is the sovereign states, were central to international law, and no supreme institution transcending states was possible. According to this school of thought, the role of international law was confined to regulating specific rights and obligations among nations. Law should not deal with such issues as war, disarmament or collective security, nor should it set guidelines for the conduct of nations. Thus, the traditionalists did not consider multilateral treaties such as the Pact to be legally binding, but merely statements of policy. In addition, the traditionalists were pessimistic about the possibility of abolishing war through a legal framework, and favored instead legal regulation of the conduct of war through the laws of war.

During the interwar years, international law showed signs of change, but this trend was not readily accepted by all scholars and all countries. Eventually, the trend prevailed, however, culminating in the establishment of the United Nations and the promulgation of its Charter. These new international instruments offer hard evidence that the traditional school of international law, which held that war was legal and that there

---

[4] *Ibid.*, vol. 17, p. 42177.
[5] Wright, "The Present Status of Neutrality," 411.

was no possibility of international organization, had not carried the day. The establishment of the United Nations vindicated the reformers' contention that the system of the League itself had not failed, because much of the framework of the United Nations was inherited from the League. For reformers, the most welcome accomplishment of the United Nations Charter was that it brought to completion the outlawry of war. Wright himself argued that by prohibiting the threat or use of force in international relations the Charter vindicated a "new international law."[6] The use of the term "force" instead of "war" in the Charter enlarged the scope of military actions to be prohibited. In addition, the concept of collective security was articulated more clearly in the Charter than it had been in the Covenant of the League of Nations.

The greatest contribution made by the reformers is not to be found in the United Nations, however, but in something far more consequential yet intangible: the introduction of humanitarian principles into international relations. In a broad perspective, they helped to ground the principle of the universality of humankind in a legal framework. They believed that moral and ethical standards should transcend national boundaries and be applied to the entire "family of nations." They challenged the absolute notion of national sovereignty and sought the common good for all mankind.

The legacy of their ideals and efforts has been far-ranging. In 1925 James W. Garner wrote that war would not be abolished as long as it was considered the exclusive concern of belligerents. War had to be treated as the concern of all countries.[7] The idea evolved into the concept of collective security embodied in the United Nations Charter. Later, when the Cold War made the application of this concept impractical, those countries that thought it necessary for the United Nations to assert its role in resolving conflicts contributed to create UN peacekeeping activities. Paul Reinsch had pointed out the lack of appropriate rules to question the legality of the Treaty of Annexation between Japan and Korea in 1910, arguing that traditional international law authorized Japan's imperialistic designs.[8] In 1960, almost half a century later, the United Nations adopted the Declaration on the Granting of Independence of Colonial Countries and Peoples, which proclaimed that colonies had the right to assert their

---

[6] Quincy Wright, *A Study of War*, abridged edition, 1964 (Chicago: Midway Reprint, 1983), p. 185.

[7] Garner, *Recent Developments in International Law*, pp. 814–815.

[8] Reinsch, "The Concept of Legality in International Arbitration," 610.

independence. Likewise, at the 1932 meeting of the ASIL, the question of whether treaties signed under duress were binding had been discussed in relation to the validity of the Twenty-One Demands. At that time, opinion had been divided.[9] In 1969, however, the Vienna Convention on the Law of Treaties clearly established that a treaty signed under duress was voidable.

Yet the traditionalists' concerns about the new international law were not groundless. The traditionalists held that collective security was not only an "unachievable rainbow," because not all countries would agree to participate, but also dangerous, because it required all nations to go to war and would therefore expand conflicts. Moreover, the problem of how to determine who was the aggressor in a conflict had yet to be resolved. Looking at occasions on which the concept of collective security has been applied in the postwar period, one can see that these concerns have largely been vindicated. In the case of the Korean War, in which the UN forces sought to challenge the aggressor, the UN army was far from a collective force, consisting primarily of troops from the United States. Even though the UN action had legal sanction, the conflict was in reality no different from previous wars, except for the fact that it had been waged under the name of the United Nations.

Furthermore, ideas and methods of the traditional school were not abandoned completely. Bilateral treaties and agreements among nations were still an effective way to regulate relations. Just as the traditionalists had argued, the basic purpose of international law lay in its function of regulating relationships among sovereign states. To this day, sovereign states remain the basic unit of international relations. And in spite of the trend toward regional and global integration, the number of sovereign states has continued to increase. The new international law did not take the place of the old. Instead, international law was transformed and its scope expanded, in large part by the concept of the "family of nations" and by the abolishment of the legality of war.

Some later scholars pointed out that international law went through a process of transformation during this period. Ian Brownlie, for instance, maintained that a feature of the first half of the twentieth century was "the decisive change" from a legal regime of "indifference to the occasion for a war" to that of "substantial limitations on the competence of states to resort to force." As evidence of the change, Brownlie cited the examples of the Kellogg–Briand Pact, the Non-Recognition Doctrine, the

---

[9] *Proceedings, ASIL* (1932), 45–53.

state practice from 1928 to 1942, and the UN Charter.[10] As my work has demonstrated, progressive international lawyers, with their definite sense of resolution and commitment, played an indispensable role in driving and carrying out this change.

Even at that time, the international law community at large was fully aware of what was going on in their field. No remark more candidly expressed lawyers' awareness than that of Carl Christol of the University of South Dakota at the Eighth Conference of Teachers of International Law held in April 1946. Recalling past events, he stated, "At a meeting of the Society of Law (I believe it was the one held in 1925) there were two schools of thought represented, the one believed that international law that existed prior to World War I could very well be neglected and that the international law that was in the making since the war was all important." However, the idea was "vigorously" contested by the other group. While the first group, "consisting largely of younger men," argued for the importance of the League, the PCIJ and the International Labor Organization, "the other group held, however, that the time after the war was still so short, that nobody knew how these new institutions and these new covenants would work."[11] It is significant to note that Christol, a South Dakota-based scholar who was not teaching at a major school in the East Coast or in a major city, had a good grasp on the movement.

This book is not primarily and explicitly committed to the theoretical endeavor of probing lawyers' role as social engineers. Instead, it intends to present a lively biographical narrative of the international lawyers who were involved in this movement. Yet, possibly and presumably enough, it may involve implications about social engineering, and can relevantly suggest the hypothesis concerning the role of lawyers in introducing changes in international law. If lawyers strive to act as social engineers, it is possible to argue that there exist five factors or levels to achieve the goal of changing norms.

1. [International lawyers' will and attitude]
   An examination of personal papers and correspondences written by international lawyers concretely and vividly illustrates their determination, position and attitude toward international law. Reform-minded lawyers believed that international law can and should contribute to peace and stability of the world.

[10] Ian Brownlie, *International Law and the Use of Force by States* (Oxford: Clarendon Press, 1964), pp. 424–425.
[11] *Proceedings, Eighth Teachers* (1946), 59–60.

2. [Legal scholarship]

   Even if lawyers had progressive views on international law, they had to articulate their views in the form of scholarship. For example, Wright presented a thesis on the Stimson Doctrine that captured wide attention at that time. Beyond their published works, the lawyers' academic activities included discussions held at the ASIL, the International Law Association and the Conference of the Teachers of International Law and Related Subjects. These discussions indicated their academic orientations, quite often signaling which topic within their academic purview should be given primary importance.

3. [Lawyers' activities and efforts in influencing policy makers and public opinion]

   Reform-minded lawyers were not hesitant in spreading their views to policy makers as well as to the general public. As Wright wrote, "law ultimately rests on the support of public opinion, and international law can rest only on the support of world-wide public opinion." But that support "will not be forthcoming unless publicists and educators give their best efforts to the task, unless the jurists continually re-examine the sources of law and interpret its rules and principles with an understanding of ever changing needs."[12] In fact, Wright's efforts in influencing policy makers were effective, as expressed clearly when Borchard observed with disdain in 1941 that "now the Quincy Wright School is in control in the Department of State, so that we have a continuity of official attacks upon international law."[13]

4. [Policy makers' attitudes and state practices]

   The three factors noted above – scholars' will, their scholarship and their activities – focus upon lawyers as actors. However, there is a need for lawyers' efforts and initiatives to be channeled into and accepted by policy makers themselves and subsequently elevated into actual policy. The two successive secretaries of state, Henry L. Stimson and Cordell Hull, and to a lesser degree yet, Robert H. Jackson, showed their acceptance, appreciation and sometimes critique of lawyers' arguments.

5. [The diplomatic and international scenes]

   If a state(s) seeks to establish a new norm in international law, conflicts can occur. Certain states may oppose the new norm. The case over

---

[12] Quincy Wright, "International Law and the World Order," in Walter H. C. Laves, ed., *The Foundations of a More Stable World Order* (University of Chicago Press, 1940), pp. 107–134.

[13] Borchard to Moore, March 22, 1941, Borchard Papers, Box 10, Folder 117.

the use of force and the Stimson Doctrine in my work highlights this point, in that the Japanese government opposed the emerging norm of outlawry of war.

Seen from the perspective of a contest between two different schools of international law, the interwar period can be termed as a transition. Behind the different attitudes toward international law lay a larger philosophical contest: between a nineteenth-century worldview in which international relations were seen as a contest for the survival of the fittest, and a twentieth century worldview that called for the greater application of humanitarian and egalitarian principles. Traditional international law did not question the appropriateness of one nation expanding its territory by military conquest or by threat of force. In the case of the Sino-Japanese War of 1894, the Spanish-American War of 1898 and the Boer War of 1899, the legality of waging war itself had not been questioned at all. Traditional international law suited the era of imperialism, when strong nations were allowed to expand their territory by force. But the new international law challenged the legitimacy of imperialism by making war illegal and by introducing the humanitarian belief in the equality of nations.

This contest of the ideas was played out on the international stage. Wright had once argued that "the reasons why the liberals and believers in peace in the West resent the Japanese action particularly is because it initiated the reversion to old imperialistic policies."[14] Wright held that the world had moved beyond the stage of imperialism, into an age in which countries would abolish imperialistic policies that had been supported by national power. He viewed the nations of the world as seeking to establish an international order based on the notion of law. For this reason, he saw Japanese military action in Manchuria and China as "a step backward" or at least a "setback." Japanese theorists, however, notably Sakutaro Tachi, still played according to the rules of the imperialist era, and their understanding of international law was tied to that era. Tachi did not agree that war or the use of military force had been outlawed. Those who sought an end to imperialism believed that an international legal order could take the place of military might in resolving conflicts, while those who adhered to the model of imperialism sought to expand their interests by military force. The chasm separating the reformers and the traditionalists was the same chasm that separated governments seeking international

---

[14] Wright to Tatsuji Takeuchi, February 2, 1938, Wright Papers, addenda II, Box 25.

order through the rationality of law and those seeking to protect their
interests through the use of military force.

In other words, this study shows that the various conflicts among
nations that occurred during this period can be explained in part by the
conflicting attitudes toward international relations held by national governments, which were reflected in their philosophies of international law.
In response to the devastation of World War I, the Covenant of the League
of Nations prohibited certain types of war and declared that any war was
the concern of all member states. There were nations who opposed this system, however, because the old order was more advantageous for expanding their interests and because they saw war as an opportunity rather
than an evil. Despite this resistance, the ideals of the new international
law were advanced in several important treaties and pronouncements.
The Kellogg–Briand Pact, the League's discussions and verdicts against
Japan, and the Non-Recognition Doctrine furthered the cause of the new
international law, for example, by establishing that the fruits of military
aggression would no longer be recognized as having been legally gained.
While it is true that these treaties and pronouncements, and the principles
they embodied, did not deter aggression, their very existence made it possible for the League and many nations to determine that Japan, Italy and
Germany had violated the treaties and hence were the aggressors.

The origins of World War II can be analyzed from several perspectives.
In ideological terms, it was a war between democracy and totalitarianism.
It was also a contest over the redistribution of resources. According to
the logic of international law, however, it was a war of collective security waged as a sanction against law breakers: a war between the "united
nations" and legally recognized aggressors. It was a logical consequence
of adherence to the principle of non-recognition. At the same time, it was
a contest between the traditional philosophy, which adhered to an imperialist international order, and a new opposing philosophy. Japan, Italy and
Germany attempted to aggrandize their positions by using military force,
but the rest of the world rejected this and resorted to collective force.

The movement to establish a new international law was not confined
to the United States; some British and German jurists, and scholars
from other countries like Nicolas Politis of Greece, were also committed to it. There were frequent exchanges of opinion among them. The
International Law Association regularly held conferences at several cities in Europe, while every summer the Hague Academy of International
Law invited scholars from various countries to give lectures. Throughout
this period, however, American international lawyers were the leaders

of the movement. They formed a distinct group and worked tirelessly to advance the movement. The US official role was limited, because it had declined to join the League and was not enthusiastic about international political commitments. Nonetheless, its role was more than merely symbolic, for the US government was a sponsor of the Nine Power Treaty and the Kellogg–Briand Pact, both of which were crucial in establishing the framework of the new international law. It is true that the broad and general nature of these treaties, which did not stipulate specific obligations, was compatible with the official stance of the US government. But insofar as the treaties advanced principles such as territorial integrity and the outlawry of war, the US involvement in the agreements was seen as an endorsement of the larger movement. In addition, the support of two American secretaries of state, Stimson and Hull, greatly encouraged proponents of the new international law.

The fact that American legal theorists were actively involved in the movement demonstrates that internationalism in the United States both existed and had a voice during the interwar years. The legal theorists, who attempted to establish universal principles in international relations, should definitely be counted among the internationalists. On the other hand, it is interesting to note that in the mid 1930s the traditionalists came to share the views of isolationists. The traditionalists did not believe it desirable to establish a universal order; rather, they held that agreements between nations were adequate to sustain international law.

The influence of legalism on American foreign policy is also notable in the tendency to view the Far Eastern situation in more legalistic terms than was the case in other regions. When the situation in East Asia was discussed, references to legal frameworks were more common than in discussions of the European and Latin American situations. This can be explained by several factors. Firstly, China was saddled with numerous unequal treaties, and consequently the study of treaty relations in China had a long tradition in the United States, as evidenced by Rockhill and MacMurray's works. Secondly, the United States was a party to the Nine Power Treaty, which made its commitment to the Far East more tangible, while in other regions only the Kellogg–Briand Pact linked the United States with world affairs. Finally, Japan's overt military actions were an obvious challenge to both of the treaties, and the League's verdict on Japan's violations of international law gave the United States a clear-cut picture of the legal situation. From the perspective of the new international law, the conflict in East Asia presented the perfect test.

By necessity, this study has addressed more questions than it has solved. The ongoing tension that informs the study is derived from a dualism inherent in international relations. On one hand, international relations can be viewed in terms of idealism, law and order, and in the context of a family of nations. On the other hand, these same relations can be seen in terms of realism, power politics, and the national interests of sovereign states. Achieving balance between the two is difficult, and tension is inevitable because the relationship between the two is complementary as well as confrontational.

International order cannot be established or maintained without effort; it requires the constant commitment and endorsement of sovereign states. The reformers emphasized that countries have an innate interest in preserving international order. Wright argued that the US interest in upholding the order of law was not motivated by material concerns alone,[15] while Fenwick asserted that the issue was not the rescue of China or Czechoslovakia, but the larger principle.[16] It is often difficult, however, for a country to acknowledge its interest in maintaining order, particularly when its material interests are not directly involved.

In addition, international order must at times be maintained by the exercise of power. The reformers were not very concerned about the relationship between the legal order and the use of power. But ultimately, power was indispensable in enforcing the principles of international law. The reformers argued that the Non-Recognition Doctrine was a revolution in human thought because it denied legality to any fruit of military aggression. But the verbal proclamation of this doctrine alone did not deter aggression. To make the order of law effective, enforcement by each nation was necessary. In its ultimate form, international order has to be secured by the punishment of violators.

On an intellectual level, the tension between the two forces at work in international relations appeared as a conflict between idealism and realism. In the late 1930s, a new generation of realists, such as Hans J. Morgenthau, joined the older generation of traditionalists. Together they shared the common view that the new international law was nothing more than "wishful" thinking on the part of certain scholars. In Britain in 1939, E. H. Carr published his famous book *The Twenty Years' Crisis*, in which he criticized some international lawyers for being utopians. As Borchard wrote to Moore that "Quincy Wright ought to read a little book

[15] Wright to Thomas W. Lamont, February 25, 1938, Wright Papers, Box 16, Folder 15.
[16] Fenwick, "International Law and Lawless Nations," 745.

by E. H. Carr on the twenty years' diplomacy of 1919–1939,"[17] Borchard referred to Carr's work when he criticized reformers. But it should be noted that the reformers were not utopians insofar as their views were realized in the new international organizations of the postwar period.

The Cold War was more detrimental to the new international law than World War II because it destroyed the basic premise of a community of nations by dividing the world into two camps. But the reformers did not abandon their faith. For those who had struggled through the two world wars, the Cold War was perhaps just one more challenge to overcome. In 1954, Fenwick asserted in his presidential address before the ASIL that we must discover "certain fundamental principles of justice, certain fundamental laws of humanity common to all peoples, certain basic common interests superseding their national differences."[18] Two years later, at the Society's fiftieth anniversary meeting, Wright gave the presidential address. He proclaimed, "Our task is not to discover the principles by which we can organize our friends in opposition to our enemies, but to discover the principles which all nations share, and which if maintained will constitute them a community." He acknowledged that the current situation was not favorable, noting that while the Covenant of the League of Nations, the Kellogg–Briand Pact, the United Nations Charter, the Nuremberg Charter, the Universal Declaration of Human Rights and other instruments had been adopted to prescribe the "new international law," the application of that law had been obstructed by the exigencies of international politics. Yet he did not abandon his hope, and argued for the need for a long-term historical view. He quoted Arnold Toynbee, who had proposed that 300 years from now the twentieth century will be remembered not as an age of wars but as a time "to make the benefits of civilization available to the whole human race."[19]

Now we have moved from the twentieth century into the twenty-first century. The Cold War is over, and the resurgence of the role of international law and of the United Nations is once again being debated. Ethnic conflicts have broken out, the discrepancy of wealth between industrialized and developing nations has not been solved, terrorist attacks have been launched, and a "war on terrorism" has been waged. The ideal of a

---

[17] Borchard to Moore, December 16, 1941, Borchard Papers, Box 10, Folder 118.
[18] Charles G. Fenwick, "The Development of Collective Security, 1914–1954," *Proceedings, ASIL* (1954), 12.
[19] Quincy Wright, "The Prospects of International Law," *Proceedings, ASIL* (1956), 7, 10.

humanitarian and peaceful world has yet to be realized. Human rights, environmental issues and globalization demand our attention more than ever. The humanitarian and universal ideals advocated by the new international law have survived the long and strife-ridden years of the Cold War and are being carried over into the twenty-first century. While these ideals are being sustained, it should not be forgotten that the new international law did not arise spontaneously. Rather, many international lawyers devoted the better part of their lives to establishing and defending that law. If their names are also carried into the future, my mission as a historian who traced their path will be fully rewarded.

Appendix: List of International Lawyers in the Interwar Period

International Lawyers in the Interwar Years

Reformers	Active Members of the American Society of International Law (ASIL)		Traditionalists	
Non-US				Non-US
L. F. Oppenheim (1858–1919) UK	*Paul S. Reinsch (1869–1923) University of Wisconsin	Charles Warren (1868–1954) Assistant Attorney General	Elihu Root [bullet] (1845–1937) Secretary of State	Thomas Baty (1869–1954) UK, Japan Foreign Ministry
Nicolas Politis (1872–1942) Greece, P, League of Nations	James W. Garner (1871–1938) University of Illinois		*Josh Bassett Moore (1860–1947) Columbia University, PCIJ	Sakutaro Tachi (1874–1943) Japan
Walther Schücking (1875–1935) Germany, PCIJ	Arthur Kuhn (1876–1954) League to Enforce Peace		Robert Lansing (1864–1928) Secretary of State	
Charles DeVisscher (1884–1973) Belgium, P, PCIJ, SF	Charles G. Fenwick (1880–1973) Bryn Mawr College	George A. Finch (1884–1957) ASIL, SF	*James Brown Scott [bullet] (1866–1943) ASIL, P	
Hans Wehberg (1885–1962) Germany	Manley O. Hudson (1886–1960) Harvard Law School, P, PCIJ		*Charles Cheney Hyde (1873–1952) Columbia University	
Kisaburo Yokota (1896–1970) Japan	Quincy Wright (1890–1970) University of Chicago		*Philip Marshall Brown (1875–1966) Princeton University	
Hersch Lauterpacht (1897–1960) UK	Clyde Eagleton (1891–1958) New York University, SF	Philip Jessup (1897–1986) Columbia University	*Edwin Borchard (1884–1951) Yale Law School	

Other Important Americans

Salmon O. Levinson (1865–1941) Outlawry of War	Charles Evans Hughes [bullet] (1892–1948) Secretary of State
Westel W. Willoughby (1867–1945) Johns Hopkins University	
Henry L. Stimson (1867–1950) Secretary of State	
Cordell Hull [bullet] (1871–1955) Secretary of State	
*Stanley K. Hornbeck (1883–1966) State Department	

[bullet] Presidents of the ASIL
1. Elihu Root: 1906–1924
2. Charles Evans Hughes: 1924–1929
3. James Brown Scott: 1929–1939
4. Cordell Hull: 1939–1942
* : Working Experience at US State Department (including diplomatic service)
P: Paris Peace Conference
PCIJ: Judge, Permanent Court of International Justice
SF: San Francisco Conference

Figure 1   International lawyers in the interwar years.

BIBLIOGRAPHY

Primary sources

Unpublished manuscript collections

Gaimusho Bunsho, Japanese Diplomatic Archives, Tokyo.

Papers of the American Society of International Law, the American Society of International Law, Washington, DC.

Papers of Edwin M. Borchard, Sterling Library, Yale University, New Haven, Connecticut.

Papers of James Wilford Garner, University Archives, University of Illinois, Urbana, Illinois.

Papers of Green Hackworth, Library of Congress, Washington, DC.

Papers of Stanley K. Hornbeck, Hoover Institution, Stanford University, Stanford, California.

Papers of Manley O. Hudson, Harvard Law Library, Harvard University, Cambridge, Massachusetts.

Papers of Cordell Hull, Library of Congress, Washington, DC.

Papers of Robert H. Jackson, Library of Congress, Washington, DC.

Papers of the League of Nations, League of Nations Archives, Geneva.

Papers of Salmon O. Levinson, Regenstein Library, University of Chicago, Chicago, Illinois.

Papers of Leo Pasvolsky, Library of Congress, Washington, DC.

Papers of James Brown Scott, Manuscript Collection, Georgetown University, Washington, DC.

Papers of Henry L. Stimson, Library of Congress, Washington, DC.

Papers of Quincy Wright, Joseph Regenstein Library, University of Chicago, Chicago, Illinois.

State Department, Decimal File, National Archives, College Park, Maryland.

Official documents

"Conference on the Limitation of Armament, Report of the American Delegation, Senate Document, No. 125, 67th Cong., 2nd Sess.," *AJIL* 16 (1922), 159–233.

Conference on the Limitation of Armament: Washington, November 12, 1921–February 6, 1922. Washington: GPO, 1922.

Foreign Relations of the United States.

Gaimusho ed., *Gaiko nenpyo narabi shuyo monjo* [Major Documents on Japanese Foreign Policy], vol. 2. Tokyo: Hara shobo, 1965.

   Nihon Gaiko Bunsho, Manshu Jihen Bekkan [Documents on Japanese Foreign Policy, the Manchurian Incident Supplement]. Tokyo: Gaimusho, 1981.

League of Nations. Documents and Publications, 1919–1946 (microfilm). New Haven: Research Publications, 1973.

Parliamentary Debates, House of Lords, Fifth Series. Vol. XCV. London: His Majesty's Stationery Office, 1935.

Pritchard, R. John and Sonia Magbanua Zaide, eds. *The Tokyo War Crimes Trial: International Military Tribunal for the Far East, Proceedings Exhibits and Judgment*, vol. 16. London: Garland Publishing, 1981.

The United Nations War Crimes Commission. *History of the United Nations War Crimes Commission and the Development of the Laws of War.* London: His Majesty's Stationery Office, 1948.

US Congress. House Committee on Foreign Affairs. *Exportation of Arms or Munitions of War: Hearings before the House Committee on Foreign Affairs.* 72d Cong. 2d sess., 1933.

US Congress. Senate Committee on Foreign Relations. *Neutrality: Hearings before the Committee on Foreign Relations.* 74th Cong. 2d sess., 1935.

US Congress. Senate. *Outlawry of War: A Plan to Outlaw War.* 67th Cong. 2d sess., 1922. Document no. 115.

US Department of State. *The General Pact for the Renunciation of War: Text of the Pact as Signed Notes and Other Parties.* Washington, DC: GPO, 1928.

   Notes Exchanged between the United States and Other Powers on the Subject of a Multilateral Treaty for the Renunciation of War. Washington, DC: GPO, 1928.

   Postwar Foreign Policy Preparation, 1939–1945. Washington, DC: GPO, 1949.

Periodicals

American Journal of International Law.

British Year Book of International Law.

Proceedings of the American Society of International Law.

Carnegie Endowment for International Peace, *Yearbook.*

Gaiko Jiho.

International Conciliation.

Kokusai Ho Gaiko Zasshi.

Proceedings of the Conference of the Teachers of International Law and Related Subjects.

Primary works by international lawyers

Alvarez, Alejandro. "The New International Law." *Transactions of the Grotius Society* 15 (1929), 35–48.

American Bar Association. *Neutrality and International Sanctions*. Chicago: American Bar Association, 1936.

American Committee for the Outlawry of War. "Outlawry of War." December 25, 1921.

American Relations with China: A Report of the Conference held at Johns Hopkins University, September 17–20, 1925, with Supplementary Materials. Baltimore: Johns Hopkins Press, 1925.

American Society for Judicial Settlement of International Disputes. *Proceedings of International Conference*. Baltimore: Waverly Press, 1911.

Baty, Thomas. "Abuse of Terms: 'Recognition': 'War'." *AJIL* 30 (1936), 377–399.

  "Can an Anarchy Be a State?" *AJIL* 28 (1934), 444–455.

  The Canons of International Law. London: John Murray, 1930.

  "Danger Signals in International Law." *Yale Law Journal* 34 (1925), 457–479.

  "The Free Sea – Produce the Evidence!" *AJIL* 35 (1941), 227–242.

  International Law. London: John Murray, 1909.

  International Law in Twilight. Tokyo: Maruzen Company, 1954.

  "A Modern Jus Gentium." *Juridical Review* 20 (1908–9), 109–120.

  "Naval Warfare: Law and License." *AJIL* (1916), 42–52.

  "Neglected Fundamentals of Prize Law." *Yale Law Journal* 30 (1920), 34–47.

  "The Obligations of Extinct States." *Yale Law Journal* 35 (1926), 434–437.

  "Prize Law and Modern Conditions." *AJIL* 26 (1931), 625–641.

  "The Supposed Chaos in the Law of Nations." *University of Pennsylvania Law Review* 63 (1915), 703–717.

  "The Trend of International Law." *AJIL* 33 (1939), 653–664.

  "War Problems." *Juridical Review* 26 (1914), 255–258.

Baty, Thomas and J. H. Morgan. *War: Its Conduct and Legal Results*. London: John Murray, 1915.

Borchard, Edwin M. "The Arms Embargo and Neutrality." *AJIL* 27 (1933), 293–298.

  "The Attorney General's Opinion on the Exchange of Destroyers for Naval Base." *AJIL* 34 (1940), 690–697.

  "A Century of International Law." In *Law: A Century of Progress 1835–1935*, vol. 2. New York University Press, 1937.

  "The Distinction between Legal and Political Questions." *Proceedings, ASIL* (1924), 50–57.

  "The Dumbarton Oaks Conference." *AJIL* 39 (1945), 97–101.

  "The Effect of War on Law." *AJIL* 40 (1946), 620–623.

  "The 'Enforcement' of Peace by 'Sanctions'." *AJIL* 27 (1933), 518–525.

  "Flaws in Post-War Peace Plans." *AJIL* 38 (1944), 284–289.

ed. *Guide to the Law and Legal Literature of Germany.* Washington, DC: GPO, 1912.

"The Legal Evolution of Peace." *American Law Review* 45 (1911), 708–717.

"The Multilateral Treaty for the Renunciation of War." *AJIL* 23 (1929), 116–120.

"Neutrality and Unneutrality." *AJIL* 32 (1938), 778–782.

"Political Theory and International Law." In Charles E. Merriam, ed. *A History of Political Theories: Recent Times.* New York: Macmillan, 1924, 120–140.

"Realism v. Evangelism." *AJIL* 28 (1934), 108–117.

"Recent Developments in International and Municipal Law." *Law Library Journal* 10 (1917), 21–24.

"The Resurrection of International Law." *Proceedings, ASIL* (1923), 61–70.

Review of *Maritime Trade in Law*, by Lord Eustace Percy. *Yale Law Journal* 40 (1931), 492–495.

"Sanctions v. Neutrality." *AJIL* 30 (1936), 91–94.

"The Various Meanings of International Cooperation." *Annals of the American Academy of Political and Social Science* 186 (1936), 114–123.

"'War' and 'Peace'." *AJIL* 27 (1933), 117–127.

"War, Neutrality and Non-Belligerency." *AJIL* 35 (1941), 618–625.

Borchard, Edwin M. and William Potter Lage. *Neutrality for the United States.* New Haven: Yale University Press, 1937.

Brierly, J. L. *The Law of Nations: An Introduction to the International Law of Peace.* 6th edn. New York: Oxford University Press, 1963.

Brown, Philip Marshall. "Changing Concepts of International Law." *AJIL* 34 (1940), 503–505.

"The Geneva Protocol." *AJIL* 19 (1925), 338–340.

"International Lawlessness." *AJIL* 32 (1938), 775–778.

"The Interpretation of the General Pact for the Renunciation of War." *AJIL* 7 (1929), 374–379.

"Japanese Interpretation of the Kellogg Pact." *AJIL* 27 (1933), 100–102.

"Malevolent Neutrality." *AJIL* 30 (1936), 88–90.

"Munitions and Neutrality." *Proceedings, ASIL* (1916), 33–42.

"Neutrality." *AJIL* 33 (1939), 726–728.

"The Shifting Bases of International Law." *AJIL* 35 (1941), 654–656.

"The 'Understandings' of International Law." *AJIL* 13 (1919), 738–741.

"The Understandings of International Law." *AJIL* 15 (1921), 69–70.

Brownlie, Ian. *International Law and the Use of Force by States.* Oxford: Clarendon Press, 1964.

Butler, Charles Henry. "Treaties Made under Duress." *Proceedings, ASIL* (1932), 45–48.

Calderon, Francisco Garcia. "Geneva Protocol as it Affects the Monroe Doctrine." *Current History* 21 (1925), 506–511.

Carnegie Endowment for International Peace. *Manchuria: Treaties and Agreements*. Washington, DC: Carnegie Endowment for International Peace, 1921.

Report on the Teaching of International Law in the Educational Institutions of the United States. n.p., 1913.

Chamberlain, Joseph. "The Doctrine of *rebus sic stantibus*." *Proceedings, ASIL* (1932), 59–62.

Chicago Council on Foreign Relations. *Significance to America of the Geneva Protocol*. Chicago Council on Foreign Relations, n.d.

Clyde, Paul. *International Rivalries in Manchuria, 1689–1922*. Columbus: Ohio State University Press, 1928.

Colegrove, Kenneth W. "Enforcement of Treaty Obligations: Self-help and Self-defense." *Proceedings, ASIL* (1932), 96–101.

Colombos, John. "The Pact of Paris, Otherwise Called the Kellogg Pact," *Transactions of the Grotius Society* 14 (1928), 87–101.

Condliffe, J. B., ed. *Problems of the Pacific, 1929*. University of Chicago Press, 1930.

Conference of American Teachers of International Law. Washington, DC: Byron S. Adams, 1914.

"Conference on the Limitation of Armament, Report of the American Delegation, Senate Document, No. 125, 67th Cong., 2nd Sess.," *AJIL* 16 (1922), 159–233.

"Consideration of Reports of the Subcommittees," *Proceedings, ASIL* (1922), 74–93.

Courdert, Frederic R. *A Half Century of International Problems: A Lawyer's Views*. New York: Columbia University Press, 1954.

"International Law and American Policy during the Last Thirty-Five Years." *AJIL* 35 (1941), 429–434.

Dennis, William C. "The Doctrine of *rebus sic stantibus*." *Proceedings, ASIL* (1932), 53–59.

"International Organization: Executive and Administrative." *Proceedings, ASIL* (1917), 92–101.

Review of *Foreign Rights and Interests in China*, by Westel W. Willoughby. *AJIL* 5 (1921), 628–630.

"Design for a Charter of the General International Organization (GIO)." *AJIL, Supplement* 38 (1944), 216–223.

Dicey, A. V. *Introduction to the Study of the Law of the Constitution*. London: Macmillan, 1889.

Dickinson, Edwin D. "Discussion," *Proceedings, ASIL* (1943), 46–50.

"Reports of the Round Table Conferences." *American Political Science Review* 19 (1925), 372–376.

"Discussion." *Proceedings, ASIL* (1924), 67–83, 117–125.

"Discussion." *Proceedings, ASIL* (1927), 63–81.

"Discussion." *Proceedings, ASIL* (1932), 63–66.

Eagleton, Clyde. "The Duty of Impartiality on the Part of a Neutral." *AJIL* 34 (1940), 99–104.

"Far Eastern Policy of the United States." *AJIL* 31 (1937), 665–669.

"The Form and Function of the Declaration of War." *AJIL* 32 (1938), 19–35.

International Government. New York: Royal Press, 1948.

"International Law and 'Public Order'." *AJIL* 33 (1939), 545–549.

"The Needs of International Law." *AJIL* 34 (1940), 699–703.

"Neutrality and Neutral Rights Following the Pact of Paris for the Renunciation of War." *Proceedings, ASIL* (1930), 87–95.

"Of the Illusion That War Does Not Change." *AJIL* 35 (1941), 659–662.

"Organization of the Community of Nations." *AJIL* 36 (1942), 229–241.

Eichelberger, Clark M. *Organizing for Peace: A Personal History of the Founding of the United Nations.* New York: Harper & Row, 1977.

Fenwick, Charles G. "The Authority of Vattel." *American Political Science Review* 7 (1913), 388–410.

"Denunciation of the Disarmament Clause of the Treaty of Versailles." *AJIL* 29 (1935), 675–678.

"The Development of Collective Security, 1914–1954." *Proceedings, ASIL* (1954), 2–13.

"The Distinction between Legal and Political Questions." *Proceedings, ASIL* (1924), 44–50.

"The Executive Legislative and Judicial Recognition of International Law in the United States." *Michigan Law Review* 11 (1913), 296–301.

"The 'Failure' of the League of Nations." *AJIL* 30 (1936), 506–509.

"Fuit Austria." *AJIL* 32 (1938), 312–314.

International Law. New York: The Century Co., 1924.

"International Law and International Trade." *AJIL* 29 (1935), 284–286.

"International Law and Lawless Nations." *AJIL* 33 (1939), 743–746.

"International Organization: Judicial." *Proceedings, ASIL* (1917), 65–75.

"The Legal Significance of the Locarno Agreement." *AJIL* 20 (1926), 108–111.

"National Security and International Arbitration." *AJIL* 18 (1924), 777–781.

"Neutrality and International Organization." *AJIL* 28 (1934), 334–339.

"Neutrality and Responsibility." *AJIL* 29 (1935), 663–665.

"The New Immigration Law and the Exclusion of Japanese." *AJIL* 18 (1924), 519–523.

"The Nine Power Treaty and the Present Crisis in China." *AJIL* 31 (1937), 671–674.

"Organization and Procedure of the Peace Conference." *American Political Science Review* 13 (1919), 199–212.

"An Outline of the Problems Presented in the Further Development of International Law." *Proceedings, ASIL* (1923), 47–52.

"The Outlook for International Law." *AJIL* 33 (1939), 105–108.

"The Relation of the Franco-Soviet Pact to the Locarno Treaty." *AJIL* 30 (1936), 265–270.

"The Revision of Neutrality Legislation in Time of Foreign War." *AJIL* 33 (1939), 728–730.

"Two Representatives of the Grotian School." *AJIL* 8 (1914), 38–50.

"The Sources of International Law." *Michigan Law Review* 16 (1918), 393–401.

"War as an Instrument of National Policy." *AJIL* 22 (1928), 826–829.

Finch, George A. "The American Society of International Law 1906–1956." *AJIL* 50 (1956), 293–312.

"Introductory Remarks." *Proceedings, ASIL* (1931), 1–6.

"Retribution for War Crimes." *AJIL* 37 (1943), 81–88.

"Secretary of State Hull's Pillars of Enduring Peace." *AJIL* 31 (1937), 688–693.

Garner, James W. "The Doctrine of *Rebus Sic Stantibus* and the Termination of Treaties." *AJIL* 21 (1927), 509–516.

"The Geneva Protocol for the Pacific Settlement of International Disputes." *AJIL* 19 (1925), 123–132.

International Law and the World War. London: Longmans, Green, 1920.

The League of Nations and the Monroe Doctrine. Chicago: League to Enforce Peace, Illinois Branch, n.d.

"Limitations on National Sovereignty in International Relations." *The American Political Science Review* 19 (1925), 1–24.

"Non-Recognition of Illegal Territorial Annexations and Claims to Sovereignty." *AJIL* 30 (1936), 679–688.

"Questions of International Law in the Spanish Civil War." *AJIL* 31 (1937), 66–73.

Recent Developments in International Law. University of Calcutta, 1925.

"Recognition of Belligerency." *AJIL* 32 (1938), 106–113.

Review of *Maritime Trade in Law*, by Lord Eustace Percy. *AJIL* 25 (1931), 182–184.

"Revision of Treaties and the Doctrine of *Rebus Sic Stantibus.*" *Iowa Law Review* 19 (1934), 312–329.

"Some True and False Conceptions Regarding the Duty of Neutrals in Respect to the Sale and Exportation of Arms and Munitions to Belligerents." *Proceedings, ASIL* (1916), 18–31.

"The United States Neutrality Act of 1937." *AJIL* 31 (1937), 385–397.

"Violations of Maritime Law by the Allied Powers During the World War." *AJIL* 25 (1931), 26–49.

Garner, James W. and Valentine Jobst III. "The Unilateral Denunciation of Treaties by One Party because of Alleged Non-Performance by Another Party or Parties." *AJIL* 29 (1935), 569–585.

"General Discussion." *Proceedings, ASIL* (1926), 37–57.

Hall, W. E. *A Treatise on International Law*, 3rd edn. Oxford: Clarendon Press, 1892.

Hill, David Jayne. "Legal Limitations upon the Initiation of Military Action." *Proceedings, ASIL* (1925), 95–102.

"The Multilateral Treaty for the Renunciation of War." *AJIL* 22 (1928), 823–826.

Hishida, Seiji. *Comments on John Bassett Moore's Discussion*. Tokyo: Maruzen, 1933.

"History of the Organization of the American Society of International Law." *Proceedings, ASIL* (1907), 23–40.

Hornbeck, Stanley K. "Discussion." *Proceedings, ASIL* (1917), 123–124.

Review of *International Rivalries in Manchuria*, by Paul Clyde. *AJIL* 21 (1927), 632–635.

Hsü, Shu-hsi. and Robert Moore Duncan. *The Manchurian Dilemma: Force or Pacific Settlement*. n.p.: China Council, Institute of Pacific Relations, 1931.

Hudson, Manley O. "An Approach to the Dumbarton Oaks Proposals." *AJIL* 39 (1945), 95–97.

By Pacific Means: The Implementation of Article Two of the Pact of Paris. New Haven: Yale University Press, 1935.

"A Challenge to American Lawyers." *American Bar Association Journal* 8 (1922), 83–85.

"Contemporary Development of International Law." *The Proceedings of the Second Conference of the Teachers of International Law* (1925), 83–94.

Current International Co-operation. University of Calcutta, 1927.

"A Design for a Charter of the General International Organization." *AJIL* 38 (1944), 711–714.

"The Development of International Law since the War." *AJIL* 22 (1928), 330–350.

"The Distinction between Legal and Political Questions." *Proceedings, ASIL* (1924), 126–132.

"The Geneva Protocol." *Foreign Affairs* 3 (1924), 226–235.

"The International Law of the Future." *Proceedings, ASIL* (1944), 9–19.

"The International Law of the Future." *AJIL* 38 (1944), 278–281.

"International Legislation." *Proceedings, ASIL* (1923), 52–55.

"The Outlook for the Development of International Law." *American Bar Association Journal* 11 (1925), 102–107.

"The Prospect for International Law in the Twentieth Century." *The Cornell Law Quarterly* 10 (1925), 419–459.

"Report of the Assembly of the League of Nations on the Sino-Japanese Dispute." *AJIL* 27 (1933), 300–305.

Hull, Cordell. *The Memoirs of Cordell Hull*. London: Hodder & Stoughton, 1948.

Hyde, Charles Cheney. "The Boycott as a Sanction of International Law." *Proceedings, ASIL* (1933), 34–40.

"Punishment of War Criminals." *Proceedings, ASIL* (1943), 39–46.

"Legal Aspects of Japanese Pronouncement in Relation to China." *AJIL* 28 (1934), 431–443.

"Secretary Hull on the Kellogg–Briand Pact." *AJIL* 35 (1941), 117–118.

International Law Association. *Briand–Kellogg Pact of Paris: Articles of Interpretation as Adopted by the Budapest Conference 1934.* London: Sweet & Maxwell, 1934.

Report of the Thirty-Sixth Conference (1930).

Report of the Thirty-Seventh Conference (1932).

"The International Law of the Future," *Supplement, AJIL* 38 (1944), 41–135.

Ito, N. "Le pacte de Paris et le pacte de la Société des Nations." *Revue Politique et Parlementaire* 37 (1930), 14–36.

Jackson, Robert H. "Address." *Proceedings, ASIL* (1945), 10–19.

"Address of Robert H. Jackson, Attorney General of the United States, before Inter-American Bar Association, Havana, Cuba, March 27, 1941." *AJIL* 35 (1941), 353–359.

"Nürnberg in Retrospect." *Canadian Bar Review* 27 (1949), 761–781.

Report of Robert H. Jackson, United States Representative to the International Conference on Military Trials. Washington, DC: GPO, 1949.

Jessup, Philip C. *American Neutrality and International Police.* Boston: World Peace Foundation, 1928.

"Defense of Oppressed People." *AJIL* 32 (1938), 116–119.

"A Half-Century of Efforts to Substitute Law for War." *Recueil des Cours* 99 (1960), 3–20.

"In Support of International Law." *AJIL* 34 (1940), 505–508.

"International Law and Totalitarian War." *AJIL* 35 (1941), 329–331.

"Is Neutrality Essential?" *Proceedings, ASIL* (1933), 134–142.

Neutrality, its History, Economics and Law. New York: Columbia University Press, 1936.

"The New Neutrality Legislation." *AJIL* 29 (1935), 665–670.

"Some Phases of the Administrative and Judicial Interpretation of the Immigration Act of 1924." *Yale Law Journal* 35 (1926), 705–724.

"Toward Further Neutrality Legislation." *AJIL* 30 (1936), 262–265.

Kellogg, Frank B. *The Settlement of International Controversies by Pacific Means: An Address by the Honorable Frank B. Kellogg.* Washington, DC: GPO, 1928.

"The War Prevention Policy of the United States." *AJIL* 22 (1928), 253–261.

Kelsen, Hans. "Recognition in International Law: Theoretical Observations." *AJIL* 35 (1941), 605–617.

Kuhn, Arthur. "The Economic Sanctions and the Kellogg Pact." *AJIL* 30 (1936), 83–88.

"Lytton Report on the Manchurian Crisis." *AJIL* 27 (1933), 96–100.

"Observations of Foreign Governments upon Secretary Hull's Principles of Enduring Peace." *AJIL* 32 (1938), 101–106.

Kunz, Josef L. "The Law of Nations, Static and Dynamic." *AJIL* 27 (1933), 630–650.

"The 'Vienna School' and International Law." *New York University Law Quarterly Review* 11 (1934), 370–421.

Kuratowski, Roman K. "International Law Conference of the Grotius Society." *AJIL* 38 (1944), 474–475.

Lauterpacht, Hersch. "The Law of Nations and the Punishment of War Crimes." *British Year Book of International Law* 21 (1944), 58–95.

"The Pact of Paris and the Budapest Articles of Interpretation." *Transactions of the Grotius Society* 20 (1935), 178–206.

Lawrence, T. J. *A Handbook of Public International Law*, 10th edn. by Percy H. Winfield. London: Macmillan, 1925.

"The League of Nations and the Laws of War." *British Year Book of International Law* 1 (1920–1), 109–124.

Levinson, Salmon O. "Abolishing the Institution of War." *Christian Century* 65 (March 22, 1928), 377–378.

"The Legal Status of War." *New Republic* 14 (March 9, 1918), 171–173.

The Outlawry of War, December 25, 1921, American Committee for the Outlawry of War.

The Outlawry of War. Washington, DC: GPO, 1922.

"A Proposed Treaty to Outlaw War." *Christian Century* 63 (December 26, 1926), 1581–1582.

Lippmann, Walter. "The Outlawry of War." *Atlantic Monthly* 132 (1923), 245–253.

"The Political Equivalent of War." *Atlantic Monthly* 142 (1928), 181–187.

MacMurray, John V. A. "Opening Remarks of the Presiding Officer." *Proceedings, ASIL* (1932), 37–45.

ed. *Treaties and Agreements with and Concerning China 1894–1919*. New York: Oxford University Press, 1921.

McNair, Arnold D. "The Stimson Doctrine of Non-Recognition: A Note on its Legal Aspects." *British Year Book of International Law* 14 (1933), 65–74.

Manning, C. A. "The Proposed Amendments to the Covenant of the League of Nations." *British Year Book of International Law* 10 (1930), 158–171.

"Meeting of the Committee for the Advancement of International Law." *Proceedings, ASIL* (1921), 83–101.

"Meeting of the Committee for the Advancement of International Law," *Proceedings, ASIL* (1992), 37–41.

Merriam, Charles E., ed. *A History of Political Theories, Recent Times*. New York: Macmillan, 1924.

Miller, David Hunter. *The Drafting of the Covenant*. New York: G. P. Putnam's Sons, 1928.

The Geneva Protocol. New York: Macmillan, 1925.

"Minutes of the Meeting of the Executive Council, April 17, 1919, International Law and the Peace Settlement." *Proceedings, ASIL* (1919), 45–64.

Moore, Frederick. "The Far Eastern Settlement of the Conference of Washington." *Proceedings, ASIL* (1922), 26–36.

Moore, John Bassett. "An Appeal to Reason." *Foreign Affairs* 11 (1933), 547–588.

"The New Isolation." *AJIL* 27 (1933), 607–629.

"Post-War International Law." *Columbia Law Review* 27 (1927), 400–412.

Morgenthau, Hans J. "Positivism, Functionalism and International Law." *AJIL* 34 (1940), 260–284.

"The Problem of Neutrality." *University of Kansas City Law Review* 7 (1939), 109–128.

Morris, Roland S. "The Pact of Paris for the Renunciation of War: Its Meaning and Effect in International Law." *Proceedings, ASIL* (1929), 88–91.

Morrison, Charles Clayton. *The Outlawry of War*. Chicago: Willett, Clark, & Colby, 1927.

Niemeyer, Gerhart. "International Law and Social Structure." *AJIL* 34 (1940), 588–600.

Law without Force: The Function of Politics in International Law. Princeton University Press, 1941.

Nippold, Otfried. *The Development of International Law after the World War*. Oxford: Clarendon Press, 1923.

Observations of the Japanese Government on the Report of the Commission of Enquiry. Tokyo: League of Nations Association of Japan, 1932.

"Opening Discussion by Professor James W. Garner." *Proceedings, ASIL* (1926), 27–31.

Oppenheim, Lassa Francis. *Die Zukunft des Völkerrechts* [The Future of International Law]. Leipzig: W. Engelmann, 1911.

The Future of International Law. Oxford: Clarendon Press, 1921.

International Law, 3rd edn. London: Longmans, Green and Co., 1920.

The League of Nations and its Problems. London: Longmans, Green and Co., 1919.

"The Science of International Law: Its Task and Method." *AJIL* 2 (1908), 313–356.

Politis, Nicolas. *Neutrality and Peace*. Washington, DC: Carnegie Endowment for International Peace, 1935.

The New Aspects of International Law. Washington, DC: Carnegie Endowment for International Peace, 1928.

Pollock, Frederick. "Cosmopolitan Custom and International Law." *Harvard Law Review* 29 (1916), 565–581.

"Methods of International Arbitration." *Law Quarterly Review* 140 (1919), 320–333.

"The Sources of International Law." *Columbia Law Review* 2 (1902), 511–524.

"The Work of the League of Nations." *Law Quarterly Review* 138 (1919), 193–198.

Pound, Roscoe. "Grotius in the Science of Law." *AJIL* 19 (1925), 685–688.

"Philosophical Theory and International Law." *Bibliotheca Visseriana* 1 (1923), 71–90.

"Professors and Instructors of International Law (1911–1912)." *Teaching of International law at the Educational Institutions in the United States* (n.p., April 18, 1913).

Pugsley, C. D. "Discussion." *Proceedings, ASIL* (1917), 118.

Quigley, Harold Scott. "Legal Phases of the Shantung Question." *Minnesota Law Review* 6 (1922), 380–394.

"The Scope, Organization and Aim of Courses in International Law in Relation to Other Courses in International Subjects." *Proceedings of the Second Conference of the Teachers of International Law and Related Subjects* (1925), 7–12.

"Enforcement of Treaty Obligations: Self-help and Self-defense." *Proceedings, ASIL* (1932), 90–96.

Ralston, Jackson H. "The Codification of International Law." *Proceedings, ASIL* (1910), 34–42.

Democracy's International Law. Washington, DC: J. Byrne, 1922.

"How Fundamental International Law is to be Discovered." *American Law Review* 56 (1922), 236–249.

Review of *International Law and the World War,* by James Wilford Garner. *AJIL* 15 (1921), 621.

Review of *International Law,* by Charles G. Fenwick. *AJIL* 18 (1924), 853–855.

Reinsch, Paul S. *An American Diplomat in China.* Garden City: Doubleday, 1922.

Colonial Government: An Introduction to the Study of Colonial Institutions. New York: Macmillan, 1916.

"The Concept of Legality in International Arbitration." *AJIL* 5 (1911), 604–614.

"Failure and Successes at the Second Hague Conference." *American Political Science Review* 2 (1908), 204–220.

"International Administrative Law and National Sovereignty." *AJIL* 3 (1909), 1–45.

"International Unions and their Administration." *AJIL* 1 (1907), 579–623.

Public International Unions: Their Work and Organization. Boston: Ginn and Company, 1911.

Review of *International Law*, by Thomas Baty. *AJIL* 5 (1911), 268–270.
Rockhill, William Woodville. *Treaties and Conventions with or Concerning China and Korea, 1894–1904, Together with Various State Papers and Documents Affecting Foreign Interest.* Washington: GPO, 1904.
Root, Elihu. "International Law at the Arms Conference." *Proceedings, ASIL* (1922), 1–12.
"Letter of Honorable Root to Honorable Will H. Hays, March 29, 1919." *AJIL* 13 (July 1919), 568–587.
"Opening Address." *Proceedings, ASIL* (1921), 1–13.
"The Outlook for International Law." *Proceedings, ASIL* (1915), 2–11.
"The Need of Popular Understanding of International Law." *AJIL* 1 (1907), 1–3.
Schüking, Walter and Hans Wehberg. *Die Satzung des Völkerbundes.* Berlin: Franz Vahlen, 1921.
Scott, James Brown. "Conference on the Limitation of Armament and Problems of the Pacific." *AJIL* 15 (1921), 503–510.
"International Law in Legal Education." *Columbia Law Review* 4 (1904), 409–422.
"International Organization, Executive and Administrative." *Proceedings, ASIL* (1917), 101–107.
"The Legal Nature of International Law." *AJIL* 1 (1907), 831–866.
"The Place of International Law in Legal Education." *American Law School Review* 1 (1903–4), 154–157.
"The Progress of International Law During the Last Twenty-Five Years." *Proceedings, ASIL* (1931), 2–34.
"The Study of Law." *The American Law School Review* 2 (1906–7), 3–4.
"The Work of the Second Hague Conference." *AJIL* 2 (1908), 1–28.
Shotwell, James T. *On the Rim of Abyss.* New York: Macmillan, 1936.
War as an Instrument of National Policy and its Renunciation in the Pact of Paris. London: Constable, 1929.
Significance to America of the Geneva Protocol. Chicago Council on Foreign Relations, n.d.
Snow, Alpheus Henry. "International Law and Political Science." *AJIL* 7 (1913), 315–328.
Stimson, Henry L. "Bases of American Foreign Policy during the Past Four Years." *Foreign Affairs* 11 (1933), 383–396.
"Neutrality and War Prevention." *Proceedings, ASIL* (1935), 121–129.
The Pact of Paris: Three Years of Development. Washington, DC: GPO, 1932.
Stoner, John E. *S. O. Levinson and the Pact of Paris.* University of Chicago Press, 1942.
Stowell, Ellery C. *International Law: A Restatement of Principles in Conformity with Actual Practice.* New York: Henry Holt and Company, 1931.
The Legal Advisor of the Department of State. Washington, DC: Digest Press, 1936.

Trimble, E. G. "Violations of Maritime Law by the Allied Powers during the World War." *AJIL* 24 (1930), 79–99.

Turlington, Edgar. "Treaties Made under Duress." *Proceedings, ASIL* (1932), 49–53.

The University of Chicago, Norman Wait Harris Memorial Foundation, "Reports of Round Tables, 1936: Neutrality and Collective Security."

Warren, Charles. "Belligerent Aircraft, Neutral Trade, and Unpreparedness." *AJIL* 29 (1935), 197–205.

"Congress and Neutrality." In Quincy Wright, ed. *Neutrality and Collective Security*. University of Chicago Press, 1936, 109–153.

"The Lack of Preparedness in International Lawyers." *Report of Proceedings of the Thirteenth Annual Meeting of the American Branch of the International Law Association* (1934), 31–44.

"Prepare for Neutrality." *Yale Review* 24 (1935), 467–478.

"Troubles of a Neutral." *Foreign Affairs* 12 (1934), 377–394.

"What are the Rights of Neutrals Now, in Practice?" *Proceedings, ASIL* (1933), 128–134.

Wehberg, Hans. *The Limitation of Armaments*. Washington, DC: Carnegie Endowment, 1921.

The Outlawry of War. Washington, DC: Carnegie Endowment for International Peace, 1931.

"Restrictive Clauses in International Arbitration Treaties." *AJIL* 7 (1913), 301–314.

White, Thomas Raeburn. "Limitations upon the Initiation of War," *Proceedings; ASIL* (1925), 102–111.

Wickersham, George W. "The Pact of Paris: a Gesture or a Pledge?" *Foreign Affairs* 7 (1929), 356–371.

Wild, Rayson S. "What is the Trouble with International Law?" *American Political Science Review* 32 (1938), 478–494.

Williams, John Fischer. *Chapters on Current International Law and the League of Nations*. London: Longmans, 1929.

"La Convention pour L'assistance Financière aux États Victimes D'Agression." *Recueil des Cours* 34 (1930), 81–174.

"The New Doctrine of 'Recognition'." *Transactions of the Grotius Society* 18 (1932), 109–129.

"A 'New' International Law." *International Law Association, Report of the Thirty-third Conference* (1924), 434–450.

"Some Thoughts on the Doctrine of Recognition in International Law." *Harvard Law Review* 47 (1934), 776–794.

Willoughby, Westel W. *China at the Conference*. Baltimore: Johns Hopkins Press, 1922.

"Far Eastern Policies of the United States." *AJIL* 34 (1940), 193–207.

Foreign Rights and Interests in China. Baltimore: Johns Hopkins Press, 1920.

Japan's Case Examined. Baltimore: Johns Hopkins Press, 1940.

"The Legal Nature of International Law." *AJIL* 2 (1908), 357–365.

"Principles of International Law and Justice raised by China at the Washington Conference." *Proceedings, ASIL* (1922), 19–24.

The Sino-Japanese Controversy and the League of Nations. Baltimore: Johns Hopkins Press, 1935.

"The Study of the Law." *Virginia Law Review* 6 (1920), 461–481.

Woolsey, T. S. "A Code of International Law – Is It Possible?" *Yale Law Journal* 12 (1902), 57–62.

"Lecture on International Law." *Yale Law Journal* 8 (1899), 387–402.

Wright, Lord. "War Crimes under International Law." *Law Quarterly Review* 62 (1946), 40–52.

Wright, Quincy. "American Neutrality." *Southern Review* 3 (1938), 747–761.

"Article 19 of the League Covenant and the Doctrine *Rebus Sic Stantibus.*" *Proceedings, ASIL* (1936), 55–73.

The Causes of War and the Conditions of Peace. London: Longmans, Green, 1924.

"Changes in the Conceptions of War." *AJIL* 18 (1924), 755–767.

"Collective Rights and Duties." *Proceedings, ASIL* (1932), 101–109.

"The Concept of Aggression in International Law." *AJIL* 29 (1935), 373–395.

The Control of American Foreign Relations. New York: Macmillan, 1922.

"Denunciation of Treaty Violators." *AJIL* 32 (1938), 526–535.

"The Distinction between Legal and Political Questions with Especial Reference to the Monroe Doctrine." *Proceedings, ASIL* (1924), 57–67.

"The Effect of the War on International Law." *Minnesota Law Review* 5 (1921), 436–458; (1921), 515–539.

"Effects of the League of Nations Covenant." *American Political Science Review* 13 (1919), 556–576.

"The End of a Period of Transition." *AJIL* 31 (1937), 604–613.

The Existing Legal Situation as it Relates to the Conflict in the Far East. New York: Institute of Pacific Relations, 1939.

"How Should the Neutrality Act of August 31, 1935, Be Revised?" *Georgetown Law Journal* 24 (1936), 416–423.

"International Law and the World Order." In Walter H. C. Laves, ed. *The Foundations of a More Stable World Order.* University of Chicago Press, 1940, 107–134.

"International Law and Commercial Relations." *Proceedings, ASIL* (1941), 30–39.

"International Law and the Totalitarian States." *American Political Science Review* 35 (1941), 738–743.

"The Interpretation of Multilateral Treaties." *AJIL* 23 (1929), 94–107.

"The Kyoto Conference of the Institute of Pacific Relations." *American Political Science Review* 24 (1930), 451–457.

"The Law of the Nuremberg Trial." *AJIL* 41 (1947), 38–72.

"The Legal Foundation of the Stimson Doctrine." *Pacific Affairs* 8 (1935), 439–446.

"The Legal Liability of the Kaiser." *American Political Science Review* 13 (1919), 120–128.

"The Legal Nature of Treaties." *AJIL* 10 (1916), 706–736.

ed. *Legal Problems in the Far Eastern Conflict.* New York: Institute of Pacific Relations, 1941.

"The Lend Lease Bill and International Law." *AJIL* 35 (1941), 305–314.

"The Manchurian Crisis." *American Political Science Review* 26 (1932), 45–76.

"Meaning of the Pact of Paris." *AJIL* 27 (1933), 39–61.

"Munich Settlement and International Law." *AJIL* 33 (1939), 12–32.

"National Attitudes on the Far Eastern Controversy." *American Political Science Review* 27 (1933), 555–576.

"National Sovereignty and Collective Security." *Annals of the American Academy of Political and Social Science* 186 (1936), 94–104.

ed. *Neutrality and Collective Security.* University of Chicago Press, 1936.

"Neutrality and Neutral Rights Following the Pact of Paris for the Renunciation of War." *Proceedings, ASIL* (1930), 79–87.

"The Outlawry of War." *AJIL* 19 (1925), 76–103.

"The Path to Peace." *World Unity* 13 (1933), 135–148.

"The Present Status of Neutrality." *AJIL* 34 (1940), 391–415.

"The Prospects of International Law." *Proceedings, ASIL* (1956), 2–11.

Research in International Law since the War: A Report to the International Relations Committee of the Social Science Research Council. Washington, DC: Carnegie Endowment for International Peace, 1930.

"Responsibilities of the United States in the Post-War World." *Free World* 5 (1943), 35–48.

Review of *Japan's Special Position in Manchuria*, by C. Walter Young. *AJIL* 26 (1932), 217–220.

"The Rhineland Occupation and the Enforcement of Treaties." *AJIL* 30 (1936), 486–494.

"Stimson Note of January 7, 1932." *AJIL* 26 (1932), 342–348.

"Some Legal Aspects of the Far Eastern Situation." *AJIL* 27 (1933), 509–516.

A Study of War. University of Chicago Press, 1942.

A Study of War, abridged edition, 1964. Chicago: Midway Reprint, 1983.

"The Test of Aggression in the Italo-Ethiopian War." *AJIL* 30 (1936), 45–56.

"The Transfer of Destroyers to Great Britain." *AJIL* 34 (1940), 680–689.

"The Understandings of International Law." *AJIL* 14 (1920), 565–580.

The United States and Neutrality. Public Policy Pamphlet, no. 17. University of Chicago Press, 1935.

"War Criminals." *AJIL* 39 (1945), 257–285.

"The Washington Conference." *Minnesota Law Review* 6 (1922), 279–299.

"When Does War Exist?" *AJIL* 26 (1932), 362–368.

Where the League of Nations Stand Today. The Day and Hour Series, no. 9. University of Minnesota Press, 1934.

Yokota, Kisaburo. "The Recent Development of the Stimson Doctrine." *Pacific Affairs* 8 (1935), 133–143.

Young, C. Walter. *The International Relations of Manchuria.* University of Chicago Press, 1929.

Japan's Special Position in Manchuria. Baltimore: Johns Hopkins Press, 1931.

"Sino-Japanese Interests and Issues in Manchuria." *Pacific Affairs* 1(7) (1928), 1–20.

Zimmern, Alfred. *The League of Nations and the Rule of Law, 1918–1935.* London: Macmillan, 1935.

"The Problem of Collective Security." In Quincy Wright, ed. *Neutrality and Collective Security.* University of Chicago Press, 1936, 3–89.

Japanese materials

Gaimusho hyakunen-shi hensan iinnkai, ed. *Gaimusho no Hyakunen* [The Japanese Foreign Ministry's Hundred Years], vol. 2. Tokyo: Harashobo, 1969.

Kamigawa, Hikomatsu. "Fusen joyaku no kachi hihan" [Critics on the Value of the Kellogg–Briand Pact]. *Gaiko Jiho* 572 (1928), 61–69.

Royama, Masamichi. "Fusen joyaku to Taiheiyo no shorai" [The Kellogg–Briand Pact and Future of the Pacific]. *Chuo Koron* 43 (October 1928), 18–30.

Tachi, Sakutaro, *Beikoku gaiko jo no shoshugi* [Principles of American Foreign Policy]. Tokyo: Nihon hyoron sha, 1942.

"Eikoku no shin Monro-shugi sengen oyobi Fusen joyaku no jikko" [New British Monroe Doctrine and the Effect of the Kellogg–Briand Pact]. *Gaiko Jiho* 577 (1928), 1–4.

"Fubar-shugi (ichimei Suchimuson-shugi) no jittai" [Nature of the Hoover Doctrine (in other words) the Stimson Doctrine]. *Gaiko Jiho* 674 (1933), 185–212.

"Fusen joyaku no kokusaiho-kan" [View of International Law in the Kellogg–Briand Pact]. *Kokusaiho Gaiko Zasshi* 27 (1928), 919–937.

"Fusen joyaku no shin kaishaku o ronnansu" [To Refute the New Interpretations of the Pact]. *Gaiko Jiho* 752 (1936), 1–30.

Heiji kokusaiho ron [International Law of Peace]. Tokyo: Nihon Hyoron sha, 1930.

"Jiei-ken gaisetsu" [An Overview on the Right of Self-defense]. *Kokusaiho Gaiko Zasshi* 31 (1932), 315–340.

"Kokusai Renmei no honshitu ni kanshite" [The Essential Characteristics of the League of Nations]. *Kokusaiho Gaiko Zasshi* 20 (1921), 520–536.

"Kyukoku joyaku" [Nine Power Treaty]. *Gaiko Jiho* 794 (1938), 1–29.

"Manshu to Panama" [Manchuria and Panama]. *Gaiko Jiho* 698 (1934), 1–14.

"Monko kaiho–shugi o ronzu" [To Discuss the Monroe Doctrine]. *Gaiko Jiho* 724 (1935), 1–23.

"Monro shugi no tetteiteki kenkyu" [A Comprehensive Analysis of Monroe Doctrine]. *Gaiko Jiho* 770 (1937), 1–39.

"'Nachisu no kokusai ho kan" [The Nazi View of International Law]. *Kokusaiho Gaiko Zasshi* 36 (1937), 1–30.

"Oppenheim kyoju to sono chosho kokusaiho" [Professor Oppenheim and his Work *International Law*]. *Kokusaiho Gaiko Zasshi* 20 (1921), 241.

"Saikin Manshu jihen ni kanrenshite Fusen joyaku o yomu" [Reading of the Pact in Connection with the Current Manchurian Incident]. *Gaiko Jiho* 649 (1931), 1–8.

Senji kokusaiho ron [International Law of War]. Tokyo: Nihon Hyoron sha, 1931.

Shina jihen kokusaiho ron [International Law and the Sino-Japanese War]. Tokyo: Shoka-do, 1938.

Yanagisawa, Shinnosuke. "Fusen joyaku no seiritusu to Beikoku no sekinin" [The Kellogg–Briand Pact and American Responsibility]. *Gaiko Jiho* 570 (1928), 86–96.

Yokota, Kisaburo. "Manshu jihen to Fuba shugi" [Manchurian Incedent and the Hoover Doctrine]. *Kokusaiho Gaiko Zasshi* 32 (1933), 46–86.

"Senso no zettaiteki kinshi, saikin no Renmei Kiyaku kaisei-an" [The Absolute Abolishment of War: A Recent Proposal to Revise the Covenant of the League]. *Gaiko Jiho* 632 (1931), 14–31.

"Stimson shugi to sekai no taisei" [The Stimson Doctrine and the World Trend]. *Chuo Koron* 48 (May 1933), 24–36.

Watashi no Issho (My Life). Tokyo: Tokyo Shinbun Shuppankyoku, 1976.

Secondary materials

Ambrosius, Loyd E. *Woodrow Wilson and American Diplomatic Tradition.* Cambridge University Press, 1987.

Armstrong, David, Theo Farrell. and Hélène Lambert. *International Law and International Relations.* Cambridge University Press, 2007.

Baxter, R. R. "The Retirement of Miss Eleanor H. Finch as an Assistant Editor of the *Journal*." *AJIL* 66 (1972), 815–816.

Beck, Robert J. "A Study of War and an Agenda for Peace: Reflections on the Contemporary Relevance of Quincy Wright's Plan for 'New International Order'." *Review of International Studies* 22 (1996), 119–147.

Bederman, David J. "Appraising a Century of Scholarship in the *American Journal of International Law*." *AJIL* 100 (2006), 20–63.

Bodendiek, Frank. "Walter Schüking and the Idea of 'International Organization'." *EJIL* 22 (2011), 741–754.

Brynes, Kendal C. "Status of the Rules of War in International Law." Unpublished Ph.D. thesis, University of Chicago, 1952.

Bucklin, Steven J. "Quincy Wright's Blueprint for a Durable Peace." *Mid-America* 76 (1994), 227–240.

"The Wilsonian Legacy in Political Science: Denna F. Fleming, Frederick L. Schuman, and Quincy Wright." Unpublished Ph.D. thesis, University of Iowa, 1993.

Bull, Hedley. *The Anarchical Society: A Study of Order in World Politics*, 3rd edn. New York: Columbia University Press, 2002.

Burks, David D. "The United States and the Geneva Protocol of 1924: 'A New Holy Alliance'?" *American Historical Review* 64 (1959), 891–905.

Burley, Anne-Marie Slaughter. "International Law and International Relations Theory: A Dual Agenda." *AJIL* 87 (1993), 205–239.

Carr, E. H. *The Twenty Years' Crisis 1919–1939*. London: Macmillan, 1939.

Carty, Anthony. "Hersch Lauterpacht: A Powerful Eastern European Figure." *Baltic Yearbook of International Law* 7 (2007), 1–28.

Chickering, Roger. *Imperial Germany and a World without War: The Peace Movement and German Society, 1892–1914*. Princeton University Press, 1975.

Clude, Jr. Inis L. "The Heritage of Quincy Wright." *Journal of Conflict Resolution* 14 (1970), 461–464.

Current, Richard N. "The United States and 'Collective Security'." In Alexander DeConde, ed. *Isolationism and Security: Ideas and Interests in Twentieth-Century American Foreign Policy*. Durham, NC: Duke Univeristy Press, 1957, 33–55.

Davis, Calvin DeArmond. *The United States and the First Hague Peace Conference*. Ithaca: Cornell University Press, 1962.

The United States and the Second Hague Peace Conference: American Diplomacy and International Organization 1899–1914. Durham, NC: Duke University Press, 1975.

Davis, Christopher Mark. "War and Peace in a Multipolar World: A Critique of Quincy Wright's Institutional Analysis of the Interwar International System." *Journal of Strategic Studies* 19 (1996), 31–73.

DeBenedetti, Charles. *Origins of the Modern American Peace Movement*. Millwood: KTO Press, 1978.

Delbrück. Jost. "Law's Frontier – Walther Schüking and the Quest for the *Lex Ferenda*." *EJIL* 22 (2011), 801–808.

Deutsch, Karl W. "Quincy Wright's Contribution to the Study of War." In Quincy Wright, ed. *A Study of War*. University of Chicago Press, 1964.

"Quincy Wright's Contribution to the Study of War." *Journal of Conflict Resolution* 14 (1970), 473–478.

Divine, Robert. *The Illusion of Neutrality*. University of Chicago Press, 1962.

Second Chance. New York: Atheneum, 1967.

Doenecke, Justus D. *When the Wicked Rise: American Opinion-Makers and the Manchurian Crisis of 1931–33.* Lewisburg: Bucknell University Press, 1984.

Dubin, Martin David. "The Carnegie Endowment for International Peace and the Advocacy of a League of Nations, 1914–1918." *Proceedings of the American Philosophical Society* 123 (1979), 343–368.

"Elihu Root and the Advocacy of a League of Nations, 1914–1917." *Western Political Quarterly* 19 (1966), 439–455.

"Toward the Concept of Collective Security: the Bryce Group's 'Proposals for the Avoidance of War,' 1914–1917." *International Organization* 24 (1970), 288–305.

Fabian, Larry L. *Andrew Carnegie's Peace Endowment.* Washington, DC: Carnegie Endowment for International Peace, 1985.

Ferrel, Robert. *American Diplomacy in the Great Depression.* New Haven: Yale University Press, 1957.

Peace in their Time. New Haven: Yale University Press, 1952.

Finch, Eleanor H. "Quincy Wright." *AJIL* 65 (1971), 130–131.

Fleming, Denna Frank. *The United States and World Organization 1920–1933.* New York: Columbia University Press, 1938.

García-Salmones, Mónica. "Walter Schüking and the Pacifist Traditions of International Law." *EJIL* 22 (2011), 755–782.

Grewe, Wilhelm G. *The Epochs of International Law,* translated and revised by Michael Byers. Berlin and New York: Walter de Gruyter, 2000.

Griggs, Emily Hill. "A Realist Before 'Realism': Quincy Wright and the Study of International Politics between Two World Wars." *Journal of Strategic Studies* 24 (2001), 71–103.

Hazard, John N. "Quincy Wright." In Edward Shils, ed. *Remembering the University of Chicago.* University of Chicago Press, 1991, 558–567.

Henderson, Gordon Grant. "International Law in American Foreign Policy: A Study of the Role of International Law in the Making of National Policy in Ten disputes between the United States and Great Britain in the Period 1919 to 1930." Unpublished Ph.D. thesis, Columbia University, 1962.

Herman, Sondra R. *Eleven Against War.* Stanford: Hoover Institution Press, 1969.

Hillmann, Robert P. "Quincy Wright and the Commission to Study the Organization of Peace." *Global Governance* 4 (1998), 485–499.

Hoopes, Townsend. and Douglas Brinkley. *FDR and the Creation of the U.N.* New Haven: Yale University Press, 1997.

Iriye, Akira. *After Imperialism.* New York: Atheneum, 1978.

Janis, Mark Weston. *America and the Law of Nations 1776–1939.* Oxford University Press, 2010.

The American Tradition of International Law. Oxford University Press, 2004.

Jeffery, Renee. "Hersch Lauterpacht, the Realist Challenge and the 'Grotian Tradition' in 20th Century International Relations." *EJIL* 12 (2006), 223–250.

Jones, Dorothy V. *Code of Peace: Ethics and Security in the World of the Warlord States.* University of Chicago Press, 1991.

Josephson, Harold. *James T. Shotwell and the Rise of Internationalism in America.* Rutherford: Fairleigh Dickinson University Press, 1975.

"Outlawing War: Internationalism and the Pact of Paris." *Diplomatic History* 3 (1979), 377–390.

Kennan, George F. *American Diplomacy 1900–1950.* University of Chicago Press, 1951.

Kennedy, David. "The Disciplines of International Law and Policy." *Leiden Journal of International Law* 12 (1999), 9–133.

"When Renewal Repeats: Thinking against the Box." *New York University Journal of International Law and Politics* 32 (2000), 335–500.

Kenny, James Thomas. "The Contributions of Manley O. Hudson to Modern International Law and Organization." Unpublished Ph.D. thesis, University of Denver, 1976.

Kingsbury, Benedict. "Legal Positivism as Normative Politics: International Society, Balance of Power and Lassa Oppenheim's Positive International Law." *EJIL* 13 (2002), 401–436.

Kirgis, Frederic L. *The American Society of International Law's First Century 1906–2006.* Leiden: Martinus Nijhoff Publishers, 2006.

Kneeshaw, Stepehn J. *In Pursuit of Peace: The American Reaction to the Kellogg–Briand Pact, 1928–1929.* New York: Garland Publishing, 1991.

Koskenniemi, Martti. *From Apology to Utopia: The Structure of International Legal Argument.* Cambridge University Press, 2005.

The Gentle Civilizer of Nations. Cambridge University Press, 2001.

Kuehl, Warren. *Seeking World Order: The United States and International Organization to 1920.* Nashville: Vanderbilt University Press, 1969.

Kuratowski, Roman K. "International Law Conference of the Grotius Society," *AJIL* 38 (1944), 474–475.

Lachs, Manfred. *The Teacher in International Law.* The Hague: Martinus Nijhoff Publishers, 1982.

Landauer, Carl. "The Ambivalence or Power: Launching the *American Journal of International Law* in an Era of Empire and Globalization." *Leiden Journal of International Law* 20 (2007), 325–358.

Lauterpacht, Elihu. *The Life of Hersch Lauterpacht.* Cambridge University Press, 2010.

The League of Nations in Retrospect: Proceedings of the Symposium. Berlin: Walter de Gruyter, 1983.

Leffler, Melvyn P. *The Elusive Quest*. Chapel Hill: University of North Carolina Press, 1979.

Marchand, Roland. *The American Peace Movement and Social Reform, 1898–1918*. Princeton University Press, 1972.

Meiertöns, Heiko. *The Doctrines of US Security Policy: An Evaluation under International Law*. Cambridge University Press, 2010.

Mitoma, Glenn Tatsuya. "Civil Society and International Human Rights: The Commission to Study the Organization of Peace and the Origins of the UN Human Rights." *Human Rights Quarterly* 30 (2008), 607–630.

Moynihan, Daniel Patrick. *On the Law of Nations*. Cambridge, MA: Harvard University Press, 1990.

Murase, Shinya. "Thomas Baty in Japan, Seeing through the Twilight." *British Year Book of International Law 2002* 73 (2003), 315–342.

Nurnberger, Ralph Dingmann. "James Brown Scott: Peace through Justice." Unpublished Ph.D. thesis, Georgetown University, 1975.

Oliver, Covey T. "Reflections on Two Recent Developments Affecting the Function of Law in the International Community." *Texas Law Review* 30 (1952), 815–842.

Onuma, Yasuaki. "Japanese International Law in the Prewar Period: Perspectives on the Teaching and Research of International Law in Prewar Japan." *Japanese Annual of International Law* 29 (1986), 23–47.

Patterson, David S. "The United States and the Origins of the World Court." *Political Science Quarterly* 91 (1976), 279–295.

Pugach, Noel. *Paul S. Reinsch: Open Door Diplomat in Action*. Millwood: KTO Press, 1979.

Roscher, Bernard. "The 'Renunciation of War as an Instrument of National Policy'." *Journal of the History of International Law* 4 (2002), 293–309.

Ross, Dorothy. *The Origins of American Social Science*. Cambridge University Press, 1991.

Russell, Ruth B. *A History of the United Nations Charter: The Role of the United States, 1940–1945*. Washington, DC: The Brookings Institute, 1958.

Sacriste, Guillaume. and Antonie Vauchez. "The Force of International Law: Lawyers' Diplomacy on the International Scene in the 1920s." *Law and Social Inquiry* 32 (2007), 83–107.

Schachter, Oscar. "The Invisible College of International Lawyers." *Northwestern University Law Review* 72 (1977–8), 217–226.

Schild, Georg. *Bretton Woods and Dumbarton Oaks: American Economic and Political Postwar Planning in the Summer of 1944*. London: Macmillan Press, 1995.

Schlesinger, Stephen C. *Act of Creation: The Founding of the United Nations*. Boulder: Westview Press, 2003.

Schmoeckel, Mathias. "The Internationalist as a Scientist and Herald: Lassa Oppenheim." *EJIL* 11 (2000), 699–712.

Schulzinger, Robert. *The Making of the Diplomatic Mind.* Middletown: Wesleyan University Press, 1975.

Slaughter, Anne-Marie, Andrew S. Tulumello and Stepan Wood. "International Law and International Relations Theory: A New Generation of Interdisciplinary Scholarship." *AJIL* 92 (1998), 367–397.

Smith, Bradley F. *The American Road to Nuremberg: The Documentary Record, 1944–1945.* Stanford University Press, 1982.

  The Road to Nuremberg. New York: Basic Books, 1981.

Spiermann, Ole. "Professor Walther Schüking at the Permanent Court of International Justice." *EJIL* 22 (2011), 783–799.

Steinberg, Richard H. and Jonathan Zasloff. "Power and International Law." *AJIL* 100 (2006), 64–87.

Stevens, Robert Bocking. *Law School: Legal Education in America from the 1850s to the 1980s.* Chapel Hill: University of North Carolina Press, 1983.

Stoner, John E. *S. O. Levinson and the Pact of Paris.* University of Chicago Press, 1942.

Strum, Harvey. "Henry Stimson and the Nuremberg War Crimes Trial." *Mid-America* 65 (1983), 3–13.

Suganami, Hidemi. *The Domestic Analogy and World Order Proposals.* Cambridge University Press, 1989.

Sutherland, Arthur E. *The Law at Harvard: A History of Ideas and Men, 1817–1967.* Cambridge, MA: Belknap, 1967.

Swift, Richard N. "Clyde Eagleton." In Warren F. Kuehl, ed. *Biographical Dictionary of Internationalists,* Westport: Greenwood Press, 1983, 231–232.

Tams, Christian J. "Re-Introducing Walther Schüking." *EJIL* 22 (2011), 725–739.

Thompson, Kenneth W. "Policy and Theory in Quincy Wright's International Relations." *Journal of Conflict Resolution* 14 (1970), 479–486.

Thorne, Christopher. *The Limits of Foreign Policy.* London: Hamish Hamilton, 1972.

Vitas, Robert A. *The United States and Lithuania: The Stimson Doctrine of Non-recognition.* New York: Prager, 1990.

Wæver, Ole. "The Sociology of a Not So International Discipline: American and European Developments in International Relations." *International Organization* 52 (1998), 687–727.

Walters, F. P. *A History of the League of Nations.* London: Oxford University Press, 1952, 2 vols.

Zasloff, Jonathan. "Law and the Shaping of American Foreign Policy: From the Gilded Age to the New Era." *New York University Law Review* 78 (2003), 239–373.

  "Law and the Shaping of American Foreign Policy: The Twenty Years' Crisis." *California Law Review* 77 (2003–4), 583–682.

Japanese materials

Ichimata, Masao. *Nihon no kokusai hogaku o kizuita hitobito.* [The Scholars who Established the Study of International Law in Japan]. Tokyo: Nihon Kokusai Mondai Kenkyujo, 1973.

Ishimoto, Yasuo. *Churitsu seido no shiteki kenkyu* [A Historical Study of Neutrality]. Tokyo: Yuhikaku, 1958.

Matsui, Yoshio. "'Nihon gunkoku-shugi no kokusaiho ron' – Manshu jihen ni okeru sono keisei" [The Understanding of International Law by Japanese Militarism – its Development in the Manchurian Incident]. In *Senji Nihon no Ho-taisei* [Japanese Legal System under War]. Tokyo: University of Tokyo Press, 1979, 361–405.

Nakai, Akio. *Doitsu jin to Suis jin no senso to heiwa* [War and Peace among the Germans and Swiss]. Tokyo: Nansosha, 1995.

Ohata, Tokushiro. "Fusen joyaku to Nihon" [The Kellogg–Briand Pact and Japan]. *Kokusai Seiji* 28 (1965), 72–86.

Onuma, Yasuaki. "Harukanaru jinshu byodo no riso – Kokusai renmei kiyaku heno jinshu byodo teian to Nihon no kokusaiho kan" [The Distant Ideal of Racial Equality – Japanese Proposal of Racial Equality Clause in the Covenant of the League of Nations and Japanese Views of International Law]. In Yasuaki Onuma, ed. *Kokusaiho Kokusai rengo to Nihon* [Japan and International Law, the United Nations]. Tokyo: Kobundo, 1987, 427–480.

Senso sekinin-ron jyosetu [A Study on the Concept of War Responsibility]. University of Tokyo Press, 1975.

Sogawa, Takeo. "Senkan ki ni okeru Kokusaiho" [Study of International Law during the Interwar Period]. *Horitsu JIho* 50 (1978), 51–66.

Uchiyama, Masakuma. "Manshu jihen to Thomas Baty hakase" [The Manchurian Incident and Dr. Baty]. In *Gendai gaiko shiron.* Tokyo: Keio Tushin, 1971, 179–210.

"Yokota Kisaburo sensei ni kiku" [An Interview with Professor Yokota Kisaburo]. *Hogaku Kyoshitsu* 28 (1983), 6–42.

INDEX

abolition of war, 71, 72
aggression, definition of, 72
American Bar Association, 30
American Bar Association Journal, 184
American Committee for the
    Outlawry of War, 75
American constitutional system of
    government, 27
American Diplomacy 1900–1950, 2
American foreign policy, influence of
    legalism on, 213
American Group of
    Interparliamentary Union, 80
American Journal of International Law
    (AJIL), 1, 14, 15, 27, 68, 128, 184
American Open Door Policy, *see* Open
    Door Policy
American Political Science Association
    (APSA), 28, 54, 73
American Political Science Review, 18,
    28, 188
American Society for the Judicial
    Settlement of International
    Disputes, 15
American Society of International Law
    (ASIL), 1, 4–5, 12–15, 20–21,
    24–26, 29–31, 35, 47, 50, 54,
    56, 60–63, 66, 78, 81–82, 107,
    111, 120, 125, 126, 137–41, 151,
    155, 163–65, 167, 168, 173, 184,
    186–88, 195–96
    Article 2 of, 13, 14
American Union for Concerted Peace,
    164
Annexation, Treaty of (1910), 207
Anti-Trust Law, 34
arms and ammunition, sale of, 137

arms-embargo bill, 123, 124
    against supply of arms to Bolivia,
    135
    views of Stimson and Wright *vs.*
    Moore and Borchard on,
    124–31
Askwith, Lord, 135
Association for International
    Conciliation, 41
Atlantic Charter, 186
Austin, John, 16

Baty, Thomas, 40–41, 97–98, 118,
    171–73, 205
Bingham, Hiram, 124
Boer War (1899), 211
Bolivian–Paraguayan dispute, 135, 150
Borchard, Edwin M., 69, 96, 124–31,
    141, 148, 203, 215
    views on international law, 17–21
British Yearbook of International Law
    (1944), 190
Brown, Philip Marshall, 22, 44–46, 53,
    61, 72, 73, 119, 126, 138, 166,
    167, 170, 171, 202
Brownlie, Ian, 208
Budapest Articles of Interpretation
    (1934), 83, 135–36, 140, 152,
    169, 170, 193

Canadian Bar Review, 184
Canons of International Law, The
    (1930), 98
Capper, Arthur, 123
Carnegie Endowment for International
    Peace, 19, 27, 99, 101, 104, 116
Carr, Comyns, 205